# OUR

# LADY

## OF

# PERPETUAL

# HUNGER

A MEMOIR

## LISA DONOVAN

PENGUIN BOOKS

PENGUIN BOOKS
An imprint of Penguin Random House LLC
penguinrandomhouse.com

First published in the United States of America by Penguin Press,
an imprint of Penguin Random House LLC, 2020
Published in Penguin Books 2021

Some names and identifying characteristics have been
changed to protect the privacy of the individuals involved.

ISBN 9780525560968 (paperback)

THE LIBRARY OF CONGRESS HAS CATALOGED THE HARDCOVER EDITION AS FOLLOWS:
Names: Donovan, Lisa, 1977– author.
Title: Our lady of perpetual hunger: a memoir / Lisa Donovan.
Description: New York: Penguin Press, 2020.
Identifiers: LCCN 2019049571 (print) | LCCN 2019049572 (ebook) |
ISBN 9780525560944 (hardcover) | ISBN 9780525560951 (ebook)
Subjects: LCSH: Donovan, Lisa, 1977– author. |
Women food writers—United States—Biography. |
Cooks—United States—Biography.
Classification: LCC TX649.D66 A3 2020 (print) |
LCC TX649.D66 (ebook) | DDC 641.5092 [B]—dc23
LC record available at https://lccn.loc.gov/2019049571
LC ebook record available at https://lccn.loc.gov/2019049572

Printed in the United States of America
1st Printing

Designed by Marysarah Quinn

PENGUIN BOOKS

# OUR LADY OF PERPETUAL HUNGER

Lisa Donovan is a James Beard Award–winning writer who has redefined what it means to be a "southern baker" as the pastry chef to some of the South's most influential chefs. She has been formative in developing, writing, and establishing a technique-driven and historically rich narrative of traditional southern pastry. Donovan is a regular contributor to *Food & Wine* and she has been a featured speaker at René Redzepi's globally renowned MAD Symposium. Her work has appeared in *The Washington Post*, *Eater*, *Lit Hub*, and *Saveur*. *Our Lady of Perpetual Hunger* is her first book.

\* \* \*

## Praise for *Our Lady of Perpetual Hunger*

### NAMED A FAVORITE BOOK FOR SOUTHERNERS IN 2020 BY *GARDEN & GUN*

"Donovan is such a vivid writer—smart, raunchy, vulnerable, and funny—that if her vaunted caramel cakes and sugar pies are half as good as her prose, well, I'd be open to even giving that signature buttermilk whipped cream she tops her desserts with a try. . . . *Our Lady of Perpetual Hunger* is about the multiple hungers that Donovan has been driven to satisfy in her life—for wonderful food, certainly, but also for love and community and for gratifying work that can support a family."
—Maureen Corrigan, NPR

"Donovan is an all-around perfect person, and this book tells the story of one of my favorite people." —Matty Matheson, *New York Magazine*

"Donovan documents her struggles in a male-dominated field—her mixed-race heritage, her own experience with abuse and assault, and how she put her life back together through the salvation of food."
—Zibby Owens, *Good Morning America*

"*Our Lady of Perpetual Hunger* from southern pastry royalty Lisa Donovan won't steer you wrong [with this] heady cocktail of love, family, food, and the fire that drives her personal and professional journey. Donovan really knows how to wring out the marrow in a story, how to bring you into a world that is etched and fleshed out with tremendous skill and a singular voice." —*Thrillist*

"With anger, honesty, wit, and passion . . . [and] an impeccable blend of deadpan humor, candor, and righteousness, Donovan critiques not only the rampant sexism in haute cuisine, but also the misogyny prevalent in our culture at large, not shying away from depicting her experiences of domestic-partner abuse, rape, and gender-based pay disparity. . . . Assertive and empowering."

—Kathleen Rooney, *Star Tribune* (Minnesota)

"As much a manifesto as a memoir—in the tradition of Anthony Bourdain's *Kitchen Confidential*—Donovan's testimony is beautifully written, fresh, and powerful. . . . A straightforward, no-holds-barred account of a difficult journey described in vivid, eloquent prose showcasing equal parts strength, anger, persistence, earthy humor, and, eventually, something like grace."

—*Chapter 16*

"Donovan's story is that of a pastry chef working her way up in an often inhospitable industry, but it's also about a woman creating her own narrative and grappling with the ways that the choices of the women who came before her—both personally and professionally—affect her life."

—*Eater*

"The pastry chef Lisa Donovan knows the insides of some of the South's top restaurant kitchens even better than people *think* they want to know them. In her moving, real-talk memoir, the James Beard Award–winning writer describes beautifully the current, sometimes painful moment that southern writers, editors, and chefs—perhaps especially women—have found themselves in as the world at large seems enamored by southern food."

—*Garden & Gun*

"Like Donovan's famous desserts, *Our Lady of Perpetual Hunger* takes simple ingredients—a woman's life, a journey into motherhood, a romance, a family legacy—and transforms them into something delectable, delicious, and downright inspiring."

—*Shelf Awareness* (starred review)

"Donovan . . . reveals the struggles and hard-fought lessons that have made her the courageous woman that she is today . . . written in a fierce and visceral style. . . . In a world that all too often credits male chefs for the culinary contributions of women and people of color, [*Our Lady of Perpetual Hunger*] is a valuable addition to the culinary memoir canon."

—*Booklist*

"Donovan . . . chronicles her career as a chef and her unrelenting passion for the culinary arts, but she also digs into her family history, offering keen reflections on the intersections of race and gender and spirited discussions of work, class, and opportunity. . . . [*Our Lady of Perpetual Hunger*] is not just a lively story of a talented pastry chef at the top of her game; it's also a profoundly relatable memoir of the pervasive pushback against female success. [She has a] fresh voice with a recipe for empowerment."
—*Kirkus Reviews*

"[A] fiesty confessional . . . Donovan's candid, passionate memoir will resonate with anyone who has worked in a professional kitchen, and particularly women."
—*Publishers Weekly*

"An absolutely stupendous memoir . . . defines a philosophy that I value very much: good old American pragmatism—what is most useful is most truthful. . . . She's an amazing chef, an amazing person, an amazing mom. . . . [Now] the world will finally get to see what an unbelievable writer she is. She is gifted in ways that most people, even good writers, are not. . . . [Donovan] finally has a platform to let the world know just how talented she is."
—Dave Chang, author of *Eat a Peach*

"Lisa Donovan's writing has such intensity and assertiveness. It spikes the adrenaline and creates tension in a way that feels almost athletic. And it's through this toned and visceral prose that we are forced to reckon with Donovan's most essential recipe: that respect is bred from unflinching truth and raw honesty. In life, and on these pages, [she] charts a path of personal growth with brave transparency, eloquently acknowledging that life's greatest challenges are not circumstances but callings."
—Ashley Christensen, James Beard Award–winning chef

"The first time you meet Donovan you want to pull up a stool, pour a drink, and listen to every story she has to tell. It turns out you don't need the stool or the drink. This is a woman you will be happy to get to know."
—Ruth Reichl, author of *Save Me the Plums*

"*Our Lady of Perpetual Hunger* is more than the story of a woman who finds her own voice in the patriarchal world of professional cooking. It's also the story of making a life—a life of love, of community, of commitment to the flame of creativity that somehow manages to burn against all odds. Lisa Donovan has written nothing less than the story of making a life in our times."
—Margaret Renkl, author of *Late Migrations*

"Lisa Donovan is one of the country's great pastry chefs, but this isn't a story about food, really. It's about the strength of womanhood and motherhood. It's about staring down the betrayals that women face. And it's about the redemptive power, not of food itself, but of finding common cause in feeding others."     —Francis Lam, host, *The Splendid Table*

"A critique of the 'world that men made,' a pledge to the women who came before her, and a challenge to work in new ways, *Our Lady of Perpetual Hunger* blazes a path of self-discovery that manages, as great memoir must, to serve readers more than self. Lisa Donovan knows things we need to know."     —John T. Edge, author of *The Potlikker Papers*

"In *Our Lady of Perpetual Hunger*, Lisa Donovan writes a line I kept returning to: 'I had vigor, the kind you could taste.' I could taste the writing in this book. Her breathless descriptors conjure heat and possibility, her incisive memories capture the dank and earthen bits. To give a book life, a wise writer understands her myths must die. This book's heart is its truth, one woman's unyielding look in the mirror and well beyond it. Donovan's ultimate embrace of the human who stares back at her is a kind of freedom for us all."
     —Osayi Endolyn, James Beard Award—winning writer

"Yes, it's about love, family, food, and one woman's personal and professional journey. But more than all that, *Our Lady of Perpetual Hunger* is about life force, the unquenchable flame within us that demands to survive and thrive. It could only be written by Lisa Donovan, and it should be read by everyone."
     —Mary Laura Philpott, author of *I Miss You When I Blink*

"Lisa Donovan writes with a voice that is both bruised and tender in *Our Lady of Perpetual Hunger*. In tracing her path to food, Donovan honors the women who shaped her philosophy in the kitchen, reminding us of the necessity of women telling their stories in a world so eagerly determined to erase them. We are quite lucky to live in a world where [she] has written her own story with such grace."
     —Mayukh Sen, author of *Taste Makers*

FOR

**JOHN,**

MY

CHAMPION

She was an American girl

Raised on promises.

—"AMERICAN GIRL,"

TOM PETTY & THE HEARTBREAKERS

# CONTENTS

# OUR
# LADY

OF

# PERPETUAL
# HUNGER

# 1

# BUOYANCY

## *Fruit*

I HAD THE KIND OF MANGO between my fingers that you really have to suck on before you can even start to bite the sinewy flesh, otherwise you risk losing all its juices down the length of your arm—and, occasionally, clear into your armpit, depending on your position at the time.

In the South, we call this a "trash-can" fruit—usually a peach—because at a certain time of the year, they are so perfectly and impossibly ripe, almost gnarly in their fecundity, that you have to stand over a trash can to eat them. But I wasn't in the South. Not my South, anyway. I was sitting in the passenger seat of an old pickup truck in Costa Rica, letting the juices flow. I had a warm beer between my knees and my bare, dirty feet firmly propped up on the sun-bleached red-now-pink vinyl dashboard as if they had been there my entire life. I bounced up the side of a mountain staring at my long toes, which landed somewhere between elegantly Romanesque and boyishly ugly. They're feet that I usually didn't take the time to look at, much less admire. They took a different shape that day with the dark, volcanic beach sand still between my toes and their arches just a bit more pronounced for some reason.

She startled me, the woman I had become, the woman I hadn't paid attention to for so many years between the baby raising and the decades of standing on those strong feet in a kitchen and the fast adaptability to make it all work, with her lean legs, her high-arched feet, her sticky mango-covered hands, and the way she took big, satisfying swigs from a body-temperature beer. She didn't even like beer. She also never felt this kind of distilled sense of being beautiful, not in her real life. She was always the smart one, the interesting one, the one who could crack a joke to make all the boys blush and bust out into a holy-shit-who-said-that kind of laughter. But she learned long ago that she would not float through this world on her beauty.

Yet there she was. There I was. A beautiful—pretty, even—girl in a tattered sundress, with little rosebud lips, dark olive skin, and good, strong eyes that scared me a little when I caught myself in the side mirror.

I was far away from the story of myself: a steep, uphill climb, with a baby on my hip, and then two, and an early-onset high expectation for my life that I was not willing to forsake. I worked for a career that I loved, one in which I was celebrated and one where I did work that made me proud. I followed a path that became clear only as I placed one foot in front of the other and said yes, very often with unknown outcomes. I can take credit for paying attention, working hard, and knowing the values I wanted to honor. I've come equipped with a kind of compass, one that is utterly mysterious in its origin but always overrides fear and doubt and is, thankfully, nearly always accurate and persistent as fuck. And with it, I found a home in my work. I found beauty there. I found moments that defined something about my life, something about what I knew I needed as a human to move forward while still being present and useful in the moment. A lot of those moments happened standing behind a prep table, next to an oven, with spatula in hand.

In the morning, there is a quiet light and an almost ethereal hum in a restaurant kitchen. This moment is one of the pastry chef's many rewards. Unlocking the door, the first one in after a night of clatter and shouting, whispered cursing, eye-rolling, loud laughing, sweating, slamming and pounding, the aftereffect leaves a crisp silence—a silence that might be alarming if I didn't know it was all going to be over sooner than I was ready for. It's a kind of postapocalyptic silence, after the fallout but just before the zombies show up.

There are hardly ever windows in these kitchens. The glow and hum do not come from anything celestial or planetary but from the equipment. The lowboys creak and buzz, keeping all the leftover mise en place cool in their quart containers with their perfectly cut blue-tape labels on their collars, looking like little schoolboys standing at attention with their perfectly pressed lapels. The soft-serve machine aches because it is never used properly and is grossly mistreated throughout the night. The dishwashing machine taps at random moments, waiting to be turned on, waiting to be ridden hard for seventeen hours straight like the monster that it is. And the elephant of the walk-in cooler makes a noise so deep and constant that it doesn't register until one day it breaks down, revealing itself as the audible baseline of the whole kitchen, the tail end of a Buddhist prayer bell that grounds everyone, that serves as the key of collective energy for the entirety of a space.

I would take my time in those early moments. I never rushed it.

Those mornings fell between my life as the mother of two young kids, as the wife of a really good human who needs conversation much more than I ever do, and as the head of my own department with three

cooks under me who were all novices at pastry. There was also the oc-
casional cook from the line who was being punished. The line is where
service is executed, where all the action happens every night. Pastry
was sometimes treated like the cargo hold of an airplane, for the storage
of things that were not useful and for people who were doing penance
for lack of preparation or other general fuck-off behavior. My already
weak managerial skills, pressed to the max. So those small moments to
make coffee, to write prep lists, to gather my thoughts, to try to fit my
heart back into the equation, became more essential to me than sleep or
water. It became my ritual, my morning prayer. "*Tea and oranges that
come all the way from China*," lulled Leonard Cohen as I tasted my bitter
coffee, black with no cream, no sugar, just dark and hot and strong and
pushing my eyelids higher with each sip.

When my career was at what most considered its pinnacle, those
early-morning moments became necessary. I would thumb through
recipes that I had spent the last decade writing and developing. I would
try to make time to look through at least one beautiful book by someone I loved and admired. I would play with fruit for as long as I could.
After all the checklists were checked, deliveries were signed for, orders
were placed, and schedules were written, fruit was the first thing I
would touch. Prepping and trimming and snacking while I had my
coffee gave me a quiet moment and a memory recall that I needed. The
methodical pace of tending to a few flats of strawberries or peaches or
damson plums—my favorite of all the fruits—became the only time I
still felt like a cook in my day-to-day life. A good piece of fruit, or
several hundred good pieces of fruit, could inspire me to make a cold,
frozen honey parfait so light and so nearly something that felt just like
honey air on your tongue that it did not disrupt the fruit's pure ripe-
ness. Or I'd rework my favorite pâte sucrée to have a beefiness that
might carry the sometimes off-putting taste of a pawpaw, and exper-

iment until learning that buckwheat or a toasted chestnut flour rounds out nicely that nearly mineral taste that those unusual and sometimes curiously disgusting fruits have. Fruit is titillating, little pockets of juicy potential, full of an almost sexual promise of pleasure. It could make me change my mind and better my plans. The winter I first processed a few hundred pounds of apples, I spent the whole time dreaming about what they might become, my hands working faster and more efficiently with each step, peeling and coring and dicing and settling the pieces into an ice-cold lemon-water bath, feeling a kind of calmness, knowing I was in the right place, doing the right work. Those meditations sealed my fate as a pastry chef. Those moments became the ones I looked for when I found myself in a job that seemingly had very little to do with them.

My refusal to do work that felt empty, coupled with my intense work ethic, created a beautiful collision of opportunities. It allowed me to drink bottles of wine with my heroes until the morning light, cook in kitchens with people I never dreamed of having the privilege to know, and it allowed me to continue to learn and to work—the only two things I really ever wanted in the first place. And I was good. That I know. My food is good. I'm not reinventing anything. I'm not competing to be the "best." My food is thoughtful and, hopefully, comforting, and that's what always mattered to me. It's intentional. In fact, my food is likely the sincerest intention of my many sincere intentions. After all these years, I think it may damn well be the very best of me. Something as simple as baking can save you. It saved me, again and again. There were moments of discovery when my hands were working pie dough, moments of grace and patience found in the learning, moments of perseverance in a cast-iron cornbread, moments of focus and intelligence and confidence in my research and recipe writing. The work was always what I was after, and I found so many rewards there.

Though as I bounced around in a squeaky but steadfast truck in a jungle, seatbeltless and sun-kissed, I was not feeling saved by anything, most especially my career. Javier was bouncing next to me in the driver's seat with his hand jiggling on the deteriorating stick shift. He had been a complete stranger only a week prior, there was an entire language between us, and yet at that moment in time he was undeniably my closest friend. Javier embodied what I saw as a distinctly Costa Rican trait—he was either sixty years old or six hundred years old. His enthusiasm and kindness catapulted him clear out of how I normally categorized a person. The lines on his face seemed like a landscape, yet the light in his eyes was similar to that of my teenage daughter, bright and effervescent, bubbly, even. There was something to his face and, I would soon discover, to his entire person that would continually set me at ease. I trusted him almost immediately—and trust was not something I came by easily at that time. I had become very skeptical on the inside and fantastically rigid on the outside.

Kindness, or even *thoughtfulness*, was a scarce quality in my world. The industry in which I had spent the last fifteen years making my way had become a markedly fucked-up cast of angry, drunken, ego-driven, and deeply sad people. Their marriages were falling apart, their careers hinged on other people's money, and their restaurants were being run by unqualified, young cooks because the new expectation (and intention) was to be famous, to damn near immortalize yourself. Not to be good. I found myself at the supposed height of my career with no direction, no leadership, and drowning in a wave of bullshit that was seen, from just far enough away, as success. My cooks were suffering. My food was not good anymore. I was not learning a damn thing. I decided to leave the career I had worked years to successfully build. By the time I found myself riding shotgun to Javier, I had more than my share of baggage to sort through.

I had watched people who loved the work as much as I did get turned inside out on a daily basis, only to be used up and barely wrung out before they were used up again, with no consideration for their young hearts. I was supposed to be fine with how their eagerness to learn and their willingness to work hard were exploited. I was supposed to listen to all the managers, all men who had very little to lose and everything to gain, talk about how expendable they (we) all were every Monday at ten a.m. I succumbed, too: became mean in ways I had never been, short-tempered in things that normally were teaching moments, overwhelmed by how much of it was slipping through my fingers.

How had wanting to make good pie come to this? I developed a deep sadness brought on by the sudden realization of how the world of cooking, something that brings people with giant hearts into a kitchen, something that is ultimately rooted in caring for others, had, in a shockingly short period of time and right before my eyes, become something that chewed you up but never spit you out—a thing that just kept you in its mouth like tobacco, sucking the juices out of you, building up a cancer inside our industry. And then, when there was no more creativity or enthusiasm to keep you going, you'd quit, somehow thinking you'd been the one to fail.

I could no longer watch kids who had just pulled six doubles in a row get brutally lambasted, lowboys pounded on, pans banged in their faces, because they messed up out of sheer exhaustion. I was demoralized by hearing the head chefs of our kitchen sit in the office making jokes about everyone under their tutelage: about their faces, their awkwardness, their fuckability, their punishments. I felt pain when I would hear them talk about how "intimidation" and "fear" were the keys to functional leadership. This was not my world. I could no longer reason out my place there. I could no longer justify my own poor leadership. I could no longer justify the threadbare support system. I could no longer justify the late nights (who am I kidding: early mornings) when I'd have to carry my absurdly intoxicated chef up the stairs to his apartment and take off his boots and put him to bed instead of putting my own children to bed because I had become a surrogate sister and wife as one of the only women crazy enough to work under or even tolerate his famously wild and destructive personal and professional habits. I wanted to learn. Also, I cared about him, and as women our value and our worth are usually also tied up in our emotional availability to our leaders, especially in an industry as intimate as the restaurant one. But mostly, I could no longer justify or tolerate my own acquiescence. I was sorting through my own bullshit and how I had, somewhere in the timeline of my life, made a silent agreement that these were the rules I had to play by.

Eventually, I ended up so tasteless and worthless as a cook, and as a human, that I actually began to believe that it was my lack of talent and aptitude that caused my undoing. I left feeling an exhaustion so deep inside of me, I couldn't begin to take it apart or find a fix for it.

By the end, as I was writing a letter of resignation from my kitchen table while my kids slept in the room next to me, my heart was sitting somewhere between my alcohol-soaked liver and my anguished, knotted-up, constipated-for-years gut. For the first time in my life, I felt that I had not chosen the right path. Even in my tumultuous and complicated past, at least I could see the reason, the lesson, the eventual gifts brought by a misstep. But this? I could find no reasoning for it. I had let everyone down. I had let myself down.

Javier didn't know any of this. Costa Rica wasn't full of broken chefs all trying to simultaneously survive and outdo one another, building worlds for themselves that were heavy burdens for everyone around them, building walls around their financial and cultural successes that were impossible for women and brown and black people to penetrate, even though the narrative they were selling was mostly ours. Costa Rica was not full of people pretending they were happy, opening restaurant after restaurant, each one more soulless than the last, to prove their value to their investors. There was no one trying to play out some rock-god fantasy of immortality, or running away from their demons, which probably all came in the form of insecurity and ego and greed backed by restaurant groups helmed by wealthy board members all voting for you to make more money, to reach a steeper bottom line, to worry less about community (unless it pays!), less about quality (unless it pays!), less about hospitality (unless it pays!), and, in all the ways, to worry less about the quality of life for your workers, heartbreakingly, unless it pays.

I tolerated all the times I was told to "wait" to make a better living, "wait" to be supported, "wait" to be promoted, "wait" to make a fair wage, after too many months, years, of doing "favors" and being a team player. I was always willing to take a chance, to dive in and prove my worth. But it was never met with equity. It was only met with a gaze that told me I should feel lucky just to be there.

When you realize you are embedded in a corporation, and not in a company that prioritizes its people or even its supposed task of hospitality, you realize that you will never be worth enough for them to support you the way you deserve to be supported. When you have wealthy partners who are somehow willing to spend hundreds of thousands of dollars on light fixtures, or handmade linen napkins from their best friend in Charleston, and truly, horrendously bad art before they even open their doors, but cannot see their way to paying their cooks a living wage or establishing health-care benefits for them or supporting them as human beings rather than merely as a means of profit, you take an already complicated and outdated caste system of workers and destroy the fibers that keep them tethered to their already complicated work.

Food doesn't lie. And when miserable people are cooking it, your whole restaurant will reek of that misery. I became determined to build my own bakery in Nashville, right around when I knew I needed to leave Husk, where I had been building my pastry program alongside Sean Brock, and make my own way by building my own place where I could create a culture that was right and correct. This was when I realized that the people who were investing in restaurants were destroying the very heart of them, and taking chefs down mentally, physically, and spiritually in the process. These types of "partners" want everything you've worked for and the talent they can't open the restaurant without. They demand that you fill 150 seats in a two-million-dollar renovation and be open every possible hour of every possible day instead of the moderate, thoughtful place that serves its community with quality and skill and provides a good living and a good life for its employees, the place that was your original vision—the vision they promised you would be able to execute when they first sniffed you out and told you they were so interested in helping you become "more." Then they make you work for ten years before they'll even consider giving you ownership shares. They end up partaking in the culture of their restaurants simply to make their presence and power known, to remind you who you serve, and to have street cred with their other rich friends as a newly minted member of the cool-kids club; and however kind they may seem to your face, you should never mistake that you are expendable if it costs them too much. It will say so in the contract.

You get commodified. And you start to believe you have no other options. You do this in the name of survival and growth, and eventually, you can't even find your way back to your own kitchen, to your own work, or to any of the reasons that had taken you that far.

My shame eventually turned to anger. Resilience, normally my stalwart sidekick, my one constant, had abandoned me. I wish I could say that I had placed some value on my own inherent worth and self, but no. I moved forward because, at the time, I had a ten-year-old girl watching my every move, and I was bound to reclaim some amount of my original power that I had somehow, somewhere relinquished without really giving my consent.

Don't feel sorry for me. I reclaimed it all.

But in the early moments of arriving in Costa Rica, I still felt a longing for my work as a dull ache deep in my body that I can identify only as heartbreak. This longing led to Costa Rica, where I was to host a culinary workshop: a gig I dreamed up with a friend of mine who is one of the few (and perhaps only) very outwardly spiritual yoga instructors whose company I enjoy. I tentatively packed my tool kit—a waxed denim wrap full of spoons, spatulas, peelers, knives, bench scrapers, and disposable piping bags—in my suitcase along with my aprons. My tool kit is like my partner; pastry chefs are notoriously considered the isolationists in a kitchen, working in a way that is hardly simpatico with the rest of the ebb and flow of the busy space, and I feel lost without mine. It was the first thing I decided I didn't want to see for a while because I was full of "fuck it" and "fuck you." I had put it away, literally far away, in the attic, because I really believed myself to be done. Looking at the weathered leather straps that have my initials, "LD," stamped into them, and the tired fabric that felt earned just hurt my feelings. I melodramatically had sequestered the thing to a box upstairs and, thinking I'd never go back, decided that I needed to allow myself to mourn it, this loss of a work I loved. Getting it back out to go to Costa Rica was not easy. I was not ready, but I suppose I am not one to sit around and wait for the spirit to move me.

Once in Costa Rica, my hands were no longer idle. My arms felt useful and strong. My brain buzzed with the potential of everything and it felt pure, almost as if seeing the pathetic underbelly of the hospitality industry had never settled in my gut. Almost. The shadows were still there. I still had a lot of work to do to find the actual light to change that and I knew it.

The villa we rented for the workshop sat perched on a mountainside in the jungle overlooking the Pacific Ocean, where we could hear howler monkeys shaking the limbs of faraway trees, and we breathed in a kind of fresh air that made you feel like you'd been living in a dark, dank hole your entire life. Here, I spent my days cooking out of a kitchen that had optional walls that could be slid away to open the space up to vast expanses of jungle, with food so fresh and ripe and clean and remarkable that your brain had a hard time computing how it could possibly be real. There were no packages. There were no jars. Food came from the trees, from the ocean, and from bins on tables that old people tended on the side of every busy road in the valley. In order to take away the green banana flour that the woman in the bright blue dress (worn for so long that it looked as much a part of her body as her hair) had spent her morning grinding and toasting, you had to bring a jar of your own.

This is not to say that packaged foods are not available; grocery stores abound. But these were not the foods I looked for. These were not the foods I asked Javier to show me. Like any cook worth her salt, I was drawn to the baskets full of sugarcane, the tables covered with buckets filled with every kind of flour from sweet potato to yucca and ziplock bags with spices like black cumin and cocoa powder with flecks of seed bark not yet sifted out. My days with Javier were spent driving around to every good mango or guava pod tree he knew and every fishmonger's house and every market he preferred. With each early hoot and holler that invariably came rustling out of the fog and the foliage along with the sun each day, Javier would show up to take the yoga students to the beach to do all the yoga things and say to me, "Then you and I make mangoes!" It was impossible to maintain skepticism, no matter how stupidly I tried.

We spent hours climbing trees and picking fruit from the roof of Javier's truck. We became pretty acrobatic together in order to reach the highest fruits from the tallest limbs, and when we succeeded, he would boast loudly in Spanish to the monkeys who had a long and hilarious history of ransacking his truck: "Now I take what is yours, babies!"—yet every single time, bowing and blowing them a kiss and telling them that he loved them, his eyes flashing as he laughed and jogged quickly away, as if the monkeys were going to leap out at any moment to snatch back the fruit we had just claimed. Javier 1, monkeys 10, seemed to be the perpetual score.

Before that week, I had never seen a guava pod, a thing I now think about nearly daily because I have yet to find something I enjoy quite as much. It looks like a giant and leathery sugar snap pea, some as long as the length of my arm. When you tear them open—not neatly, mind you, they do not acquiesce—you are gifted with seeds covered in the whitest, softest flesh that feels, in your mouth, just sweet enough, supple and utterly delicious. I became very good at spitting those seeds out of Javier's truck across the jungle. I definitely increased the population.

I enjoyed these fruits so much that on the third day, Javier arrived with the sun and walked through the door with both arms full of giant pods. He was elated and proud. He worked hard at happiness and succeeded quite skillfully. We off-loaded them into the kitchen, and I teetered, in my broken Spanish, about all the things I could do with them—wondering out loud how best to harvest the fruit off the seeds without putting them in my mouth—when he grabbed my hand and said, *"Más, mi amiga! Más!"* He had filled the entire bed of his truck with guava pods that morning, apparently while the rest of the world slept.

"You are simple, Lisa, Scorpio sister. It is fine."

We each had about a 30 percent mastery of the other's language yet somehow discovered that we shared a birthday with many years between them. He loved that we were "practically twins," but most certainly "Brother! Sister!" and thus the same. He did seem to understand something about me, beyond a kind of horoscope nonsense. When he said these words to me for the first of many times, he followed them up with "Yes? You see my words?" I did. I saw them. He would often repeat them to remind me after long moments of silence on our drives together.

We were quickly running out of days in Costa Rica. The weather had been miraculous, probably very typically so, and after many miles of hiking damn near every mountain on that coast, my body was sore but in the most rewarding and satisfying way. I was the kind of tired you hope to be at the end of each day, when you know your sleep will be deep and you'll wake up the next day ready and willing. I was having those tomorrows, in fact, the ones without the gloom of what the day might hold. Mornings were full of joy and enthusiasm instead. My resolve was waning. The stored damage in my gut was breaking into little bits inside me, the plaque around my heart dissolving. I was shitting. I was pumping blood. I was alive after all. Imagine that.

On our second-to-last day, I awoke and stood alone in the kitchen. I opened the doors, exposing the entire house to the thicket of trees, a shocking greenness that made my glasses useless—my vision seemingly perfect for the first time since I was small. My bare feet were now thoroughly the color of the earth; I hadn't worn shoes for days. My hair was in a kind of makeshift turban that I had copied from some old

Liz Taylor pictures, but I'm fairly certain I looked more like Miss Hannigan. I laughed at myself in the mirror and touched my face, glad to see the wrinkles around my eyes again. I saw a kitchen full of papayas, guavas, flours, spices; remembered the fish—a collection of beautiful red snapper that Javier's cousin had caught for me—waiting for me in the cooler; smelled the coffee from the early yoga risers, all full of their proper spiritual feelings and good yoga vibes or whatever yoga people do and feel; and stood listening to the racket of the hills.

I took my clothes off that morning, unwrapped my short hair from the cloth, and stepped slowly into the water. I floated on my back for a long time, no one in the house, no one for miles as far as I knew. My breasts and my face bobbed above the water while the rest of me felt the softness that comes from being naked and the weightlessness that comes from being submerged, neither rooted nor mobile, a stillness that used to scare me. And I stayed there like that for some time that day, in a jungle all alone with myself.

I had lost the narrative. I was trying to fit myself into something that was not built for me, and I had tried to do that for a really long time. The world that men made had finally used up and exhausted every bit of me. I had thought I could keep my head down and go through it to get beyond it. But, instead, that world, the one built around ego and greed and rooted in misogyny, got in. And then I ran because I was ashamed and angry about it all. I blamed myself.

I almost gave up.

Almost.

But I didn't.

I was simple.

It was simple.

It was all very simple.

I remembered. I remembered what I had meant to do, where I had started and what it was all for. I remembered that one facet of an industry that ultimately is so good should not have the power to take me out of the game. I had resisted the dirty power of men's egos for as long as I could remember, walking away when I was taken for granted and never looking back. I did not have to give away my gifts because of a broken world that turned me inside out and made me nearly unrecognizable to myself. In fact, I needed to stand in the middle of that world and do it the way I had meant to all along.

I put my clothes back on, my skin still wet, my hair dripping salty water down my back, my entire body feeling as wide as that capable, beautiful, and deeply vast Costa Rican sky. Then I pulled seven snapper fish onto the kitchen island, sharpened my knife, remembered where I came from, the shit I had taken in my life, the wrongs I had made right time and time again, and I got back to fucking work.

# 2

## A BEGINNING

*Wheat*

M Y STANDARD UNIFORM in the summer of 1999 was denim coveralls, rolled up like in the Bananarama "Cruel Summer" video because, really, it had been my only standard of fashion at that point in my life (and, honestly, still is). My hair, which reached past my waist when down, was always twisted up in a messy bun that rested on top of my head—a throwback to my days as a serious ballet dancer (read: a girl who danced and took herself very seriously)—armpit hair nearly as long, perfectly round glasses on my sleepy brown eyes, and a pair of white Jack Purcells on my feet. I had my little blue Honda hatchback, a car that I bought from my big brother, David, after he surprised us all a few years earlier and boarded a big navy ship at the age of eighteen, leaving me only a sad, short note and his childhood teddy bear on my pillow to say goodbye. On a June day that summer, the back seat held one bag from Winn-Dixie with three items: bread flour, rye flour, and buttermilk. Next to it was a pile of laundry that I kept in my car because I had a habit of long drives and, at the end of them, sleeping in my car wherever I ended up.

I could lay the back seats of that little Honda down and tuck myself in under the hatch, where I kept a pillow and a jug of water, no one ever the wiser.

Once or twice a week, I would get off work from waiting tables at TradeWinds—a twenty-two-seat Italian cigar den housed in a double-wide trailer on a dirt hillside corner of the adjacent town of Valparaiso—around midnight and just drive. Something as basic as a good song or album would spark it. I'd be so wired from running plates of chicken principessa and linguine con vongole around these twenty-two seats for eight straight hours that I was nowhere near in the mood to go home and sleep. So I'd drive. I would drive right past my house, right past my town, toward someplace else. Some days I'd wake up in parking lots in Marion, Alabama, or Slidell, Louisiana, just because I didn't want to stay where I was from and I didn't know how to stop once I started driving. In the mornings I'd be woken up by the sound of big trucks delivering trees to the garden centers or the clatter of store shopping carts abandoned during the night being collected from the parking lot. I'd open my eyes, splash some rose-scented witch hazel on my face, throw on a fresh shirt from the pile, put on some lip gloss, and drive back home with a particularly shitty cup of gas-station coffee and, if I was lucky, a fresh Krispy Kreme right off the delivery truck. I was that girl at the age of twenty. Warm, wildly detached, prone to walkabouts, gentle, hairy.

But I was never aloof. Which is how, that summer, I found myself pulling up to a house I thought I'd never see again. It was a house in Niceville, Florida, and inside was a room made just for listening to music. Stuart Petermann greeted me at the door with his usual steadfastness. He was the stepfather of an on-again, off-again boyfriend. I guess I'm being purposefully dismissive here. It was actually pretty serious, the relationship, but it was on-again, off-again. The boyfriend's name was Phillip, and he was someone I was oddly committed to for such a young person, and when my better sensibilities would kick in, in an on-again, off-again way, I would repeatedly try to shake him and leave many, many times over several years. I had done the normal thing and gotten close to Phillip's family. Stuart had, despite any encouragement I had or had not given him, behaved like a father to me. He was an Old World, utterly precise, and somewhat cold Eastern European man, thick with the traditional girth for the cold nights back in his homeland, I assumed, cartooned with a gray mustache and plump, rosy cheeks. He had no accent, except when he pleased, which led me to believe with absolute certainty and to this day that he was, in fact, a spy.

When I arrived, his face was adequately solemn for the occasion, head a little bowed, lips pursed to invisibility under his perfectly measured mustache. I had just dissolved my relationship with his son and it was, I thought, finally final. As Stuart's protocol required, he had invited me over to say goodbye and impart one last piece of whatever wisdom he deemed I needed in my young lady life. It was a simple yet grand gesture and one that spoke to the finer points of his strict manners. Everything in his world was kept in cold, intellectualized order.

Stuart taught me how to set a formal table. Or, at least, how to sit at a formally set table. I watched him give a toast properly, stuffy as they always were, by clinking delicately on his crystal wineglass with a salad fork and his pinkie erect, full of intention. He knew about wine and which food to drink it with, and guests were not given a choice. I learned that there is some kind of beauty in such regimentation but that, ultimately, the way Stuart went about it wasn't for me. I appreciated his penchant for fineness, for quality, for how beautiful a perfectly polished silver spoon was and what it implied to me, the guest.

That information stuck. There was something so rigid about his delivery, though, protocol overwhelming every gesture—a kind of militant hospitality. Never an unironed napkin. Never a seating arrangement without rules. I learned at his table that a shiny spoon does not a beautiful experience make.

Still, on that day I followed Stuart's rules. On that day, I honored his request and sat with him in the room made just for listening to music.

The lights were dim, and I realized we were alone. There was a slight undertaker vibe to the whole thing, his body big and slow moving, but I wasn't going to say anything, polite as my mama had taught me to be. He took my hand and I felt a deeper sense of discomfort. He had never done that before. In fact, I couldn't remember ever making any physical contact in our nearly three years of knowing each other, other than very proper handshakes and royal-style kisses on cheeks and whatnot. Stuart released my hand and said, "Take a seat, Lisa. I want to say something to you."

I crossed my arms and stood at the window for a moment instead, watching a mother duck usher her babies into the water by doing nothing more than floating her own way away from the shore toward the dark belly of the bay, still full of mood from the storm the night before. They all followed, one little baby duck after another just instinctively wanting to be near her wherever she was going, and for some reason I felt like I was watching some kind of miracle. I felt a deep and unusual yearning that I did not really understand. A strange ache came over me and I almost started to cry. But then Stuart's voice reminded me where I was.

"Please sit down, dear."

I shook off the mood he was setting for me, blaming him for my weird and overreaching sentimentality toward some ducks that I'd seen a million times before. I usually prefer to wallow in my own variety of melancholy, and his was not suiting me in that moment. I was not quite sure what to expect next, so I went "accommodating as fuck" until I could read the room a little better.

"Yes! Of course!" I chirped.

Stuart sat in the armchair closest to me and leaned in. Our knees were nearly touching, and I started keeping personal-contact score with him. Already he'd exceeded his limit. He put his hand on my knee, a third offense, and said, "I thought I might say goodbye. There's a lot to say, so much I want to impart to you, but there is someone who can do it better than I can." He winced and squinted his eyes at me and nodded.

He had an orchestrated way, every time, of putting on music from his incredible and impressive record collection. We had been in this room before with Phillip many times, and I knew the drill. I immediately recognized the routine and it put me at ease. He ran his hands across the alphabetized wall of albums that were all tucked into a built-in shelf until he got to the letter he was aiming for. He wandered all the way down to the letter *S*. Stevens, Cat. *Tea for the Tillerman*. One of my favorite albums, which I knew by heart. I relaxed even more for some reason, suddenly feeling like I wasn't alone with Stuart any longer.

He placed the album on the display shelf and picked up the oval, red velvet brush and then lifted the lid to the record player. While he went through these flourished motions, I started to worry about the buttermilk in my car. Even buttermilk can't withstand the summer heat of June in Florida. I had biscuits to make for family meal that night at TradeWinds and I had no money to replace rotten ingredients. I thought about the ducks again and distractedly looked back toward the window, wondering where they were, if they had made it across.

Stuart walked over, as if he had rehearsed, right as Cat started in with his "La-la-la-la-la-la-la-la, la, la / La-la-la-la-la-la-la-la, la, la . . ." and sat down. He bowed his head, his knees against mine again. I swallowed hard, my eyes were nearly as big as my glasses, and I could not rearrange them no matter how hard I tried because it was all happening so fast. With a steadfast swoop, Stuart gathered my hands in his and, as Cat Stevens started singing, stared at me right in the eyes. "Now that I've lost ev-ry-thing to yo-ou / You say you wanna start somethi-ing ne-ew," and then as Cat crooned, Stuart gazed and winced at me, mouthing every word of Cat's warnings and grievings and arrogant assumptions, as if I were leaving *him*, not his son, as if I were some lost cause worried about who was going to buy me pretty clothes, or as if I were completely unaware until that moment that the world was, I do declare, hard for a woman.

At any rate, it continued.

Through the entirety of the song.

I found myself looking around as if there were someone there who might save me.

His grip got firmer on my hands. My eyes got wider.

Two minutes, I thought.

This song is definitely only about two minutes. I can do just about anything for two minutes.

Every word was an opportunity for Stuart to show the elasticity of his face, and every pause a reflective prayer. I've never had my eyes so looked into before or since.

"Good fucking god" is the only articulate thought I remember having.

And then it was over.

He got up, walked over to pull the needle off before a new song started, and solemnly turned to me from the record player with the vinyl in his hand to put back into its sleeve.

Before he could say a word, I shouted, "Buttermilk!"

"What's that?" he said, seeming disappointed that I had no remarks on what I had just experienced.

"I have buttermilk. In my car. It's hot. I should . . . go."

But before I could make my clumsy escape, he walked over to me, and before I could stop him, I found myself face-deep in his grayhaired chest, his buttons open just enough that I had to sputter the fuzz out of my mouth as he hugged me for the first and last time.

"GoodBYE, Lisa. Good. Bye." And with my shoulders in his hands, he nodded that it was now the correct, and proper, time to make my exit.

I did not know what to say, so I said, "Yes, OK, thank you," and walked as casually as I could toward the door, not wanting to alarm anyone by being hasty, most of all myself. I got to my car, stuck the key in the door, and looked back at the house. He was standing there, waving with one arm up above his head, slowly and rhythmically, as if I was far off in the distance on a ship about to set sail.

The car was hot, but it was good relief from the cold cave of the music room, blasted with typically over-the-top Florida airconditioning. I felt queasy and I could smell the buttermilk from the front seat. I could tell that it was wang-y by only ten minutes or so, still salvageable, I thought, and decided my biscuits would not be ruined. My already powerful sense of smell had been unusually keen for a few weeks. I thought maybe it was the impending shift of the seasons or maybe there had been a literal sea change and the air was brighter or cleaner or something. I put the car in reverse and went home to my house on Cotton Avenue to spend the rest of my morning undoing some man's weird baggage and assumptions and bullshit advice by, as per usual, sticking my hands in some flour. These moments alone and appalled were some of my first baking lessons.

THE BLUE HOUSE on Cotton Avenue was mine for a few years. Inside of it, I lived with a cat named Sonny, my truest confidant and most protective friend. Sometimes, my then-ex-boyfriend would live there as well, as it technically belonged to (his) Grandma Jo. Phillip's grandmother was a Filipino tailor who ran that family with something of an Imelda Marcos spirit, amassing great sums of money by sneakily buying property with her earnings from sewing patches on soldiers' uniforms and selling lumpia on holidays—all behind her abusive first husband's back. She would use this private means of independence to control situations, to wield power, and to manipulate when she was underestimated or undervalued as a brown female immigrant, which meant nearly every situation in which she found herself. She was a boss with mad tailor skills. I respected and loved her immensely.

When the blue house was mine, NPR played on a battery-powered radio and the house was always in some state of renovation or disrepair. My windows were always open so Sonny could come and go as he pleased, which he did, usually with a bird or squirrel in his mouth. He meant this as a form of rent, but I never had the stomach to dispose of them any more ceremoniously than flinging them back out of the window with a long-handled colander that quickly got retired from cooking. Because of the open windows, my house always smelled like an open-air market. There were only three tiny houses on that street right in the center of town, a place with the standard suburban set of fast-food joints and big-box grocery stores. The trio of houses, oddly placed a few blocks between the Ruby Tuesday and the O'Reilly

Auto Parts store, were all former military homes that had been bought and moved to that empty lot next to the bayou by a tractor (and by Phillip's industrious grandmother) in the 1950s from the air force base five miles away. They were all stationed in a row, and I was in the middle.

On the left of me was an Italian sandwich shop run by a real asshole from New Jersey named Al who just happened to make a good meatball. Al was proof that sometimes knowing how to make a good sandwich is all a person needs to get by in this world. There was a forever waft of "gravy" and baked bread and other delicatessen sundries that perpetually snaked its way over to my yard and into my windows.

Some mornings I would wake up to Al and his wife, Ellen, screaming at each other about watering the plants or making the pickles. Ellen once threw a pot full of water, chicken bones, carrots, onions, and, I suppose, garlic out of the window while she shouted, "I TOLD YOU TO NEVER PUT GARLIC IN THE GODDAMNED STOCK, AL! THIS MARRIAGE WAS OVER BEFORE IT EVEN STARTED!" Her sharp voice and tonality were not a common thing to hear shouted around what was, essentially, lower Alabama. They had thick, sharp accents that had nothing to do with the lull and marble-mouthed mumble of Florida. They were very Italian and very much from somewhere else, somewhere I had never been. I would close my eyes really tight during those morning fights—Cotton Avenue filled with the scent of tomato sauce and cheese melting and meat grilling—and, before admitting I was awake, pretend I was in New York. I had not yet been to New York, but from a very early age I knew it was a place I was meant to be. For a long time, my only way of being there was by daydreaming about it. Pretending I had New York before I actually did essentially sums up how I've lived my whole life. You can get through a lot of bullshit with that kind of romance.

On the other side of me on Cotton Avenue lived a good friend who roasted coffee beans out of his house to supply to a few local coffee shops. A single, kind, balding, middle-aged man who used to own a coffee shop in town, he had the nickname "Honey Bucket" bequeathed to him from his days in the air force as he apparently had an uneasy stomach, especially on flying machines. The inside of his house consisted solely of a bed and a giant coffee roaster. Eventually, he got a couch where we could get high together while the coffee roasted, drowning out the smell of marijuana that Al surely would've called the cops on us for. Honey Bucket used to be my boss at the coffee shop. He was a good boss and I was a good employee. But, ultimately, he became my friend. A real friend. It counted for something because I didn't have too many of those at that time in my life. My best friends from high school were off being brilliant in Paris or discovering San Francisco and Portland and even finding their way in my New York—because that is what dynamic, smart, artistic teenagers who knew better did after graduation. I'd get letters, postcards, and, finally, emails from them telling me about the things they'd seen, the boys they'd fucked, the girls they'd kissed, the bottles of wine they'd numbered. I read all these love notes while I was shacked up on Cotton Avenue, Al denying me yellow mustard ("garbage") on my sandwich to one side of me, and on the other, a cautionary tale of a kind and loving friend who was ten years older than me who was making the best of things, living in Niceville fucking Florida.

My parents fell in love in Niceville some thirty years earlier, when it was mostly still a small town adjacent to a desolate, romantic coastline with emerald waters and healthy sand dunes. Then, while my father served in the army, we traveled the world together as a family, starting our lives with a collective wild spirit that eventually, for them, quieted. In the middle of my junior year of high school, something urged them back to that place, something that they must have been romanticizing since the day they left it. And so we packed up our dogs and things and left the foothills of north Georgia, a place I had come to love with people I did not want to live without. Niceville was the first town I ever lived in that felt wholly and destructively permanent in my army-brat life, the one that felt like it would never end. No three-year limit to that tour. No reassignment. Just the perpetually oppressive heat. The continuous view of strip malls. The Goo Goo Dolls on repeat in every store I walked into. Britney Spears look-alikes everywhere. The elderly people, bless 'em, just waiting to die by killing time in a Subway sandwich shop with bad lighting while eating a tuna-fish hoagie every day at the same time. The young people who had no interest in leaving the county limits, who spent most of their free time in Kmart buying shit to pile on top of the other shit they bought last week. The constant waft of dirty oil in the air from KFC and the Coffee Shoppe fryers that never got cleaned. The mullet. The mullets. All of it. Forever and ever, amen.

Somehow, my parents' collective fear of all that could go wrong in my life after I graduated convinced me that I should remain in that place, go to a community college, tuck in, take it easy, go slow, avoid mistakes. They have never known what to make of my ambition or, for that matter, my personality. My whole life was a dance between their fear and my eagerness to do all the things I carried in my mind and in my heart. When I applied to the summer dance program at the Tisch School of the Arts at NYU when I was fifteen and still living in Dahlonega, Georgia, at a time when you had to research any and all extracurricular programs at the local small-town library and hand-write an actual letter and rent a video recorder from your high school and buy VHS tapes with your babysitting money to record your-self dancing in your basement to send in for an audition—I did so privately and secretly—my parents balked when I got accepted with a partial scholarship, my mom telling me she wouldn't be alive when I returned and my dad fretting about murder and rape and money and eventually just not talking about it at all, denying it ever happened, leaving me to sit around a country town for an entire summer watching my brother and his best friends skateboard and listen to the same Jane's Addiction album over and over and over again. My whole young life was them being equal parts proud and terrified of and for me—the fear always outweighing the pride, mind you. It was no different when it came to leaving for college.

So I enrolled in a community college and embarked on the most significant period in my life where I proceeded to actively let myself down, denying the voice inside of me that has always read the compass correctly. I knew better. I've always known my potential, always knew I could work hard enough to make everything OK. My parents nervously laughed it off until they realized one day that I was serious about who I was. That it, that I, couldn't be helped. I'd love to say that I gave everyone the middle finger and was a righteous feminist who couldn't be held down from the start. That came later, but not too late. During that small chunk of time, however, I tried to appease. I really cared about doing "right" by everyone, most especially my family. I tried to make sure no one got hurt, even if it meant tempering my spirit. It was the biggest bunch of bullshit I'd ever believe in.

THE POSTCARDS AND LETTERS from my friends stung. Deeply. But most especially the ones from Paris, where two of my best friends were living together for a summer, eating cheese and being wild and trying to love me through the disappointing decisions we all knew I was making. They knew the impact these postcards would have on me, so they sent them en masse, and the effect was not lost on me. I longed for travel. I longed for good food and conversation. I longed to be with people my own age in places I had never been, or at least places that weren't as heartbreaking as Niceville.

I missed Europe, where I had been raised for most of my life—having formative experiences with chocolate and bread and gummy bears, even, seeing bare-breasted women on the beach and in shampoo advertisements, staving off pedophilic Italian men who touched my hair without permission, secretly kissing both translucently blond-haired, blue-eyed boys and dark-skinned, Afroed or box-braided girls, none of whom spoke a lick of English, behind the pommes frites stand at the *schwimmbad*, all of our upper lips reeking of curry ketchup, our skin collectively pruned and tanned from the hours spent under water playing tea party or having handstand competitions in the chlorinated water, wrinkling our tender skin and singeing our eyes until they were red and itchy for hours.

After Germany, after we chiseled away the Berlin Wall with our bare hands and a hammer and my dad had no more wars to fight, the eighties were over and we moved to north Georgia, to that small, backward town called Dahlonega. There I met wildly interesting people who listened to great music, bands like Big Star and early Talking Heads and Velvet Underground and real B-52's (the old, good shit) and took me to see weird shows at no-name places in Atlanta and introduced me to the punk scene in Little Five Points or took me to batshit-crazy insider art shows with drag queens and tap-dancing hillbillies in the middle of crop fields outside of Athens or took me cave spelunking in abandoned mine shafts on their father's cow farm or gave me LSD to take at their parents' biker-gang parties in mountainous creek-side backwoods with the Allman Brothers on full blast from propped-up speakers among the trees and at least ten bonfires going at any given time. I really enjoyed the whole living thing. I was ready to go anywhere and do anything. My wildness had found its way and its place. I was full of it, that thing that you cannot define but that keeps you from sleeping because it is a wild riot in your head day and night.

And then, at seventeen, I was upended, plopped straight into a haze of mediocre suburban malaise and delayed trends and borrowed and sometimes stolen cultures from people and places that actually mattered.

Before things got bad with Phillip, he had been the most interesting person I had met in Niceville. Our courtship included getting up at three a.m. to get to the beach by four a.m., where we would ride two ATVs down forty miles of the Gulf Coast during the sea-turtle nesting season. Phillip was a budding environmental scientist, doing his research on oceanic conservation efforts. We would build fences around the nests to protect the eggs from coyotes and track the gestation period. It was a crapshoot, though. We had to get there before the eggs were ready to hatch and remove the fences so that the baby turtles could make it to the ocean. Once or twice, we not only made it just in the nick of time to make sure the babies weren't hindered by our fences, but in time to watch them make their way to the light. There were times when the fences were useless in the face of clever wildlife and we lost hundreds, maybe thousands, of eggs. His sensitivities were deep, and these kinds of things mattered to him. We took care of a local woman's horses together, a job Phillip had had since he was a young boy. We brushed them and fed them daily and cleaned their stalls every other day. There were stray cats that made a home in the stables and we took care of them, too. I watched my own Sonny being born in that barn, the runt of the litter, dismissed by the five other siblings who had a stronger clamor for the teat than he did, Sonny always being left in the hay, or in my hands, until a nipple would free itself up.

A year after I arrived in Niceville, I graduated, and when the friends that I did make left town, I found it hard to connect with new people. Then, when a potential new friend did pop up, a dark side became known about Phillip, the first sign being the extra deadbolts that were added to the door of the house we occasionally shared on Cotton Avenue. He developed an increasing and alarming need to control my every move, and his insurmountably deep insecurities kept everyone, including his oldest friends, at bay. Folks stop coming by when word gets around a small town that your unhinged boyfriend literally chased after the car as you rode down the street to have a cup of coffee with a person you just met. Or that he stood in the middle of the road to stop a car you had just gotten into to go hiking with someone whom he was certain you were having an affair with—even though that person was a sweet gay boy who only wanted to show you the red-cockaded woodpeckers he was studying and tracking for the Audubon Society. When I had to casually tell a woman to "just floor it" after he had jumped on the hood of her car to stop me from leaving to get lunch one day, I realized that my new normal was not only embarrassing but growing dangerous.

I have a picture of myself in the kitchen on Cotton Avenue, taken the week before I met with Cat Stevens and Stuart Petermann, the day after I decided my tenure with Phillip was definitively over. I'm standing in front of my old two-burner stove making a pie. The pie doesn't look very good. In the picture, it is rolled out into the pie tin, the dough slouching over the edges slack and definitely not cold enough, and definitely not rolled out with any precision. But it overflowed with plums tossed in sugar and, I'm sure, vanilla bean and a little shake of cinnamon, because, even before I had the confidence of a professional, I have always found these things to be the warmest, nicest set of flavors when combined. My figure is slim and I'm barefoot. I'm wiping my hands with a towel and appear to be in the middle of saying something that I think is funny—to whom, I'm not sure. I can't remember who took the picture. But there are stacks of books on the counter and I look happy, despite the actual desperation of the times. It was a ramshackle kitchen and I barely knew what I was doing, in the kitchen or in life. But that kitchen, the one that had little black sugar ants perpetually crawling around the perimeter, which I could never bring myself to kill, was one of the only places where things made sense to me. It was where I found a sense of control over my life that seemed otherwise embedded in other people's troubles and fears. In a kitchen, though, I could try to get everything right. I could rely on just what my hand knew.

I've built a lot on what that girl in the photo knew, and didn't know. There are some constants from those moments that are still in my hands today, in every kitchen I step into, in every class or workshop I teach, in every menu I write. What I know of cooking can't be condensed into a magazine article. It doesn't work. But when I need her, the girl in that photo can still manifest. I'm always relieved to know she's still in there, because the person I was back then, teaching myself to bake despite it all, remembering how watchful I was and how I learned to follow my intuition by way of food—the lesson becomes one bigger than technique.

I will teach you about flour and butter and what to do with them, yes, because learning about those two things will tell you everything you need to know about what makes a good pie. But, more important, understanding what the variables you cannot control might do to them is the true gift of a southern baker. Knowing those two ingredients and how to manipulate them with intuition, by watching and feeling, in the southern heat, the sticky humidity, knowing what the temperature of my hands on any given day might do, started to become second nature to me in that kitchen. Knowing that flour has one duty—to absorb moisture—and that it sitting on the countertop of that open-windowed house could change everything was a key lesson to my later work in a fancy, professional, climate-controlled kitchen. Knowing that butter is made by beating the water out of cream—informing you that you should not "overwork" it, especially on a warm Florida day in a kitchen without air-conditioning, thus releasing more water—and that the more the butter releases its water before it is ready to (in the oven as fast, hot steam), the more your flour will do its job and absorb it all, making your dough tough and chewy instead of flaky and beautiful. You learn, after these moments of dedication, that your dough should look marbled with the sweetest yellow swirls, indicating that your butter is coolly and quickly worked in.

This is practically all you need to know. I've said those words now to many cooks over many years, and I've tried to convey this idea in several recipes in several books that don't even belong to me. But lately, because I don't quite know when everyone got so intimidated by cooking and learning how to make something they love, my answers alongside these technicalities have become something that reminds me of that picture: just play some ELO, drink a bottle of wine, smoke some weed, do whatever your equivalent of letting go is, and enjoy making the goddamn pie. That's it. Think about what tastes good. Think about what you like. Remember how to play. Enjoy the fact that you don't know everything. I'm not being hyperbolic. Read all the cookbooks and follow all the recipes you want, take heed of everything I've said, yes, great, that is practice. But when it comes time to cook, enjoy yourself, for Christ's sake. Let yourself be a person you once were before the world and Instagram and expectation and all the other bullshit crept in. It's food. It's supposed to feed you.

· · ·

THAT PICTURE: I can remember the exact moment it was snapped, despite the fact that I can't recall who was behind the camera. I can remember what I was feeling, what my kitchen smelled like, and which season it was. I can remember vividly that I had a new dent in my left shin and that the night before I had spent a few hours in the emergency room. (Shins are funny in that they are a bone that can withstand an incredible amount of trauma without breaking. The dent will last forever, but otherwise you'll be tip-top, as good as new as soon as the pain stops.) I can remember that the picture was taken the day before I made the decision to finally leave that house, that man, and that town, and started packing up my belongings from the house on Cotton Avenue. That pie would be, I thought, the last thing I baked in that kitchen.

The picture was taken the day after Honey Bucket's surprise birthday breakfast and the subsequent incident that sent me to the hospital. I wanted a grand gesture for him. I had a key to his house, and we (me and a few of his friends from TradeWinds) thought it'd be funny to wake him up really early by sneaking into his bedroom around seven a.m. with a bottle of champagne and shouting "SURPRISE!" startling him, underwear-clad and all, from a dead sleep. He'd be rewarded with a giant spread of cinnamon rolls and quiche and coffee and cake I had made. It was absolutely the kind of thing that I loved planning and I knew he would be a good sport about it. I loved him, and I loved hosting meals and surprising people and finding reasons to bake, so I selfishly wrapped every good thing I could into that morning. We nearly pulled it off. He was good-natured about the surprise, and while he was getting dressed, I realized we had nothing to light his birthday muffins with, so I had to return to my house next door to get some matches.

Phillip was waiting for me inside, angry that I was gone when he had woken up—even though he had been invited—angry that I looked so happy, angry that I was being so flippant about a thing like looking for matches when he clearly wanted to know who I thought I was. He turned all the deadbolts, put the keys in his pocket, and, in true Phillip fashion, said that the others could find their own matches because we had things to talk about. One thing led to another, keys were fought over, and when I went to jump out of the window—sadly, a maneuver I had done a time or two before—he grabbed me and threw me so hard against the futon and the coffee table that my poor shin busted. Though I hadn't realized it, nearly an hour had gone by and a knock came at the door. It was Bucket, looking worried. He came in, I sat on the couch (the one Phillip had just shattered my shin on) and tried to look as casual as I could. Phillip, naturally, explained it all away, handed Bucket some matches, and tried to send him on his way.

I'll never forget the look on Bucket's face as he turned to go, asking me if I wanted to come with him. It was a look I decided I never wanted to see directed toward me again. It was one of deep concern, of pity, of helplessness. I sent Bucket home, said I'd be right over, but never returned. Instead, I sat on that couch trying to figure out what to do with my leg and my life. Phillip did the predictable thing and cried, fell at my feet and begged me for forgiveness. This was our ugly routine. Him trying to possess me entirely and me forever trying to make the best of every situation life presented to me, as if I had no choice. I think on many levels I had been shown only how to play defense, never offense. In my defectively hopeful way, I really thought I could bring out the best of him, of that town, of that potential life. Army brat that I ever will be, I bolstered myself again and again, my dad's voice ringing in my ears, "Happiness is a decision you make, not a location." This mantra was proving to be entirely untrue and ineffective for living and finding the life that I wanted. I felt trapped in other people's darkness, and at that point in my life, I was nothing but light, bright, and determined. I was constantly having to protect what made me different from all those people. It was like they wanted to eat me alive, feed on that light, and I was letting them. It makes me sad to think about that girl. It's the only thing I ache over still. I have no feelings about the other people who were involved back then, truth be told. But her. I feel a sense of loss for her to this day.

Phillip was getting ever darker in his need to control everything in my life and darker in his threats to hurt himself if I left. But the injuries to me, mostly emotional up to that point, were escalating. The complexities of our living situation didn't help. I was afraid that he would fulfill his promise to kill himself if I left—when you're not yet twenty you believe liars like that. I, stupidly, felt that living with him as a friend as we transitioned out of a relationship was the easiest way, but it was proving horrific.

I kept wondering how and when the next flare-up would happen, when the next embarrassing moment would reveal itself to me, and I could not wait to get my shit together enough to get the hell out of there and never look back. My friends had come and gone; several attempts at packing me up and taking me with them proved unsuccessful. The question often gets asked how a woman like me could ever have been with a man or in a situation like that. The likely reality is that most women you know *have* been in a relationship or, at least, a situation like that—with men who are mentally unfit and who think they deserve all of you. A strange looming lack of self-worth, putting myself and my needs last, after every other person in my life, tethered me to him longer than I care to admit.

If I learned anything from being with Phillip, it is, as my dad always said, that happiness is in fact a decision. But sometimes that decision means burning everything you know to the ground and re-setting the scene the way you knew it could be—essentially, getting away from everything and everyone holding you back while you still have your senses about you. Sometimes happiness means walking away from the place you call home and rebuilding from scratch with nothing but your own two hands to rely on. I decided to be happy and then I set out to make it so.

# 3

## A PIVOT

*Wine*

I MADE THREE DOZEN BISCUITS the day I left Stuart Petermann's house and packed them into a metal, vintage bread box (because I was very cute back then). I took them to work, where my second family, the one at the restaurant, waited with a giant rondeau full of pasta and gravy on the stove, ready to eat, and two flats of strawberries, which I quickly trimmed and sliced and sugared with the help of One-Eyed Sam, my dear friend who was the dishwasher every night except Sundays. We were like old ladies, me and Sam, gossiping together, talking shit together, giggling together, and dancing together every night to Etta James. He was someone I trusted, and he was someone with whom I made a lot of staff-meal strawberry shortcakes during the summers.

TradeWinds was an oasis for me. It was run by a man named Tom D'Eufemia. Tom single-handedly introduced me to restaurant culture and everything you might imagine that entailing. I was just a waitress in his trailer restaurant, yet he was fiercely protective of me and taught me everything I know about Italian wine. He knew about finer wines and we drank plenty of them, but he argued that there was not a damn thing wrong with a good, sturdy, not-in-any-particular-way-special bottle of plain old table wine. And that, in fact, in order to really appreciate those nice, fancy things, you should make a habit of drinking the others with just as much reverence so as not to get too ahead of yourself in life. Tom was not a chef, he only liked good things. He was a true bon vivant. He had been a mechanical engineer his entire life, and this restaurant was his retirement gig. He was tall and salt-and-pepper-bearded with a kind of pigeon-toed walk, always with old Sperry Top-Siders that looked like he had worn them every day since the seventies and glasses that sat perched on the tip of his big, beautiful, arched nose. Tom was one of the few folks I opened up to about how my life really was back then—little was said, a thing I appreciated, but much was understood. He had no patience for "that Phillip guy" and would jokingly ask, often, if now was the time that he could get the kitchen boys to "take care of some things." This was my first kitchen family. Tom raised me, gave me my first bottle of Montepulciano to nurse, taught me how to walk across a busy floor and know what every single person in every single seat needed even before they knew they wanted or needed it. Is John Toner, the BMW-riding instructor, fishing around his moto gear looking for his cigar? Fetch an ashtray. Is six-year-old Sammy fussing in his mom's arms because he's tired and his parents are trying to finish their bottle of Sangiovese to celebrate their anniversary? Maybe warm up some milk with sugar and cinnamon for him. Did someone move their food around their plate, not really eating it, for the first five minutes of it being served? "Maybe they want something else, go on and ask 'em, Lis." His was the kind of hospitality that resulted in people forgetting their manners, people forgetting themselves because the feeling was so buoyant that you'd end up laughing ugly with gravy on your face and not even care. I learned what generosity meant and that it had nothing to do with material gifts, that it was a kind of spiritual calling for some of us, that unrequited giving of self.

The food was good, don't get me wrong. But, really, people came to the restaurant because the whole place was an extension of Tom's good and boisterous heart. He was very affectionate toward me and I toward him. We always kissed hello, sometimes on the lips, but in the most familial, unpretentious, sloppy, Italian way. He smoked cigars and made the finest Neapolitan-style pizza I've still ever had from a simple deck oven that he had the trailer retrofitted with. Eventually, he upgraded to a wood-fired oven, and it's a miracle we never burned that double-wide down. At times, he would just sit there, sipping on a singular glass of wine that was never empty—because I took good care to make sure it was always replenished, a small genuflection of respect—sucking on a fat cigar (which were wetter than his kisses), legs crossed lady style with an elbow perched on his knee, the cigar dangling between three fingers, watching the dining room and the kitchen tick and ready for a laugh or a fight at any given time. I learned to be quiet there. I learned that less talk meant more impact. I was young and I'm certain I talked too much and anytime he heard me oversharing with a customer he would tell me in a low whisper, "Listen, Lis, you gotta remember to keep your shit between you and your asshole—especially on my floor," and it's still some of the best advice I've ever been given. He was from Tarrytown, New York, Italian-mouthed and tenderhearted, and didn't hesitate to throw someone out of his restaurant by the scruff of their neck for not acting right. Luckily, we mostly had regular customers who knew the drill—you ordered good wine, you took your time, you were nice to your server (me), and you looked away when loud arguments broke out in the kitchen, no matter how heated it got.

Tom had a temper but only about things he knew in his core were wrong. He lived by a certain code, one that I later realized became embedded in me, too. You do right. You act right. You work hard. You play hard. You treat people with respect. He had no patience or tolerance for people with bad manners. And he really had no patience for cutting corners. He hired a motley crew of derelicts who were otherwise out of place in that town or in the world and we all worked hard for him. We each had an entire soap opera of our own happening outside of that trailer: a twenty-seven-year-old cook on parole after five years in prison; a classically trained but very young chef from Chicago who had come home to be with his parents because his little sister, just a freshman in college, was the victim of a fatal drunk-driving accident; a once-retired grandmother now hostess who had to adopt her junkie daughter's kids and was starting over as a new parent at sixty-five years old with new bills to pay; a dishwasher with only one eye who never told you any of his real stories but who seemed to have lived harder than anyone else in the place; and me, a girl so ashamed of her ambition that she was letting some boy bust up her shins and break her spirit whenever he felt like it.

Sam knew what my life was, too, and he had the good grace not to ask about it. He had a rocks-in-a-tumbler growl to his voice, one that made him sound like he was mad at you all the time. And I think he probably was mad at most people most of the time for lots of good reasons. On that particular day, though, we spoke about my plans, my dreams, and the new apartment I had just put a deposit down on in Tallahassee. I was going to have a place of my own, me and Sonny; I was going to go to a real college with real challenges; and I was going to relish every single moment of getting there. I told Sam that my new apartment had a balcony, one that was high enough for me to see a pretty clock tower from, and he warned me, should I end up missing him too much, not to jump off it. I promised him I would be careful. And that I would call and write often—as I accurately translated that as the only sufficient means he had to tell me he was sad to see me go. He was on a very short list of people I wondered if I could live without.

We were about two hours away from opening and about an hour away from family meal. I still needed to make whipped cream while the strawberries macerated. I got out the cream and tripped over a milk crate, making my wounded shin zing just a bit, jerking me out of my stupor but also serving as a kind of victorious reminder of what my life was no longer going to be. I was in the kind of headspace that encouraged daydreaming and goofy grins that made everyone wonder. I spent the hours at work packing my things on Cotton Avenue and unpacking them in Tallahassee in my mind—what to take, what to leave behind, what to give away to friends, what to burn sacramentally in a colossal bonfire by the ocean to appease whatever gods or ancestors might be keeping track of whatever good fortunes I might have mistakenly taken for granted all those lost years. My days of lamenting my place or my decisions were over. A spark had been reignited, right around when I tried to jump out of the window for the last time. I broke loose from some weird baggage I had been carrying for other people, and I felt lighter and freer than I had in some time. I had vigor, the kind you could taste.

I STARTED WHISKING THE WHIPPED CREAM, two quarts by hand with a whisk the size of my arm. Long strokes at first, then shorter strokes, then longer strokes, then shorter. I had strong arms and wrists and the whisking took very little time back then. It was a small thing, but I made pretty whipped cream, the kind that is soft but firm, lactic and not too sweet, with just a bit of vanilla bean peppered throughout. I was in the zone, a little cream splattered on my glasses, absorbed in the motions, when I felt Tom next to me where Sam had been just ten minutes earlier.

"Hey, listen, your mom is on the office phone. She sounds upset. Do you want to take it?"

I appreciated Tom's forever understanding that no one had to deal in other people's shit unless they wanted to. I liked that he had given me a choice. Did I want to manage my mom right then and there? I had options, according to Tom. Options and choice felt like such a novelty for me, honestly, but suited me just fine at the moment. "Do you want to take it?" made me feel like a grown-up.

But of course I wanted to take it. It was my mother, after all, and I didn't feel much like a grown-up anyway. As it turned out, it wasn't a phone call about her shit. It was a phone call about my shit.

I said, "Yeah, of course, hold the line for me, I'll be back in a minute." I wiped the cream from my hands, handed the whisk to Sam, knowing he was going to overbeat it without even meaning to, and cleaned my glasses with my shirt as I walked back to the office.

The phone was an off-white wall-mounted rotary deal with a very long cord so that Tom could walk around the office and take inventory while he talked long distance with the wine distributors. I turned the corner and grabbed the receiver, which was teetering on top of the dial pad.

My mom did sound distressed, but not at all in the way I had imagined or was accustomed to. I could tell, somehow, even over the phone, that she was flushed, stammering over her greeting to me, not sure if she could be as emotive, whatever emotion she was feeling, as she wanted to be. My mother is seldom measured. Yet here she was, asking me to sit down.

"Mom? You OK? Is Dad OK? What is going on? I don't have time to sit down."

And then she giggled. She actually giggled.

"Mom. I'm at work." I was not amused, and at this point Tom had sat back down at his desk about ten feet from the phone.

"I know, I know, I know, I know," she said really fast. "I just don't know where to start."

"Well, start somewhere," I said, mostly for Tom's benefit. He cared very little that I was on the phone but cared totally that I was in his space.

"Dr. Spellman called with your physical results!" she literally shouted, more nervous than I'd ever heard her before.

I had to get a physical for admission into Florida State University. Blood work, vaccines, all the routine things.

"Here, let me play you the voicemail because . . . well . . . just HOLD ON!" she said, again shouting. Two or three of the longest minutes of my life unfolded then and there while my mother rewound the tape recorder and missed it by two messages and then fast-forwarded and then rewound again.

I held the phone up so I didn't have to hear the excruciating fumbling that was happening on the other end, rolled my eyes toward Tom, and leaned my forehead on the wall, twirling the phone cord between my fingers—a habit I'd had my whole life.

Tom poured me a very full glass of wine and walked out of the office with a laugh.

"OK! Here it is. I'm putting you on speakerphone."

The tape started to play, and it was, indeed, Dr. Spellman.

"Hello, Lisa! Just calling to let you know the results of your physical are TIP-TOP! You're as healthy as they come, no surprises there. And also to say CONGRATULATIONS! Looks like you're going to have a baby! Let's get you in for some prenatal care!"

*Click.* My mom pushed stop on the answering machine.

That click lingered in the air like a goddamn zeppelin that had just exploded.

"You there? Lisa? You still there?"

I was, but I had slid down the wall, my back pressed up against it for stability, and was instantly splayed out on the floor with an overfull glass of wine between my legs and a twenty-foot phone cord dangling from above like a noose. The lights seemed dimmer, my mouth was dry, I couldn't really find my way out of the shock enough to make words.

Immobilized as I was, my brain worked fast. I went straight to denial; he must have mistaken me for someone else, he must have grabbed someone else's piss or blood. But I kept thinking about the ducks from earlier and my achy boobs and the weird sense of smell that nearly kept me up at night and the fact that during our entire apartment-hunting trip, I had made my mom stop four different times at Hardee's for jalapeño poppers. I knew it was true. I knew that those ducks floating over the dark, shitty, storm-churned water were some kind of annoyingly trite foreshadowing from the universe and that I had been in denial even then.

"Lisa? Hello? This is OK. We're OK! You're going to be OK!" my mom said as softly as she could but still with an air of excitement in her voice that I was not ready for. I was grateful for her voice on the other end of the phone, but my knee-jerk reaction was to hang up as quickly as possible. I remembered all the baby clothes she had been stockpiling (in my closet, no less) for years, hoping this moment would come. I loved her, but I resented how much I knew she was likely relishing this moment, especially on the heels of my impending departure, which was most certainly in question now.

"Mom, OK. Yes. I have to go. I'm OK. We'll talk when I get off work. I'm OK."

I stood up, hung up the phone, and felt my face and eyes burn with emotion the way they can only when your body feels pure terror. Before I realized what was going on in the room around me, I felt Tom's hand on my back. I turned around and he knew, he always knew everything, which saved me from having to say more than I wanted. I had no more defenses. I had no more resolve. I fell into his chest, went completely limp, and cried. I cried about twenty years' worth of hot, fierce tears, most of them accumulated over the last four or five. I was angry. I was scared. In an instant, I was back to square one. Tom held me up and did not say a single unnecessary word but only a hushed "Hey, you're OK, silver girl, you're OK."

He called me silver girl when he knew I needed it. It was his pep talk to me. He thought the Simon & Garfunkel song that it came from was melodramatic, and I said that life is sometimes melodramatic, Tom. Sometimes you need a sweepingly overorchestrated song, one that is way over the top, to remind you that everyone is going through the same shit, and hell, Tom, maybe they even have it a little worse. He came to work one day and said, "Fine, I listened to that song again and it's not as bad as I remembered." And for the first time he called me by the name, "Not bad at all, silver girl."

Tom pulled me off his chest, kissed me on my wet cheek, and said, "You ready to get back to work?" because he knew that's what I needed.

I handed him the glass of wine, went out front, and tied on my apron, not knowing then that tucking myself behind that soft canvas and tying those strings double-wrapped around my waist would be the thing that would save me time and time again for the rest of my life. Service was starting. It was time to go.

# 4

## ARRIVAL

*Bitter Chocolate*

THE NURSERY ON COTTON AVENUE that my parents and I put together was full of John Lennon drawings, little yellow crocheted things, and a used crib that Sonny the cat was very fond of. I never made it to my new apartment and I never saw the clock tower from that high balcony ever again.

I kept waiting tables at TradeWinds. Tom changed the smoking policy for me, and he only had to kick out a few guys who refused to put out their cigars while I was on shift. Only one put up a good enough fight that Tom eventually had to grab him by the scruff of his neck and physically throw him out, shouting as he closed the door behind the man who was then lying in the gravel parking lot with white ashy soot all over his cheap suit, "For the last time, Lisa's pregnant, you ugly motherfucker."

I waited tables until I could no longer fit between them, which was happening faster than I had anticipated because I was also baking more than I ever had before. I suppose I was nesting, fluffing the house for a new person and also learning the very important lesson of how to provide for something besides a cat. Phillip's family let me stay in the Blue House throughout my pregnancy even though Phillip had taken a job in Savannah, a position my dad got for him after we learned we'd be tethered to each other in some financially obligatory ways potentially forever. We were not officially "together," but our new roles as parents meant that some accommodations to our relationship had to be considered. And while it might have been riddled with shitty memories, the house provided a simple and beautiful space for me to be alone with myself. In those moments, I baked. I always ended up with enough to feed a whole mess hall full of families. I gave away whatever I could, and the things I could not give away I ate. I was very hungry and very happy to do so. Not surprisingly, once I came to terms with the situation, being pregnant seemed to be right up my alley. My body took shape beautifully and quickly and it felt as if I were a natural at the whole thing. Even on the mornings when I woke up to areolas the size of my face and more hair on my body than ever before, I took utter joy in it all, fascinated by the sheer and pure strangeness of the changes, of the bloom that looked different every day. My body wasn't just made for it the way that women's bodies are "made" for it. My body seemed to be trying to win some kind of fertility award. I was like a goddamn totem of female flourish. Ripe, full, ample. I was mother goddessing all over the place, still in a pair of denim coveralls and sneakers, at that.

BEING PREGNANT FELT like a time to square some things away with myself, to reconcile the time I wasted and actively move forward. It also made me think about my girlhood—about all the things that made me and were also likely to blame for my urges and constant daydreams and wanderlust. Nearly all my memories centered around food and the people who provided it for me—it was a constant reel in my mind and it was full of hyper-real detail and sensory recall that left me literally and figuratively hungry. I remembered the many family trips to Salzburg from our home in Bamberg, where I would eat mostly bread and the beautiful, dense, and rich cakes—flavors that my brother hated and that my parents thought were stodgy but that I thought were incredible. For a kid raised solely on Little Debbie and Hershey's, the taste of a real cocoa-bean chocolate was exotic. Even when it was too dry on the palate, too bitter to the tongue, it felt worthy of my attention. I was excited by it, would push it on anyone traveling with us, and would be disappointed when no one felt as completely enthralled by the new tastes as I was.

One winter, a young GI named Ruiz (everyone was called by their last name in the army, and to this day, I don't know what his given name was) who was traveling with me and my parents, whom I might have had an age-inappropriate crush on, handed me a chocolate from the shop he had just been in, told me to try it, and waited with a sideways grin, laughing and winking when I bit into the pure grain alcohol in the center that tasted of almonds and cherry, new and unknown to me. It was pure wonder and raw fucking life stuff. He thought I would balk and held out his hand and a napkin for me to spit it out, but my eyes only got wider and then teary from the heat of the liquor. Then, in one swift turn, I about-faced and walked into that same store and spent the remainder of my loose pfennigs and marks on four more and ate them as slowly and methodically as I could—trying to determine what those flavors, the pungent fake almond and cherry, were.

I spent the rest of that day keeping count of how many of those chocolates were left in my fanny pack and pressing my chocolate-covered fingers on the glass of every cake case, asking the attendants in my clear German for the name and flavor of each layer.

The only person as excited as I was about it was the gracious and very pretty bakery attendant who allowed me to hold an ingredient inquisition. I held her hostage until she could please tell me not only what every single flavor laid before us in the case was, but also, if you don't mind, dear lady, what the flavor was inside of the chocolate in my fanny pack. I was not shy and not embarrassed about insisting on conversations with strangers. I still remember that woman's friendly face every time I make anything that remotely smells of almond or cherry, because I must have shoved it in her face three or four times before she realized that I was not going to leave until I had answers. She held the bottom of my hand and brought it close to her face, politely smelled the half-eaten chocolate with a bit of a purse to her lips to hide how wretched the experience of a sticky American kid shoving gnawed-on chocolate in her face must have been, and eventually said, *"Mein schatzi, das ist nur kirsch und mandel. Jetzt geh weg."* ("My dear, that's just cherry and almond. Now go away.") And I did.

These were the moments I obsessed over in the early months of my pregnancy. On trips to the library, I would collect every baking and pastry book I could find, every book that had the words "old world" or "bread" or "pastry" in the title or, good god, all three. I'd check out the max limit and hoard them in my house for months, returning to the library only to extend the check-out date or to exchange the ones I had no more use for because I had copied every single recipe that worked, edited with my changes, into a notebook. Mostly it was full of variations of brioche—savory brioche, brioche buns for sandwiches, brioche sweet rolls full of cinnamon or chocolate, brioche plain and simple with just a touch of honey glaze. This habit of obsessing over one thing and tediously recording it in a notebook is one I still have today.

Bernard Clayton Jr.'s books *The Breads of France* and *The Complete Book of Pastry* became the tomes I perched on my earth-size tummy every night when I got into bed. I started to scratch out recipes in the margins and write notes of things to try the next time I cooked for anyone who would let me. His recipes were clear but not uncomplicated, and his writing was clean and economical. He told a good story, but he was also a dedicated technical guardian. My friends would come home from college or travels over the holidays and arrive to a table full of brioche, sourdough, quick breads, and pastry. Clayton quickly became my go-to, even in later years when I wanted to get to the bottom of an old European baking problem. He wrote meticulously about ingredients before it was cool to do so, and he communicated the "why" of things—which I also found, and still find, remarkably refreshing. I discovered him way before I discovered anyone else's food writing, and to this day, I think of him fondly, though I never met him, as a first mentor of sorts.

And so I was going to college full time, working full time, and essentially coming home to an empty house and baking through the night, replacing my old habit of driving off to strange places to sleep in my car with preheating the oven as soon as I walked in the door and baking away after I showered off the spilled wine and food smells from my body. I was getting pretty good at the thing, baking, and the glow I had was more likely from butter than from the baby.

I started to build, for the first time in my life, a cozy relationship with food. I had previously vacillated between anorexia as a postpubescent dancer who could not come to terms with her broad shoulders and curvy hips and, the fear of being too big for dancing aside, the worry that I would end up bedridden by obesity, diabetic and alone with nothing but cats and a singular child to tend to my immovability. This was a nightmarish and dark fairy tale that my mind would often wander toward in quiet moments. Only I knew that I loved eating and making food just about more than anything else. It felt like a secret. I did not yet know what to do with the information that food was a priority for me, as most of my peers were off being skinny and yogic and smoking cigarettes very coolly instead of baking and eating a few thousand calories a week on bread and perfectly salted butter alone. I was definitely not doing yoga with any kind of aerobic results and was certainly not doing anything very coolly. Instead, I embraced all of it. I was not going to hinder this pregnancy with bullshit, I decided. So I cooked. I baked. I ate. And I grew a baby.

My son was born in a military hospital room full of my best girlfriends, my mom, six medical students, three doctors, two nurses, and my dad over the phone long-distance all the way from South Korea with about thirty soldiers listening to me labor on an army radio. "It's a boy!" was shouted, to our surprise, and a great round of applause was started mostly by my friends out of nervousness and relief for what they had just seen my vagina do, but continued all the way to South Korea, where my dad's voice cracked, "A BOY?!" followed by an uproarious round of "HOOAH!! HOOAH!!" from the soldiers over the phone. It was an event that marked the start of the rest of my life. Thank god there was fanfare.

Later that night, I lay alone in the hospital room with my son for the first time. The nurse tried to take him so I could rest, but one of the beautiful things about being so young when you have a child is that you might be weary, but life feels more important than sleep. I just wanted to look at him. I just wanted to smell him. There was nothing, up to this point, that made as much sense as the way he felt in my arms. A nurse had a small radio playing quietly at her station outside my door, Elton John saying things about "Don't have much money, but boy if I did . . ." I cried while he suckled, inducing cramps that were healing my womb, pain upon pain, glory upon glory, still feeling the labor while I held the born baby in my arms, slowly realizing that motherhood is all the painful tangled mess of the body and spirit, perpetually, and you can never again untie the knots. Instead, you feel it, all those feelings, all at once, at every moment, because that is the task at hand, that is the only way to get this right. To believe how everything, every moment leading up to this very second was important in getting you here. It brought you him. So you do your best for him, girl, every single moment you have available for the rest of this life. You are his forever. You are his mother.

I NAMED HIM JOSEPH for Phillip's Grandma Josephine. There were some small, beautiful parts of knowing the family that Phillip came from, and Grandma Jo was one. When people saw pictures of Josephine in her prime, they would literally gasp. She was luminous: dark skin, dark eyes, dark hair, and a perfectly placed beauty mark on the side of her mouth that Hollywood could only fake on their movie stars, strikingly gorgeous in an unequivocal way. By the time I met her, she was in her seventies and wore the same three impeccably tailored cotton blouses, the same three pairs of capri pants in the style of Audrey Hepburn, and the same two pairs of slip-on shoes in rotation.

She drove a modest car and worked every day, seven days a week, at her tailor shop, a trailer situated directly outside the military base that she had outfitted with—behind a curtain so her customers could not invade her privacy—a small cabin bed, a little couch in front of a TV, and a small kitchen with everything she needed in it, including a nearly life-size photo of an apparition of Jesus she swears she saw in person that one time she went to Jerusalem. She lived there after her husband, Eddie, died and seemed content with solitude. She had been through it all, heroically passing fruit and dried meat to American POWs in Japanese camps in the Philippines, getting caught with her hands under the gates, and then hiding in the jungle with her younger siblings strapped to her body so as not to be, literally, murdered for treason.

She was fixed and unafraid of anything by the time I met her. She would not tolerate being underestimated or undervalued. Not for a second. After she left her country, though, after she honed her grit and her fire in the face of real danger, she ended up spending a mighty long time as a new American having to tolerate exactly that. But she had a cinematic way of saying "fuck you" to people who dared underestimate her or mistake her for a fool, without ever using those words. Her whole life was Julia Roberts shouting "BIG MISTAKE" at the Rodeo Drive salesperson with just a posture or a look or a silent burning of a bridge, which she never looked back on, and it was a glorious thing to watch.

I sometimes wondered if Grandma Josephine was the reason I stuck around Phillip for so long—I loved to be around her. I knew that she was manipulative, and I knew she would do whatever she had to do to survive, but I made an agreement with myself that I would never be in a position where she had to treat me with any kind of resolution that was not one of love and care. She exhibited a loyalty to herself and to her expectations that I don't think I had ever encountered before, or, frankly, since. I valued her absolute confidence that she was always right about a person—which, mind you, she absolutely was. Josephine. The woman I named my son after became the remedy to the imposed self-doubt that people like her grandson cultivated. Her grandson seemed to be a similar version of man as her first husband, the one whom she fed through a POW fence and who brought her to the New World but who, ultimately, tried to dismantle the things that were so powerful about her, the things about her that saved his life. And when she came to live with us for a short time on Cotton Avenue after Joseph was born, when we cooked together in that kitchen making sweet coconut rice, baked in a cast-iron skillet like an upside-down cake with a sticky brown-sugar cap, she told me that I should stop being so afraid of making people angry. She said, as we sorted through mung-bean sprouts at my kitchen table to put into vegetarian lumpia for me, that I should stop being afraid in general. That life will bring you what you deserve. Grandma knew who I was. And, despite her love for her grandson, she knew the score.

I TOOK THE SUMMER OFF, just me and Joseph and Sonny on Cotton Avenue breaking in the new life we had started together. And did we ever bask. Joseph and I were lovers of the highest order. It was easy to feel purposeful and it was even easier to feel like there was sunshine permeating everything we did together. I toted him around as if he were simply an extension of myself. I used my hands to work. I planted a garden with him tucked as close to me as the wrap would allow. I poked at my sourdough starters while he nursed. I did not take this new life, either his or mine, for granted. Our lives were delightfully indulgent for a short period of time. I fussed over baking, even more so than before. It seemed that this indulgence in food, the thing I blamed on pregnancy, was actually going to stick.

I studied wild yeast while I bounced him to sleep. I lay on my side at night with a reading lamp clamped to my bed, a cat on my hip, a baby on his back next to me with my nipple in his mouth, and a book in my hand, absorbed in the idea of making and sustaining, joyfully overwhelmed by the idea that it was my job to keep something well fed. Joseph could not eat the bread, of course, but something felt right about warming the house with the smell. I guess I wanted that to be what he remembered, if he remembered anything from that time. I wanted to give him everything, even good smells. I wanted to make the world perfect and good for him, even if only through the idea of a home with a hearth that fed a whole family, not just the two of us and an old cat in a rickety wooden house with an oven older than me. I imagined it, our own house and our own oven one day, for the two of us, and bread from a borrowed oven was the only thing that made it feel real, the only thing that felt like I was getting something right for him. I worked very hard at it so that, maybe one day, it might be true.

I also had a steadfast and determined way of pretentiously wanting to make things very "correct," like most assholes do when they have their first kid. I focused on building our lives as well as I could. Most days, it seemed like the only real choice was what to feed myself and my son. Everything else was a "must." I "must" fill out student loan and grant applications. I "must" attend a dietary seminar so we can keep our food stamps. I "must" finish college so I can be a financially stable single parent. I "must" try to figure out my relationship with my son's biological father sooner rather than later so as not to emotionally damage my child. I "must" stay close to my family so that I will not be completely alone in my efforts. All the "musts," and cooking and being with my son the only chosen reasons for joy. So I did the cooking as beautifully and as sufficiently as possible.

Falling in love with food and my son at the same time was pure goodness and near repayment for what I'd lost. It was beyond frustrating to know who I was and what I was capable of, to know what my intentions had been for my life, and to feel like I was stuck in some strange, slow-moving wheel that I could not find the controls for. I found my control through food. I put my best and most sincere foot forward, and I found a deep sense of worth and value in that place.

I have just one regret. I wish I had been softer to my mom during those days of discovering this love I had. In some ways, I'm sure I hurt

her feelings during that period of becoming a mother myself by essentially eschewing everything she had ever fed us, making dismissive comments about how we never ate a fresh vegetable growing up
(we had only canned potatoes and green beans, truly) or how I would
never buy Little Debbie cakes for my kids. I mean, *how could she?* I
accused her when she would offer what I deemed "trash food" to my
son. It's easy to be unintentionally pretentious when you're so young
and dedicated and, in trying to do what is right, forgetting that your
mom and dad have actual feelings and that they likely did, and are doing, their best regardless of what your ungrateful ass thinks.

Here's the thing, though. When I was a kid, I loved what my mother
fed us. We were the envy of every neighborhood we ever moved into.
We were barely middle class, but we ate better than most families I
knew. My mother was a natural-born hostess, and we were her favorite
guests. Fried bologna finger sandwiches with toothpicks on the sidewalk outside during the summer? Check! Frozen watermelon balls
floating in ice-cold Sprite? Check! Stouffer's French Bread Pepperoni
Pizza cut into sixths and served on a chips-and-dip tray with ranch
dressing in the bowl while my friends and I watched *Labyrinth*? Check!
Oreo cookies dipped in white chocolate bark? Check! Peanut-butter
saltines dipped in regular chocolate bark? Check! Check! Check!

My friends could never believe my luck.

Occasionally, when I was very young, I would open my lunch bag
to find a can of BBQ-flavored Vienna sausages and a short sleeve of
saltine crackers. This typically meant one of two things: that my nana
had been to visit (it was her favorite snack) or that my mom was keen
on me and had splurged at the commissary. Either way, it was more
than the plain Vienna sausages with no saltine crackers or the bologna
sandwiches on yellow-mustard-smeared Bunny Bread that I was accustomed to in my day-to-day *Jem and the Holograms* lunch box. The

BBQ sausages meant something. It meant I had been thought of a little more sweetly that morning or on the day they were bought. I would hold the squat can in my hand for a minute, enjoying the anticipation of it and, indeed, feeling very lucky. I would pop the lid, the sound making a quick vacuumed hiss, and lick it carefully so as not to slice my lip or tongue, a not uncommon casualty in those days as even the peeling of a metal pudding cup lid—a thing you would be crazy not to lick until it was shining clean—would slice through you if you didn't mind its cruelly sharp edges. In the seventies and early eighties, we were mostly so skinny and hungry as a country that you didn't waste a lick of sugar. All the wars that our daddies and their daddies and their daddies fought in taught us that, mouth corner cuts be damned.

This lunch happened only when we were stateside, though. We returned from Germany to southern Georgia nearly every summer during the early 1980s. Those summers were hard on me, and they helped me develop, early on, an affinity for how nice and clean and cool and crisp and sane and normal and pretty and ancient Europe seemed by contrast. Southern Georgia was a haze of red clay, fire ants, warm oysters in old coolers, dead deer strapped to the hoods of trucks, fast food, bare feet, cutoff blue jeans, dirty hair, and dumb redneck boys whom I found myself in one too many fistfights with. The transition took some getting used to, every single time. It created a strange dichotomous tension in me that is at once restrained classicist and utter hooligan. Oddly enough, it is also the one trait I immediately recognize in most of the chefs I know and love.

The trips to southern Georgia were important for my family because it meant my dad was eligible to be an officer. The officers' quarters were the clean, tidy, bigger culs-de-sac on every military base. They had nicer cars parked in their carports, and the kids who lived there all hung out together in school. Humans are funny in that, no matter where you put us, be it the center of a big city or a military base in the middle of nowhere, people corral based on their money, how much "stuff" they have, and their status—and the kids follow their parents' lead. I thought those kids were kind of pretentious assholes and still mostly do. But it was a promising time and one that my parents worked really hard for. It meant that the extremely lean years were soon to be over, and my mom seemed proud that she could splurge on things like casseroles and TV dinners. The consistency with which she fed us was her way of loving us.

Our mealtimes together were something I did not see in a lot of other homes, and every kid was in awe of my break in the middle of a long summer day when my mom would call me in from outside and I would go running. My friends were usually just shoved out the door in the morning with a piece of fruit or a bag of chips, their parents hoping to not see or hear from them until sundown when all of us would run home as the curfew of the streetlights ushered us out of our forts and trees. But me, my name would be shouted right around noon and I would run home to a table set with a bowl of ramen noodles, the orange package that said it was "chicken," a glass of sweet iced tea, and a couple of Chips Ahoy! chocolate chip cookies, slightly toasted in the toaster oven, waiting for me in my mom's kitchen. She had a gift of generosity that had little to do with what she was serving, and she really loved a nicely set table. She gets embarrassed when I talk about the kind of food she used to give us, thinking that I am somehow making fun of it, or of her. I wish she knew that it was the best love I've ever known. It was the calling of my name when I was sweaty and hungry in the woods. It was the napkin folded next to my soup. It was the tea sweetened just right. It was her, above all. The meal was simply the moment in which I got to have her.

Most kids raised in the seventies and eighties were brought up in a world where food was either of convenience or an afterthought. The discrepancy between how much my mom wanted to provide for us and what we could afford meant almost entirely prepackaged foods. My mom will never stop thinking that talking about this is some kind of smear campaign about her role as a mother. But the majority of people born in the seventies will agree, this was simply how nearly an entire country ate in that day and age. Most of us didn't grow up in the countryside with bygone-era grandparents or parents who still knew how to farm or prepare real food picked from the ground. We were not stringing greasy beans up for the season or slicing apples to dry for keeping through the winter. Most if not all of our vegetables came from cans and our meals came from boxes and packages of some sort.

This is less a commentary about who my mother was as a cook, which she actually excels at, and more about who we were as a community of lower-middle-class southerners thrown into a military base camp with one grocery store for every person living within its gates. We thought eating dehydrated potatoes in a box with a fancy French word on it, which we grossly mispronounced (aww graw-tuhn), was getting a leg up on things. It was also, considering the climate of the time, the "contemporary" thing to do and is not too different from current communities of people who live at or below the middle-class line of American life. My mom made sure we ate three square meals every day and that we had a bowl of ice cream every night if we wanted it—even though I do not think we had the kind of money that usually afforded that kind of perk. I truly believe she spent most of our money on food, and she reveled in it. The military families, at least those who lived in the enlisted quarters, were composed primarily of people who were trying to get the hell out of Dodge. Wherever their specific "Dodge" was varied. But, not unlike my parents, the families we were surrounded by were people who did not come from much in the way of opportunity and were trying to build a better life for themselves and their kids. Scrappers marrying scrappers begetting little wild scrappers. We were an outrageous and glorious bunch of wild animals trying to make sense of ourselves in a supposedly civilized world.

THERE IS A STORY IN MY FAMILY, one I can't fully remember, that we used to eat military-issue MREs (Meals Ready to Eat) to get by during my parents' early years as, essentially, kids trying to build a life. My daddy, a freckled, shaggy, strawberry-blond-haired, shy, and sensitive boy with a crooked, snaggletoothed smile who listened to a lot of the Animals and Neil Young and Jackson Browne and who picked at a guitar some, dropped out of high school at the age of seventeen to run off with the woman who would eventually become my mom, a dark-eyed, dark-haired stunner with olive Latina skin, a wicked sense of humor, and great social aptitude. One day, they got into his white Ford Falcon and drove away to Andalusia, Alabama, where it was legal to marry anyone at any age without parental consent, and did the thing. My daddy joined the army straightaway, and when he went to boot camp, my mom tucked into a dilapidated trailer in Valparaiso, Florida, not far from where TradeWinds eventually would be, to wait for him.

The story of "them" before "us" is one I still fantasize about a lot. They both left families that were, by and large, mostly bad for them as human people, and they built an entirely new world—occasionally somewhat recklessly—that eventually made me. I was made of love and determination and passion and grit and dreams. I still see my parents' young hearts even if all the years have complicated them. I still see the two people who wanted more than the lives they were born into and who went out and made the life they wanted, together. When

I wonder about all the goddamn yearnings I have, sometimes wishing they would just sit still, for Christ's sake, I remember it's a genetic defect, or gift, depending on the day.

While I can't recall eating MREs out of necessity (though I do not doubt the story), I do definitely remember waiting for my daddy to come home from "the field"—the nonplace all military children were accustomed to having one of their parents, typically their father in my day and age, exist in for most of their childhoods. I loved when my daddy came home from the field. It was a micro-celebration every time. On his arrival, we would be gifted one MRE for my brother and me to fight over. My daddy would come home with knapsacks on his back, smelly clothes to be laundered, and at least one pair of boots that needed to be polished—a task I loved watching and participating in with all my heart. To this day, the smell of combat-boot polish and my daddy's freshly washed white undershirts (never not smelling of his scent, no matter how many times my mom put them through the machine) are my most formative smells of love.

My mom would kiss him for a long time, and he would do that thing where he would bite his bottom lip and squint his eyes at the sight of her. My brother had a few moments of peace and parental love before my mom outed him for all the bullshit he had pulled while my dad was away. And me, I would just sit back and bask in all three of them, happy just to be there, basically, with my three favorite things on the planet. I was the youngest and always bursting with such an overwhelming enthusiasm for the people I loved that it sometimes left me very quiet and beaming. If an army life imparts one thing to a kid, it is that your immediate kin are the only constants you have. I knew from a very early age that these three humans were all I could count on in this world. I would watch all their moves, their nuanced interactions; sometimes I would count their breaths during a lull in conversation because I liked watching their life, the actual life, inside them. They were the first things I ever fell in love with.

At that point in our family history, I'm certain that the MRE was a diversion, not a necessity. My dad probably used it as a tool to do more than just bite his lip toward my mom, and my brother and I never failed to take the bait. It didn't take us long to rip the impossibly thick, drab-green plastic wrapping off and begin fighting over the brick of brownie that needed to be reconstituted with two and a half table-spoons of water. Often, I would just let my brother divide it all up—never fairly, of course. But he would tell me what I could and could not eat and I usually acquiesced. For me, the novelty of the thing began and ended with the dessert, and I was smart enough to pick my battles with my brother. He was equal parts my protector and my aggressor, as most big brothers are. It seemed important to him to be an author-ity in my life, and so I let him think he was. He's also probably the reason why I am unusually tough on people and am also not wont to suffer a fool. My brother did not suffer a fool, even as a kid. He came out spitting piss and vinegar, with a deeply sensitive heart of gold. It was a weird combination, one that has always complicated his life. He literally taught me how to fight, putting me through daily sparring drills—randomly thrusting his hands up, palms toward me, and I knew immediately I was to practice my punches. I don't know whom I was preparing to fight all those years, but I've got a wicked right hook that has proved useful once or twice. I followed his lead for the first ten years of my life, and he would hold my hand and show me things. We were each other's person and I mostly liked giving him his way.

Once we got down to the Handi Wipe part of the MRE, my acqui-escence ended. There were two Chiclets tucked away in the Handi Wipe package, and they were the only thing we really fought over. Two Chiclets are the minimum number of Chiclets that one should ever put in one's mouth, yet we would have to split them, he declared. I protested; we fought. I declared that one Chiclet in your mouth is such an incredibly monumental letdown and that he had, after all, had the lion's share of the MRE. He tried, as he had every time before, to convince me that I didn't even like Chiclets. I didn't, but I wasn't about to be the sucker who let him have the entire MRE with just half a dried-up brownie in my stomach. And by the time we each had one instantly tasteless Chiclet in our mouth, my dad's boots, fresh from being knocked, were positioned in front of his chair in the living room ready for a polish.

The military ensures that you have a roof over your head, but otherwise, things were, you might say, a little rough around the edges. Some families had nice living-room sets; some had lawn chairs for furniture. Some sleepovers consisted of frozen pizza and real, name-brand Coca-Cola and moms who would blare Anita Baker or Roberta Flack in the morning to wake you up to a table set with three kinds of cereal and cold milk in a glass jug; some sleepovers consisted of hearing your friend's mom roll home at four a.m. with three guys she just met, waking you all up to have some of her leftover sandwich from Subway that had been in her purse since noon and a few Slim Jims from the gas station that she said would help "our" hangover. It was a crapshoot. And we were absolutely accustomed to all of it.

I had several worlds, from the tree house in the woods that rested in the crook of an old oak tree to the community theater that I ran to every day after school, which neither of my parents ever penetrated. I would ride my bike everywhere and, as long as I was home by sundown, no one really cared where I was.

I know everyone waxes poetically about their generation and how it was the best. I don't know if that is true for my generation, a stalwart group of individualists who give a lot of fucks about what is happening around them but zero fucks about the useless conversation that usually surrounds it. But I don't mind saying we—or at least the we I knew— had a childhood that some of our finest qualities as a culture arose out of. We hopped on bikes, put on our Walkmans, and spent our entire childhoods riding to the thing we wanted to do or see. We had Iggy Pop and the Minutemen and early R.E.M. blaring in our ears because, even though we were young, we had tough and wild big brothers to show us good music, and music was nearly, literally, all we had. We had no time to waste on television because that shit was for grown-ups, at least until MTV happened and then we gathered around televisions on rainy days and watched twenty-four hours of music videos to mimic the dance moves because, believe it or not, babies, that used to be all MTV was.

We were weird and geeky and awkward, and we reveled in it. We left the shy kids alone and knew how to include them, mostly, when they needed or wanted to be. Kids who were hearing-impaired and kids who were fully deaf went to our classes because there was no such thing in our world as either "special education" or a "gifted" class. We saw sign language and were required to pick up at least the alphabet and a few polite phrases because it was just what you did, not a novelty. We all went to school together and learned pretty early on that the world was bigger than our own immediate experiences. We watched rocket ships with actual human beings riding inside of them go into outer space as a regular event. We had teachers who believed and dreamed about their own qualities of thought and loved us, really loved us, and, moreover, loved Ray Bradbury and Edgar Allan Poe and Gregory Hines and Georgia O'Keeffe and astronauts and could not wait to tell us all about them with a light in their eyes and a quiver in their voices at the greatness of it all. We knew who the gay kids were, and even though we could never talk about it, we always protected them because some grown-ups and kids were such assholes. We practiced nuclear-bomb drills, our imaginations consumed with them and outer space simultaneously, making us constantly aware of our own mortality with our eyes turned ever upward, yet looking past the place where the bomb might enter the sky, clear toward the places, the planets, the unknown darkness, that we could dream of going to instead. We played on metal and concrete playgrounds, all of us having some kind of broken limb or scraped knee or chipped tooth at any given time. Casts were so prolific back then that we invented new ways to decorate them with different-colored masking tapes and Magic Markers. Kids walked around with headgear and pimples and notes pinned to their shirts from their parents to their teachers. We were the diamonds that came out of an entire century of war, tragedy, freedom fighters, innovation, protests, rock and roll, exploration, and self-discovery as a nation. We were gloriously unhinged and wild and free, the last of a certain kind.

# 5

## HOPE

*Fire*

W HILE I ROMANTICIZED MUCH of my childhood, by the time I was an adult and became a mother, there were definitely holes that felt vast, losses that felt historic, lying between me and the people, the women, I came from. My mother was ever present, but I could not let her in as closely as she wanted to be. I felt protective of myself, but I couldn't quite put my finger on why. Nevertheless, she and so many of the women in my life arrived squarely on time after my son was born, and I was eager to get closer, to build those relationships and find a way to understand things about myself that felt both superimposed (like caustic fear and doubt) and inherent (like ambitious enthusiasm and wildness).

One of those women was my mom's sister, my aunt Rose, who came to stay with me, becoming a nurse and caretaker for a few days—and, more important for me, a family archive I could plunge into. Aunt Rose became a significant connection to the truth of my nana, my maternal grandmother, in that family. I never wanted to make my mom cry, and so asking her was not something I was willing to risk. Breaking her heart was not something I could bring myself to do. So during those nearly twelve days of Joseph's life when Rose stayed with me in Niceville, Florida, I asked her as many questions as I could about my nana as we sat together, me nursing my son, her giving me her undivided attention, under my roof on Cotton Avenue. Rose had never made me feel anything besides beautiful, cherished, and adored—a thing every little girl needs, not from a random person but from a significant woman in her life. Rose was a beautician in the 1970s and early 1980s. She used to cut and curl my hair, paint my nails, let me play with her jewelry, teach me how to wash my face. She inserted herself into my life unlike anyone else—with kindness and a watchful eye, and with pure love and zero expectations.

There had always been a shadow of something, of someone, in my mother's family and in my own. And there was a big part of me that wanted answers about the guilt I felt for wanting more, an explanation for the outward lack of expectations for my life to be more than a wife and a daughter and a mother, answers to why I had let someone like Phillip in at all, much less given him enough space to make a child with him. For the first time, I really wanted to sit with some of the residual darkness that lingered from the loss and shame that the women in my family carried with them like totems, like a dowry, and me, seemingly the only recipient who did not want anything to do with it. If having a child gave me some kind of permission to enter, to ask questions I was never allowed to ask before, to demand answers, I realized it was my duty to do so.

MY NANA'S HANDS were nearly the same size as mine were when I was a child. The thing I remember most about them, her hands, was the crepelike softness of the skin that reached from the top of her wrists to the tips of her fingers. I used to spend a lot of time telling her how beautiful I thought her skin felt and how the almost-mother-of-pearl sheen of that crepey skin reminded me of a pretty silk scarf that I remember a neighbor lady wearing around her neck once. (I remember that scarf so distinctly because that nice lady let me touch it, and when I would not stop, she took it off and let me wear it while we both waited for my mom to come home one afternoon on Sergeant's Court in Fort Benning, Georgia.) I used to love to run my fingertips on my nana's skin, loved to kiss her hands, her soft skin to my soft lips, and sometimes I would just rub my lips on the back of her hand like a little weirdo. But she didn't care. This small, simple affection was something my nana basked in—it was a kind of love she recognized in herself, one that she offered and allowed and provided.

The first time I remember noticing her hands was one afternoon at my aunt's house. My nana made tortillas on a cast-iron skillet. I believe it was the first and only time I ever saw this happening. I remember noticing her hands as she used Saran wrap, sprinkled with water, a heavy hardcover book, and a glass tumbler as a rolling pin. She would mound the masa in her palm, place it between the plastic wrap, and press it with the book. After that, she would flatten it by rolling the glass tumbler over it, then, removing it from the plastic, she would slap it back and forth between her hands to finish shaping it, and then she would slap it onto the hot skillet. I can remember the smell of that tortilla cooking as deeply as I can remember the way her skin smelled in bed after she washed with Pond's cold cream at night. Unfortunately, I had decided at that age that I hated corn tortillas and cannot recall ever tasting one that she made. I only remember eating her flour tortillas made from flour and leftover bacon grease, which were my favorite to eat with everything, but most especially with butter smeared evenly on the tortilla while it was still warm along with a small pinch of salt. But the smell of that masa in a small kitchen in Kissimmee, Florida, from that day is one that still lives inside me, as if it were my own blood recognizing something out in the world that became richer and thicker for the experience of it in that moment.

She was my favorite part of childhood, my nana. Her father was a Mexican carpenter from Guadalajara, Jalisco, and her mother was a native woman from the Zuni tribe in New Mexico. She spoke to me in Spanish while we fell asleep at night in the canopy bed that we shared so many times when I was a young girl that I often felt scared when she wasn't there. She was the one who taught me to pray every night before I fell asleep to Jesus's mother for everyone I knew, starting with my immediate family and moving my way out into the world until I ran out of people and dogs and cats and strangers to mention. My nana picked out my first communion dress, sewed a medal of my favorite saint (Francis) into its hem, and fastened my veil onto my tiara. She hid many things in the seams of my clothes and she sewed tiny pockets into my pillowcase so that I could store treasures next to my head at night. The pocket in my pillowcase, the one she embroidered with bright, colorful flowers and cursive letters that read "Sweet Dreams, Lisa Marie," was specifically sewn on to hold my glow-in-the-dark palm-size statue of the Virgin Mary, which I used to clutch so hard and pray so many prayers to until I fell asleep that some mornings my hands would be nearly atrophied around it, bright red and sweaty and stuck in place, as if I were holding on for dear life.

My nana dropped out of school in the sixth grade. She had to pick lettuce rather than learn math or poetry or writing after her family left the small village situated just outside the Zuni reservation in New Mexico where she had been born and moved to California. She had to work to help keep her family fed. Education was a privilege. By the age of eleven, she was simply a farm worker and no questions were asked. Despite that, she had the most beautiful handwriting, which I can remember her practicing on the backs of used envelopes as we sat at her dining-room table in Live Oak, Florida, when I was a girl. The table was always full of hot sauces, ashtrays, toothpicks, pepper vinegar, and her tossed-aside envelopes with everyone's names practiced in cursive over and over. She worked hard to hide the fact that she did not have an education above the sixth grade. Our lives were full of these small secrets, all hiding her shame and embarrassment about where she came from, where we all came from.

I only learned this fact, the one about her lack of education, when I was the tender age of forty. My mother cried when she told me, hesitating because she had likely been told her whole life to never talk about it, her mother's shame, to never give proof of how poor and choiceless life had been for my nana, to never acknowledge how hard she had had to fight just to get a little of the life she knew she wanted and how little she had to settle for, convincing herself that she wasn't worth much more than what she got. When my mother told me that her mother was not allowed to go to school past the sixth grade, so much was revealed to me. I started to understand why I had corralled my feelings about my mother's family into a specific, and very protected, space in my life—a space I wasn't willing to dive into, one that I had to identify as that very "emotionally intelligent" and "spiritually important" place of "having boundaries." We carry one another's pain so deeply, the women in my family. It is like an extra organ, a broken chamber of our hearts that none of us knows how to make work, blocking the normal things that other people's hearts do. The reason I felt so far from my own mother was because I was not willing to keep telling those lies. I wanted truth. I wanted their truth. I wanted my own truth. I didn't want boundaries. I wanted things to be revealed. I had always wanted that. It was so hard to find that truth after all the time they spent burying it.

My nana was raised on a reservation out west by her brown parents whom she was not allowed to be proud of, whom we did not know growing up, whom we did not see pictures of, whose food we hardly ate, whose language we never spoke. I was raised by a mother and an aunt who were told by their own father, in angry, sharp tones, that they were "stupid" and who learned that love came with a lot of shame and an overwhelming responsibility to loathe every part of what we are made of. Hearing your mother being called "stupid" repeatedly by her own father is a scar, a deep scar, that a little girl will never know how to mend, even when she is a grown woman pretending that she has it figured out.

With all the pain my nana carried—obvious to me now as an adult with some experience in the world—one thing was unmissable about her, an anthem she spent her whole life writing and rewriting and projecting as loudly as she could and one she passed along to her own daughters: she lived for her children.

My nana was the foundation of so many things in my life, including a belief that someone is watching you at all times, usually a dead ancestor whom you shouldn't disappoint or embarrass. This is a notion that, even at my age today and as nonreligious as I am, I can't shake. Red cardinals swoop by or sit next to me for long minutes on my front porch and I know it's someone with a message. A hawk waits for me on the hood of my car after a hike and I know there is an answer or a warning somewhere in its presence. My dreams are filled with their voices. I expect my ancestors to be watching. I talk to them and feel fear when I do not feel them near me. When I do not feel my nana near me.

Her deep and nearly mystical relationship with Catholicism was unyielding. Holy water, thumbs blessing my forehead every time I so much as walked out the door to get the mail. Hell, I wore a woolen scapular with four stations of the cross on each side under my clothes as if I were a monk my entire fifth-grade year (not surprisingly, the same year she died). My family is the kind of Catholic that is different from other Catholics I've known. If you're Irish Catholic, like my husband, you understand the difference as immediately as I do. For them, drinking seems to be the replacement for mysticism, for the belief in spooky fear. It's sanctioned and encouraged to drink away the guilt and pain and sadness rather than wail or cling to your statues until your hands are damn near bloodied. I've been to Irish Catholic funerals. There is no better party around. Except for Irish Catholic weddings.

But not us. We are of Mexican traditions. My uncles usually drank at weddings and funerals, sure; that might be where the Venn diagram of all Catholicism intersects. How it played out was markedly different, however. For my family, invariably, lots of crying or shouting or fistfights would break out between them or, as happened at my uncle's funeral, a beloved dog was dragged out to the swamp and shot as revenge for something that had happened decades earlier. The women would sit around the table and talk about the past as if it were all we had, no future in store for anyone. They'd flagellate themselves with old pain, making sure to reopen the wounds of every person around them.

My nana died when I was ten. There were no more daily baptisms. There were no more medals sewn into my clothes. The chaos of my family only grew in her absence. But at ten years old, all I noticed was that a magic had died. There were no more whispers in Spanish of dreams and wishes into my ear as we lay in bed together at night. There were no more reasons to pray.

I spent most of the years after my nana died wondering. Wondering why we were all so incapable of rising from her ashes. I wanted to understand my grandparents' markedly fucked-up marriage, one that ended in my grandfather avoiding her during the final tragic and painful year of her life, her dying in a makeshift hospice room built out of Rose's garage and him living with another woman who would become his wife only three months after we buried my grandmother's body.

I still dutifully loved my grandfather, as my mother did. For years, most of what I felt from the women in my family was that pain, though, a pain that encouraged hiding, a pain that, yes, seemingly came from my grandfather, a mean and angry philandering man who slept with my nana's own sister a mere month after their wedding and who definitely had women from Vietnam to Florida under the spell of his handsome Elvis Presley–like Tupelo-Mississippi-country-boy sneer. But it was also a pain that was supported and encouraged by the country that my nana was desperately trying to succeed in, the one that allowed her to only pick lettuce at eleven years old, the one that, even in her adult years, had little regard for women in general, but most especially brown women with a Spanish tongue, except for how they could be of use to men. A great burial began with my nana. A great undoing unfolded then.

Somewhere in my childhood, I was told that the family records belonging to my nana had all been burned. Baptism records. Birth certificates. Marriage certificates. Intentionally. This is something that is argued among my aunts and uncles, but the jarring lack of information I have been able to gather about my mother's family is all the proof I need to believe it to be true. It seemed that the estimation was that it was better to be invisible than to not be white, or "American." The best chance you could give your kids was to erase the parts that had no capacity to thrive, the dark parts, the non-TV-dinner-picket-fence-Sunday-dress-tip-your-hat-to-the-neighbor parts, the parts that were not allowed to go beyond a sixth-grade education, the parts that spoke Spanish, the parts that looked different or sounded different, the parts that married a white man from Mississippi to make a better and whiter life no matter how badly he treated you, the parts that had been scrubbed out of my life like a stain. What replaced all of that was a kind of shame that has no face, a kind of small yet persistent madness in my mother's family that I never wanted to be around, never wanted to understand, until the burdens of not knowing broke my heart too much.

Everyone talked about everyone behind everyone's back and made fun of each other to their faces, and everyone assumed the worst of one another—but most especially of Aunt Rose. It was a painful thing to experience as a child, to hear people I loved so much talk about one another so (to put it plainly) meanly. But they came by it honestly, I supposed.

My grandfather spoke about everyone with such painful loathing that it became a primary language of sorts. For every sweet moment I forged with him, brushing his hair for a quarter or a dime in front of the TV at night, mimicking the acquiescence I saw the other women in my family give, there were half a dozen times I was met with loathsome disregard. I was often screamed at with pure and raw hatred for small infractions, like sticking my little finger in the jar of peanut butter when I was six. Each time, my mom just sat there acting like it was normal. And I suppose it was normal for her. Those moments were when I started having my first feelings of resentment toward her for letting someone treat me that way. I realized later, many years later, that she had been too scared to speak up, too conditioned to know that it wasn't normal or right. When I had to face my grandfather as a knocked-up college kid during a family reunion, his response was,

"Well, not surprised—your mom did such a terrible job of raising you that the only thing I *am* surprised about is that it didn't happen sooner." By then, I had categorized him properly in my head and he no longer had access to my heart. But watching him with my mother was hard, and I could never bear to hear him shout at her about what a bad mom and wife she was and how she had raised two "stupid" kids, but of course she did because she was "stupid," too.

My brother, David, went his own way, as fast as he could, and eventually he made all the men in the family proud by becoming a Black Hawk helicopter pilot. But before that he was invisible to my grandfather, an embarrassment, and my mom would get the brunt of the insults about what a terrible job she had done with both of us. While I was "in trouble," my brother was living the life of a bass player, making money as a bicycle repair guy and a bike messenger in San Diego. He was in a punk band, recorded an indie record or two, and had a body full of tattoos. He would send me mixtapes of music from California, knew all the best new bands that would reach the South's earshot only long after they had done all their best work and were too commercial to really be appreciated. I learned about the White Stripes because my brother once walked into a shitty bar in Los Angeles in 1998 and saw two drunk, scrappy musicians playing to a small crowd, and he called from the bar just to tell me how good they were. I thought he was the coolest because he was. My grandfather thought he was a failure, until he finally did the thing they could all understand: become a soldier.

My brother has his own baggage from the damage that men like my grandfather wielded with such reckless abandon. Men aren't exempt from how harmfully toxic other men can be. In fact, guys like my brother, who has a heart far more tender than mine, probably feel it much more darkly and deeply and have nowhere for it to go. I wonder often if my brother flies those helicopters so that the men in his life will finally love and recognize him. I wonder, if my grandfather had asked him just once about his music, about bicycles, about women and sunshine in Southern California, what could have been. I wonder that quite a lot. But we all managed it, we all dealt with it, as if the pain my grandfather was doling out was our birthright. No questions asked. Allowances made forever until we were all so choked with it that we couldn't even sit in a room together without nearly spontaneously combusting.

My grandfather's attitude and meanness were always done with an air of joking, so we romanticized him as some throwback Archie Bunker character—this softened the blow for us all, I think, hoping to god he was kidding about how much he seemed to hate us all, hoping to god we weren't really as small as he made us feel when we were around him. My mother was and is generously dutiful to her father, which I understand and respect and honor. But fucking Aunt Rose? Nope. She also was dutiful. But she never went down without a fight. If I had to try to figure out why I bonded so distinctly with her, this might be the reason.

Though my grandpa raised her, Aunt Rose was not his biological daughter. She was my nana's firstborn, out of wedlock (tradition!), and the eldest of my mom and my uncles. When my nana married my grandfather, he adopted Rose. He raised her as his own, so much so that I was an adult before I learned that Rose was not his actual child. After my nana died, though, that thread dissolved and I watched my aunt be made to feel more and more like the loose cannon, the one in the family whom no one knew how to manage. She was undoubtedly the outsider of the bunch—no biological imperative to be blind to the thing I could never make sense of. She was the only person who ever stood up to my grandfather—to anyone, really—on my behalf. When I

picture her, I see her with her chest billowed, her long, perfectly manicured finger pointing, and a hiss of "Dontchootalktomyniecethat-
way!" with a sharp tonality and a punctuated power that she had
cultivated from years of learning how to protect herself from the madness she spent her lifetime trying to deny. She was on guard. And I
was grateful. She never, not once, let a mean word get said about me
or about her own kids in my grandfather's presence. She resisted. She
fought back with a mark of fearlessness that I honor—because I know
she was not, in fact, without fear. But she wasn't going to let him decide what her life, or any of our lives, was worth.

WHEN AUNT ROSE STAYED WITH ME and helped care for my son,
I learned many stories about the deep trauma of their childhoods—the
life that my mom ran away to Andalusia to escape. Aunt Rose started
talking about the abuse, the affairs, the other family that potentially
existed overseas somewhere. She told me about the time my nana
apparently found letters written to my grandfather from the other
woman in Vietnam, and worse: the knots tied in the inseams of all my
grandfather's military uniforms after he arrived home from a long
tour of duty, assumed to have been put there by the woman who wrote
the letters. This was a symbol deeply understood from one mystical
brown woman to another. Whoever this woman was, this man, my
grandpa, belonged to her, and she was letting my nana know. And that
meant war.

My mom and my aunt apparently came home from school one day
to find their mother, my nana, on the front lawn standing next to a
bonfire nearly as tall as she was, built from all my grandpa's clothes
and the other woman's letters, throwing lit match after lit match into

the flames to make sure the fire did not go out. They walked by without her even noticing them, the flames shadowing her face and flickering a kind of crazy look in her eye that Aunt Rose said they had never seen before.

Aunt Rose and I had a lot of long, late-night talks when I was a new mother. And even though in the context of my time, becoming a mother at twenty-two was seen as early in one's life, it was not unusual to her or to my own mother. They had both been married and were well on their way to having their second children by the time they were that age. There seemed to be something markedly different about the world I expected for myself compared to the lives they ever would have imagined for themselves, much less have had the capacity to want. They were not young revolutionaries in the age of revolutionaries. For my women of that generation, doing what was expected of you, doing what your own mother did but hopefully a little better, was the best you could hope for. The best way they could advance their lives, to be revolutionary in their own subversive way, was by marrying men who were kind and good, which they did, and to try to raise women who had more self-worth than they could muster, which, no matter how bumpy this made life for me and my mom, they did.

I wish I had learned all of this during that week, that year, back then. Instead, I spent a lot of time angry about what I saw as some kind of historical pattern I had followed, expecting less for myself than I knew I deserved. I was pissed that baby clothes had been hung in my closet, that my aspirations had been mocked, that I had been made to feel selfish for having big ideas, and that, without meaning to, I had followed through the way they wanted. I was angry that my women had not pushed me with all their might out of that bullshit arena of low expectations and fear. I wanted someone to blame. Why didn't they love me enough to want more for me? It would take me many more years to get there, to embrace how much compassion my women deserved, to really see that I was the only one who could do this thing, this work of creating a bigger space for myself, even if facing the truth of it all might cost me everything.

# 6

## PILLARS
## AND POSTS

*Salt and Clay*

AUGUST ROLLED AROUND after Joseph's and my luxurious first summer together, and classes were starting. I had three semesters to go, and I was more determined than ever. Financially (or logistically, as I was now another person's main food source), day care made little to no sense. I had a very snug black carrier, which was basically just a cloth swatch that went around my shoulder like a beauty-queen sash. Joseph fit quite comfortably inside, either lying down to sleep or to nurse, or sitting up with just enough support to see what was going on around him. It was not a problem for me or for most people. But I could acknowledge it might present some issues when I returned to class with him in tow. This was people's education. I understood. I wasn't trying to be a dick. I just needed to get this done.

I signed up for one advanced religions class where we would be doing a close reading of the Dead Sea Scrolls and the preexisting Gospels to try to find an exegetical explanation—an X-Gospel, as the academics called it—of the New Testament. It was a lecture class with a professor whom I knew was willing to let me sneak a quiet, perfectly timed napping baby into the back of his lecture hall, close to the door in case I had to make a hasty exit. I had originally been a Religion & Philosophy major with every intention of going to graduate school for art history and technical museum studies, becoming a well-heeled egghead academic who could potentially get whisked away for far-away projects, digging in dirt and writing about, restoring, and studying relics. I wanted to handle objects that other people, people who lived thousands of years ago, had handled. It was the stories I was wrapped up in, though, not the objects. I could sit and stare at an ancient vessel for hours, just imagining who made it, who held it, who drank from it. It was always the stories I was hungry for.

With a baby in tow, no partner by my side, I spent hours looking over my transcripts to chart the fastest course to a degree and a job with some security and benefits for my son and myself. My old high school art teacher, a bright and wonderful woman who cared about her students quite a lot, kept tabs on me and hinted that she would love to help me become an art teacher. I had more art credits than anything else, and a BFA would take me an entire semester less than my original plan. So I changed my major—deciding that a BFA could still get me back to my original plan one day, maybe when Joseph was older—and signed up for two studio classes, one advanced sculpture and one clay hand-building class with a professor whose name I did not recognize. I took all the right precautions and planned feeding times and nap times and all the cursory times that go along with taking a five-month-old baby into a two-hour college class. Joseph was asleep, his fat cheeks just poking out of the discreet carrier, when I walked into my first studio class in over a year. I knew that I could focus mainly on found objects, clay and paper, avoiding any large equipment. I did not know this new professor, and which direction this was going to go in was entirely in his hands. So I was optimistic, but aware that it might be best not to make any real plans at that point.

There were people in the studio when I showed up to class early, and I assumed that I was the last one to arrive. Advanced studio classes typically have eight to ten people max, and there were already approximately that many people clamoring about in the room. It was hard for me to discern if the professor was there yet. Everyone looked around the same age except for an elderly woman named Peggy, in her nineties, whom I knew to be a nonmatriculating student who frequently audited classes to gain access to the equipment. She was a force, that Peggy, often making bizarre sculptures out of her husband's used pill bottles, one time years prior melting them into vague shapes of people and dangling them from a bed frame hoisted from the ceiling. "It's called 'Lots of People Upside Downy-ville'!" she exclaimed the day she had presented it to our class. I was definitely relieved to see her now, and my eyes lit up to hear her voice.

She rushed over to hug me and stopped just in time. "OH! You have the baby ON you! Oh, blessed be!" Everything was mostly an exclamation for Peggy, and I enjoyed it, her enthusiasm that bordered on mania. We caught up for a few moments until I noticed a looming figure behind her. When she noticed my eyes distractedly looking past her, she turned around and shouted, "OH, LISA! It's our new professor! You're going to LOVE HIM!"

We stood there, face-to-face, and he looked at me and then looked at Joseph and then looked at me again.

"Can I help you?"

"Yesssssss," I said, stammering a bit as I pulled the schedule out of my pocket so I could remember his name and introduce myself. "Are you, uhmmmmm, hold on a second, um, John Donovan?"

He was a young and not entirely unattractive guy. I was surprised by him.

"Yes. Can I help you? Are you in this class?"

"Yes, hi, I'm Lisa Rierson." I decided to aim for delightfully belligerent confidence. "Where would you like me to sit, anywhere in particular?"

"Well. I guess I'm a bit confused why you're here, you seem unprepared."

"Nope. Perfectly prepared. It's nice to meet you and if you'll just direct me to my seat, I'll stop delaying your class."

"But you have a baby there." He was being belligerent himself, but with far more authority and less delightfulness. "And this is a sculpture class. I don't think you're in the right place."

He started to walk away from me, as if it were decided that it was time for me to go.

I understood his position, but this dismissal sent me to a place, probably a place close to panic, where I found myself trying to temper the tone of my own voice, a voice that was becoming more disagreeable and sharper by the second. And, regardless of the fact that I definitely should have had this conversation with him, like an adult, prior to my arrival, in the flash of that second I changed my mind about him, out of some very real fear and frustration and, admittedly, immaturity. Defensively, I decided he was probably older than I imagined. And funny-looking, yeah, that was more accurate, I thought. And was he wearing Birkenstocks? With socks? I mean, fuck off, buddy.

Do I become an insufferable bitch if you threaten to get in my way when the stakes are high? It was a new one for me but, apparently, yes.

However, I was going to play nice so as not to get any further on the wrong side of this weird, flannel-wearing, goatee-clad guy who probably had never had a single thing go wrong in his whole privileged male life. I had him sized up. I had his number, I thought, letting myself get heated again. I was surprised by how much I really did have to steady myself. I had gotten unusually worked up in a very short amount of time. I tried to calm down because, ultimately, I was the asshole in the room with a baby. I took a deep breath and tried to plead my case with as much respect as possible.

"Listen, yes," I stammered, without missing a single soft bounce to keep Joseph from waking up while I spoke, "I understand it's not standard and that this class will likely present some challenges, but they will be my challenges and no one else's. I promise."

I had practiced that exact line in the car mirror should I need it. I was proud and surprised by the way it was just sitting there at the ready at the right time, the words knowing the exact moment to fall out of my mouth.

"But we are WELDING in this class! Do you even know what you signed up for? Do you understand that this is not acceptable for what we will be doing in this class?" he quietly shouted.

I cleared my throat and felt the indignation rise up, an indignation that I know I can't swallow when I'm faced with something or someone who underestimates me, especially a stranger assuming, and accusing me of, something as offensive as heedlessness.

"Do I understand? Let me tell you what I understand." I leaned in a little closer to him, still maintaining that slow, rhythmic bounce. "I understand that I have to take this class to graduate. I also understand that I have a baby who needs to be with me most hours of the day to eat. I further understand that this might not be what you are accustomed to, but that does not mean it is not possible. Do you understand what is going on here, or are you just the one obstacle that is going to get in my way after I have come this far to keep my shit together?"

"But, WELDING?!"

He was incredulous.

I tried to soften my shoulders.

"OK, listen. How about this: until it's an actual distraction for you, we don't talk about it again? Or we can take it to the dean right now and have a conversation about how this institution isn't interested in the success of its students."

I was being terrible. But I was not about to be shut down. I had wasted enough time in my life on clueless boys getting in my way, and this motherfucker was not about to whine about welding to me. Welding? I wanted to shout, "OH, welding? Like how my asshole WELDED itself back to my VAGINA hole after squeezing a nine-pound baby out of it five months ago?! YOU HAVE NO IDEA WHAT I'M CAPABLE OF, MOTHERFUCKER!"

But I did not.

We just stared at each other for a moment until the silence was broken.

"OH, FOR PETE'S SAKE, can we get started?!" Peggy shouted from across the room, much to my relief. "SOME OF US ARE LITERALLY DYING HERE!"

We stood there staring for another moment.

He made my pulse race and I did not like how quickly he made me generate heat. He was sizing me up, messy bun atop my head, same hairy armpits, same denim coveralls covered in paint, a baby hanging from me, my nostrils flaring from all the things I was not allowing myself to say. I could tell he didn't like the cut of my jib, either. At least we agreed on that, I thought. His trimmed goatee around a plump face that probably ate Wendy's twice a day and his boring, baggy jeans that were made for a man twice his size, his lack of a single good argument or solution in the face of an actual challenge, his very expensive flannel shirt that was the dead giveaway that he was some rich kid fresh out of graduate school. He got under my skin. Oddly, quickly. And it was strange how much I immediately cared about what he thought of me, despite my best defenses. No one had elicited that kind of response from me in a long time, maybe ever. He threatened me in ways I was unfamiliar with. I was bound to make it work, though. And, at that point, I became determined to prove him wrong.

Class proceeded. Joseph slept through it all on the first day. Eventually and slowly, John and I became better acquainted with each other and maybe even considered each other friends. Joseph was occasionally awake for some of the classes, but he was quiet and nondisruptive and, when we welded, Peggy and I took turns taking him for walks outside. When I signed up for a second semester of his class in the spring, that John Donovan guy offered an incredible olive branch on the first day of the new semester and brought some of his nephew's old wooden tools for Joseph, who was then embarking on his first birthday. "Here! Now he can pretend he's sculpting, too!"

I had been wrong about people before, but not in this way. I usually overestimated their good graces and character and was let down. With John Donovan, I was faced with a person whom I had no idea how to manage. He was not so easy. He was smart. He talked about art in a way that I was starved for. His whole face lit up when he talked about clay, when he talked about artists whom he admired. He was enthusiastic and bright. And, despite our intense first meeting, he was also very, very kind. For the first few months of our acquaintance, we had no idea what to do with each other. He challenged everything I thought I had under control and I think the same was true for him regarding me and the seeming gust of fervor and focused insanity that I carried with me at all times, everywhere I went. Neither of us was wrong about the other, oddly enough. We were both just incapable of understanding at that point in our lives that, in fact, those are the kinds of relationships that you should put squarely on the front burner of your life. All my burners were full, though. I was not interested in making the kind of room that he might require, I told myself.

Still, I found myself thinking of him when I was off campus, wondering what his opinion would be of books I was reading or paintings I was completing. I found myself leaning my ear into people's southern drawls, a thing I had never appreciated until I met John Donovan but now longed for, as his was sweet and slow and thoughtful. I caught myself staring at his hands one day in class, watched them move, wondered how soft they might be, enjoyed how deliberate they were when they worked. They seemed so capable.

When my oldest best friend came down from Asheville to help me with Joseph and life for a couple of weeks while I took my finals, she noticed immediately how frequently I spoke of him. I had no capacity to think of romance at that point, my life was not built for that, and besides, I was protecting myself from so many things, primarily from intimacy, which had not worked out so well for me up to that point. But I felt something deeply for him. He made me laugh. He made me think. He inspired me. I urged my friend, a woman I have known since I was twelve, to meet him before she went back to North Carolina. "I can't tell you why I want you to meet him, he's probably no big deal, he just feels really important to me" were my exact words to her. I did not know then that that was what falling in love felt like.

# 7

## COMING AND GOING

*Water*

THE SPRING WAS WINDING into summer, and I had been on the receiving end of a lot of pressured conversations about my "duty to build a better relationship" with Phillip. I had one more semester to finish my BFA and I was determined. Phillip's family, in a power move, convinced Grandma Jo that the house on Cotton Avenue was no longer available to me. Somehow, I had found myself opposite her—that vulnerable place I had promised myself to never occupy. She did love me, and she did offer real, honest, and sincere friendship. To a point. She still wanted what she wanted, and in her own way, she was not beneath siding with her family, despite their shortcomings and our long talks over my dining-room table.

I had resisted Phillip and all his advances—he was merely a visiting father to Joseph when he traveled from Savannah once or twice a month. He was not a bad father; he was dutiful and clearly loved the boy we had made together. I am hard pressed to say he was a "good" father, though, because being an actual good parent requires a selflessness and a deeper sense of maturity than, sadly, he was capable of. For every good moment he shared with my son, there were half a dozen humiliating experiences bordering on dangerous that unfolded around us as we tried to make sense of who he and I might be as parents together. I was still sorting through what my actual obligations were to this person and how to manage them.

Even so, in the summer of 2001, I found myself packing the house on Cotton Avenue into a small U-Haul to make my way to Savannah to spend a couple of months giving Joseph the supposedly important experience of having both of his parents under one roof. I strapped a fourteen-month-old Joseph into his car seat, put Sonny in the passenger seat, slid Joni Mitchell's *Don Juan's Reckless Daughter* CD into the deck, and headed east toward Georgia, feeling all the while like a planet slipping out of her proper orbit toward potential cataclysmia.

I AM FLAWED IN MANY WAYS, but I seem to be a pretty fair chess player in life-strategy stuff. I know how to play the long game, how to protect myself. But when I left for Savannah, I was not confident in this skill. I had done some hard math, and it seemed I had two choices. I could keep stringing out a relationship between Phillip, my son, and me for the next eighteen years—incredibly unhappily and threatening to the harmony of my child's (and my) life—or I could go with what I knew to be true in my heart as a woman and as a protective parent.

I saw an opportunity in Savannah to finally prove to everyone, including myself, that this was not, in fact, what Phillip wanted and, moreover, not what was best for me and Joseph. I was ready to expose it to everyone so that I could, without a single doubt in anyone's mind, move on to build the life that Joseph and I deserved. Also, I felt somehow that I owed it to Joseph to make damn certain that I was correct about this man.

But you can't control crazy. Ironically, it was Phillip's mother who once told me, in reference to her ex-husband (Phillip's biological father), who was involved in Phillip's life when he should not have been, that "if you're trying to control a crazy person, you are actually the crazy one." She was right, naturally. Yet it was a lesson I had to learn the hard way.

Savannah felt utterly painful at every turn. We lived in a neighborhood that was probably not dissimilar to the one I grew up in, but in a much different time. We were near an army base and we lived among young, enlisted army families. But, unlike my childhood, there was a darkness to it that, when mixed with the deep suffocation of the thick, swampy Savannah air, felt like the worst kind of smothering that refused to let up. The tragedy of my neighbors' lives crept into the tragedy of my own life every single day in a way that I was not prepared for. I had, until that point, felt like a young mother faced with hard obstacles and tough choices. I felt quite on my own in my life, with a baby to raise and an "us against the world" attitude that felt righteously silly on this street.

Here, I lived on a street with seventeen- to twenty-year-old girls, black, white, and Hispanic, already with multiple babies who were wandering, crawling around in their front yards, and in my front yard, in filthy diapers and with dirty faces and hair and feet and hands. Babies were literally put outside to cry while their mothers locked themselves inside their houses—most of them with blinds dangling from the windows and dented-in front doors from various fights with their husbands and boyfriends—while older siblings, four- and five-year-old babies themselves, cared for their siblings and tended to them the best they could.

One Tuesday, a beautiful day with a blue sky that might make someone with a better life cry, I heard a tiny knock on my front door. Joseph was napping, and I was relieved that it was such a quiet knock. I opened the door to a small girl holding a baby in a soggy diaper. I knew her, she had been over to play once or twice. She was about nine years old yet seemed older than that by decades. She interpreted all our conversations for her mother, who did not speak English. The girl spoke both English and Spanish with a pure tongue, each effortlessly native to her.

"Hello, Miss Lisa. I found this baby and thought you could help."

"What do you mean, 'you found this baby,' Tricia?" I was confused.

"Well, I was riding my bike home from Letty's house and this baby was crawling in the middle of the road by itself."

My heart did a weird thing. I got that surge of adrenaline that is usually reserved for when you or your kin are in peril.

Leticia, or Letty, as the other kids called her, lived at least three blocks away. I knew this because one day, on a long walk with Joseph in his stroller, Tricia sidled up next to me, directing us until we arrived at Letty's house, where she said, "Here's Letty's house! Goodbye, Lisa! Goodbye, José!" and disappeared into her friend's house.

"But, Tricia, that is over three blocks away! You carried this baby all the way HERE? Was no one outside with him? Are you sure no one was looking around for him?"

I knew I was panicking deep down inside, but I was trying to control my fear so as not to scare this girl who seemed capable of handling anything.

"Yes. That's right. No one was around. I even knocked on a few doors and no one answered. So I came here. I knew you would answer."

The baby was oddly calm. He had no clothes on, just the very dirty diaper. He was clearly going to need a new one and some water. It's the first and only time I ever saw a baby actually look strung out. His skin was dry. His eyes were sullen. He was plump but also, somehow, gaunt at the same time. I took him from her arms.

"Joseph is sleeping, but come in. Let's get him cleaned up and then we'll go for a walk."

Together, Tricia and I diapered, washcloth-bathed, and dressed the baby in some of Joseph's clothes. We got him a bottle of water, and, against every instinct I had, I locked my own baby, asleep and safe in his crib, inside the house and set out with Tricia to walk down the street to find the baby's home. My panic was now compounded. Was finding the home even the right choice? Who loses a baby? Who loses a baby in such a way that the baby ends up crawling down a busy neighborhood ROAD? Alone?! A road that CARS go down? How was I supposed to hand this baby off to the people who allowed that? But, ears ringing and mouth dry as ever, I kept wandering a few blocks toward Letty's house with a stranger's baby on my hip and a small girl next to me holding my hand, a girl who was expecting me to know exactly what to do, where to go, and how to fix this.

It was a series of knocks on doors. Most people didn't answer or weren't home. A few of those who did shrugged their shoulders and didn't recognize the baby. This was not a neighborhood where people had close ties. Not only did no one know this baby, but no one seemed to really care when I exclaimed "IN THE STREET!" wildly in explaining how he came to be in my possession. Strangely, I seemed to know everyone's kid. They would end up lingering in my yard and would occasionally come inside for snacks or painting. Joseph could not have cared less about their presence. And, though I don't know who attracted whom, I told myself that they were there for him.

I had been gone nearly ten minutes and was finally on the street next to Letty's street. I had to get back to my son. I was nearly nauseously uncomfortable with the fact that he was alone in the house, even only a block away. I decided that I'd hit three or four more houses and then I would get back to him. As I knocked on the next door, though, a scream came. A wail. A funeral pyre–style howl. A young woman was heading my way with her arms up to the heavens, screaming, "MY BABY!!! MY BABY!!!"

I honestly did not know what to do. I looked at the baby to, I don't know, see if he was responding to seeing this woman, some kind of validation. But he was as blank as ever. Not upset, not happy. Just mute and glazed over, just as he had been the entire time he'd been in my custody.

A woman opened the door to the house I had knocked on just before the wailing mother reached the porch.

The woman at the door looked at me and looked at the baby and said, "Why you got her baby?"

"I. I found him. I mean. She found him. And brought him to me. In the street. Alone." I felt very much like I had done something wrong, because that was the suspicion.

The mother gratefully said, "YOU FOUND MY BABY!" and quickly snatched him from my arms.

The woman at the door, like the best side character in any good story would, followed up with "Pshhhhh, Renee girl, you gotta stop losing your kids! Shit!" and slammed the door.

Renee said "Thank you" very blandly, as if I had just returned a lost scarf or hat, turned, and walked off. There was no conversation beyond our introductions. There was no curiosity about where the baby's new outfit had come from. Or the bottle that the baby had sucked dry in a matter of moments, thirsty as he was in the southern

Georgia heat. The only thing I kept thinking was that she looked just like my cousin. Irrationally, I wondered if she *was* my cousin because the brain does weird things when you are faced with such a confounding situation. And then she just walked off with him, gone before I could even say anything to her. Tricia had also left, I think fearing that we were in trouble, and so I walked back home alone.

I was angry. I was scared. I felt sorrow and grief and then immediate guilt for judging someone and then immediate indignation for not judging a woman whose baby was wandering the streets in a deteriorating diaper, a baby who seemed traumatized for no other reason, perhaps, than lack of care. I then felt guilt again. She couldn't have been more than seventeen. How did she get here? Where is HER mother? I spiraled down that hole about Renee for hours. I settled on a disquieted compassion and actually felt a kind of solidarity with those women that took the form of a subterranean rage I do not regret allowing to settle in my heart. What I know of being a woman is that the world is ready to take every last bit of you if you let it. I kept thinking, "She is doing the best she can, I know she must be doing the best she can." I needed to believe that more than I actually did. I mean, she might have just been a piece of shit, but I really needed to believe, at that moment in my life, that there was something more to it than that. It felt like it was a chance to see the truth of what the world will do to you if you are not on constant guard, ready to work and will it your way, toward your dreams, toward the life you know you and your kids deserve. I had my troubles, they were plenty, but I had not lost hope. These women seemed buried in obstacles and clearly felt out of options or choices in their lives, following some strange path that they seemed to believe, at best, that they were predestined for, and at worst, that they felt they had no real tools to find their way out of.

Back then, when I was still naïve and idealistic enough to think that a man like Phillip could be better than he actually was, I also found it hard to reconcile that anyone was ever born without the capacity to hope to the point of action, and I believed that the worse things got for a person, the more their actionable hope reserves would get activated. From the women on that street, I learned a lot about how, at a certain point of struggle, giving up, or at least putting your head down and holding on for dear life, was nearly the best you could do in moments when you felt like the hurdles were just too insurmountable. I learned about doing what you have to do simply to survive. Sometimes that is all that is possible within a moment in time. We were all there trying to survive something much bigger than ourselves on that street.

My privilege and good fortune rested somewhere between the color of my daddy's skin and my parents' radical decision to essentially run away from home, drop out of high school, get married, and raise their kids far away from what they had known. Had my parents not run off to Alabama to change the course of their own lives, I might have grown up the same way these women did, the same way most of my cousins did: in and out of jail and prison, in and out of hospitals for drugs and violence, and otherwise suffering from a genuine lack of choices—or a lack of seeing options—in life. Was this the reason Renee reminded me of my cousin? Not because of her looks but because of her strife? Was it because I will always carry the fear, the knowledge, that I am actually made of the same stuff? With circumstances always at the ready to keep me in an uneducated or uninspired life or with an abusive man, making myself smaller and smaller as each year goes by? Was there some thread that felt like it was trying to keep me there, in that space, in that story? Would that have been my fate had my parents not somehow known how to save themselves and, in the end, save me? It felt like my actual fate in that moment. Thinking back, Renee may not have looked like my cousin at all, but I did recognize her. And I made a desperate decision to honor that glitch in my upbringing, the one my cousins did not have, the one that would not allow the kind of life unfolding on that street to take hold, no matter how much it seemed to be trying to claim me.

The life my parents raised us in was different; my upbringing was full of expectation because of the world of travel and movement and bigger pictures that my parents plopped us in the middle of, despite their own fears and limited experiences. Those expectations came mostly through the hands of my teachers. I can't say that I learned much in the way of formal education, but I learned about the world, the universe, space, poetry, romance. My teachers during my childhood were beacons of hope for me. They were such bright lights and pure, unfiltered enthusiasts about the world. They all joined the DoDDS (Department of Defense Dependents Schools) system with the promise that they would travel every three years just like their students. Thus it attracted a lot of free-thinking, highly intelligent, deeply hopeful people who wanted nothing more than to see the world and be constantly challenged and pushed to grow. At times, it felt more like a cast of Peace Corps individuals—individuals, however, who needed a better salary and decent health care. People who were hopeful about the world, about one another, and about the future stood at the head of our classrooms—always dreaming with and for us and encouraging us to think about what we might be able to bring to the world. They instilled a responsibility in us to do what we were meant to do—each of us coded with different gifts and skills to better the world and to better ourselves, and it was our deepest responsibility to honor those gifts and skills. I did not learn math very well, but the horizon line and I are perpetually tethered.

. . .

SAVANNAH WAS NOT MY PLACE. That street was not my place. The man I had come to make amends with was not my home. Summer was ending, and I had, privately to myself, committed to staying through Christmas. It made sense at the time. I felt a responsibility to the "situation," but that responsibility would end before I rang in 2002, and then I could, with a clear conscience and, more important, a plan and a place to live, move along in a way that made sense for me and my son.

I did not know, however, when I made that arrangement with myself, what kind of life-altering horror and trauma that year would hold. I did not know that, on a slim blue-velvet rocker that my nana had bought for my mother in the seventies, I would hold my nursing child on my lap and watch planes fly into skyscrapers in New York. When I lay scared for a lost world, my immediate displaced sense of security and fear for everyone I loved, most of all for the baby I had just brought into this world, Phillip would say, "Pffff, why are you so upset? It's not like you knew anyone that died." The world was, nearly literally, falling down around us, and Phillip had devolved into something worse than I had remembered before I returned to him, perched at his computer every night, spilling dirty bong water on the cat and watching porn, laughing at my feelings, dismissing that there was anything more important than his high or his own sulky moods.

I could no longer find the strength to pretend that life was anything more than a disaster. Those lost babies on my street invaded my dreams. The sad, hollowed eyes of every woman I found myself around haunted my days. Every time I looked in the mirror, I searched for them inside of me, wondering when that loss of hope was going to set in, what it looked like, wondering when and if it would get me.

I started cloistering myself and Joseph inside Phillip's small two-bedroom house, retreating to the backyard only to get fresh air and play in the dirt when the sun was nearly setting and the Savannah heat was relinquishing some of its thrust. I reached a point where I had somehow erased Phillip from my emotional landscape entirely. It takes me a very long time to reach that point of no return with another human being. But when I do, it's shocking even to myself the force with which I no longer consider that person's feelings or needs. "Dead to me" is a real thing, it would seem.

By October, I knew I had to renege on the commitment I had made to see this charade through to the end of December. We ate separately. We slept separately. We even spent time with Joseph separately, though I watched Phillip like a hawk because I feared he would run off with my son. He started disabling our cars by disconnecting wires and taking out spark plugs or hiding keys so that Joseph and I couldn't go any farther than a bike could take us. He started coming home during lunch and at other random, unplanned times to "check in" and make sure we knew that he was watching us. He had not installed deadbolts as he had on Cotton Avenue—maybe because there was a child involved now—but I suspected it might only be a matter of time. He knew I was not long for Savannah. He knew I was not long for that life.

I knew I would have to be very careful about how we left. I knew that it might have to be done secretly and stealthily if I wanted to make it out with no confrontation and no interference. Essentially, I was going to have to find some control over the situation, and over myself, to get out safely. And I was going to have to learn how to fix cars.

I figured I needed to acquire parts like distributor caps and distributor rotors and spark plugs as these were routinely the parts he would remove and take to work with him. Luckily there was a mechanic we could ride my bike to. He was an old man and seemed kind, and we enjoyed our visits. He had a dog named Bob who looked to be about five hundred years old. Most of the time, Bob slept under the shade of an old Chevy pickup truck that looked like it had been parked in the same spot since the sixties. Grass had grown under it, around it, and even inside it; rust had set in everywhere and the tires were embedded in the earth so deeply that I didn't see how it could be moved even if someone wanted to. That truck was part of the landscape, and Bob lived there. The old man showed me a great many things about cars and ordered the parts I needed. I brought him cookies, and I think he knew I had no money, since I was trying to pay him with little ziplock bags full of loose change and dollar bills, so he never charged me. I ended up with a drawer full of various car parts, buried under my socks and panties, which I basically knew how to use should I ever need to.

I also decided to try to ease the tension by acting like a basic human being. I started to cook meals for all of us, including Phillip. Talked about the news, the weather, what Joseph had done that day. Small talk and roommate etiquette seemed sufficient. I needed Phillip to soften his grip. And, truthfully, I was still, maybe foolishly, hoping to leave on better terms. I saw this as being honest. I decided I didn't want to manipulate him or anyone or the situation just to work for me. I wanted to change the dynamic to be able to leave the right way. I wanted to do it my way, with integrity and grit if needed. I wanted to remind Phillip of who I was before I left. I would be the person he was trying to bury, unabashedly out loud. I would leave on my own terms and in a way that I could look back on and know was, no matter the circumstances, still full of character and, with any luck, a little grace. I would start undoing his damage right in front of him, proudly and defiantly.

He had other plans. They did not include character. They did not include grace.

The goddamned thing about a guy like Phillip, and about a lot of guys like Phillip, is that they just take what they want, what they believe to be theirs. They spend their whole lives looking for the things they believe they "deserve" and then they just take them. I could write and reckon about my young heart, a heart that wanted to make life correct and good and wanted to believe that everyone else was also aspiring to be their best selves—and mostly that is true. But it was really the grief and sadness in me that Phillip preyed on. He had access to that small sliver of shame that preexisted me, the one I was angry at my women for anointing me with. The part of me that is lace and breasts and soft skin and a cunning, sharp mind is all tied up with a deep, and oftentimes painful, darkness that is also a part of my womanhood, a beautiful, mysterious, murky swamp with one small patch of quicksand that you think you know how to navigate but that threatens to become all-encompassing terrain when a man like Phillip sniffs out its coordinates. It is the part of me that is always whispering that I am not enough, that I am no good, that I am weak, that I am only worth being near someone who could never value the better parts of me. I am diligent to keep that patch of darkness roped off, especially now, with my age and experience. But back then, Phillip mined for gold there, dug deep, used every tool in his toolbox. He worked hard, I'll give him that.

My resistance to him was always the spark that ignited his ire, his irrational need to control and possess me. In my new steadfastness to be good-hearted as I made my final exit from his life, my generosity seemed to be the worst kind of punishment for him despite my intentions. This resulted in more than a few altercations where I had to pry myself away from him physically as he mistook my friendly "hello" as an opportunity, later sneering that I was just a sinister "bitch" who was leading him on cruelly. I began to calmly make it clear that Joseph and I were preparing to leave; I got rid of some things here and there, tidied up the place, tried to gently make our way out the door. My desire to be clear and honest was conflicting daily with his inability to handle the truth.

THE NIGHT BEFORE I LEFT SAVANNAH, I made dinner, served him a plate, and let him know that the following Monday, I would be going down to Florida to visit my parents. In actuality, I asked permission. That is what I had to do. I don't like to admit it to myself, even all these years later, but it's the truth. I needed the car. I needed the car to not be disabled. I needed to leave peacefully and successfully.

My only fault was that I was telling a small fib. And he knew it. I wasn't "visiting." So when he asked when I would be back, I did not continue the lie. I said, "I won't, Phillip, and you know that by now." I implored him to be realistic about our situation. He refused to hear the real words being said to him and kept going back to his original stance, lobbing dates back at me for our potential return. "So by Christmas, maybe?" And then, after several minutes of me explaining how we could no longer live this way, he'd say, "So by the new year, then?" I became frustrated, realized that nothing was going to come of our discussion, calmly scooped up Joseph, and we said our good nights. As I started to walk away to put my son to bed, he shouted that he would "think about it"—"it" being allowing me and Joseph to go "visit" my parents. And then he offered the addendum that he'd probably just take us down there and come back to pick us up to bring us "home" after a week. He'd keep the car.

I spent about an hour tucked into the bed that Joseph and I shared. That hour was spent reading and singing Joseph to sleep. But as I lay next to his small, sleeping body to read my own book and trouble-shoot what to do now that I had confirmation that Phillip was not going to let us go easily, the door opened. Phillip stood there, and I knew immediately why he was there. He was wearing only boxers and I could tell that he was already erect, threateningly so. He estimated that I wanted something from him. This put me, in his eyes, in a vulnerable position where, as his world turned, I owed him something. No words were spoken for a moment. And then, before I could get myself upright to avoid the terrible thing that I felt pulsing between us, he was on top of me.

I fought. I fought so very hard. My legs and arms were immediately splayed and pinned, and his full weight was on top and inside of me so quickly that it was difficult, nearly impossible, to move. And there was still a part of my head, my heart, that was more worried about the child in my bed, right next to us, being woken up to this terror than the actual terror happening to me at the moment, so my thrashing and fighting were at about half strength, or at least at a very concentrated, punctuated full strength in small bursts. And Phillip knew that about me. He knew my swamp, my quicksand, and he knew that I would rather be violated than for my child to be a witness to my pain. If there had been any premeditation to this, I would guess that he had bet on me being far more docile with Joseph next to me than if he had cornered me elsewhere. That's the only kind of thinking ahead Phillip did—the kind that helped him manipulate and monopolize a situation to get what he wanted. I muttered "Stop," "Get off me," "No," and "No, Phillip, please, no" over and over until his hand covered my mouth, which was doing nothing more than sobbing pleading whispers. No one could hear me but him. He was only shielding his own ears from my voice. For weeks after, his handprint would be a bruise on my chest, my arms, and my face. The thing I remember most from that night was a train whistle blowing, loudly and furiously in the strangest way. It had never sounded like that before. When I remember my own voice that night, it sounds like that train, the screams and rattle still resonating so deeply that it makes me quake.

And I remember him saying, after he came inside me and threw my torn underwear onto my face as I quietly cried into my hands, "You deserved it."

I PACKED QUIETLY THROUGH THE NIGHT, taking only what was immediately available from our room, not the house at large, then placed the backpack and the laundry basket in the shower in the bathroom in our room and pulled the curtain to hide them, knowing that it was the one place Phillip would not look when he came into our room in the morning to inspect us before he went to work. He always left early in the mornings and that particular morning he took the car, which had been pretty badly dented on one side in an accident, not his bike. I knew this meant that he would be coming to "check in" on us frequently during the day. He knew I was a flight risk, I suppose.

I waited exactly twenty-three minutes from the moment I heard his car back out of the driveway before I got out of the bed and tried starting the other car. That was long enough that, if he had forgotten something and returned, I would be in the clear. I also suspected that he might lie in wait somewhere down the street on watch, to make sure we didn't bolt immediately after he had gone. He had left earlier than normal, and I thought it might be a trap. So I waited until I knew with absolute certainty that he would have to be in the presence of his boss:

7:30 a.m. exactly. It was a thirteen-minute drive, give or take a few; thirteen minutes, I estimated, to get everything I had packed into the car and go, should he double back to the house to make an appearance. I put Joseph in his high chair with a banana, took three ibuprofen for the terrible aches I felt from my face to my thighs, loaded the car with the laundry basket and backpack in the front seat, grabbed a few snacks and juice boxes and a giant mason jar of water, screwed the lid on, grabbed the baby, wiped his face full of banana, booped his nose, kissed his cheek, and put him in his car seat.

I don't know why Phillip always left the "good car" for us, a car I foolishly cosigned with him a few years earlier, a car we were both equally financially invested in. Perhaps he did it for visual effect, perhaps for some backward reassurance to himself that he wasn't really shafting us—never mind the pulled spark plugs and hidden car keys. But, thankfully, the morning I needed it most it was there, and in working order. I did suspect, however, when the engine turned over beautifully, instead of screeching as it had done many times before, that this was only by error or default. The sound of the engine in perfect working order made me instantly sob with relief. These are the moments when I look upward and say, "I love you, Nana," because I know better than to not recognize immediately what kind of powers are at play.

I was too scared to turn off the car once I got it going, so I put in a CD for Joseph and ran back inside to grab the cat and, as a last-minute treat to myself, a small stack of books I had been reading that were by my bedside. I threw the books on the passenger-seat floor; Sonny immediately nestled himself under the driver's seat, his normal spot; and I slammed the car door hard enough that it scared all of us. I took a deep breath and tried to collect myself for the remaining two minutes of potential "all clear" that I still had on my watch. I had to calm down. A few deep breaths and then I slowly, thoughtfully, and satisfyingly put the car in reverse and drove down that street, away from that house, away from him, away from the life that was never meant for me, and I did not even think for a moment to look back. There was not a single flinch of emotion that did not feel like full satisfaction, certainty, and fierce self-realization. I looked at myself and my son, both partially reflected in the rearview mirror, and made a distinct and silent pact with us both to never, ever doubt myself in the presence of fools again.

I ARRIVED UNANNOUNCED at my parents' house in Niceville that afternoon with a baby on my hip, a cat under my other arm, and a backpack and laundry basket full of random shit that seemed important in my haste. My father sat on the foot of my bed that night as Joseph and I slept. I woke to find him in the same place he had been when we fell asleep. He was beside himself with guilt and, I think, blamed himself for leaving me so vulnerable. Also, he was angry. I was not completely forthcoming about what had happened, but there was so much that was obvious to them, for the first time. I had never, not once in my life, come off as fragile, and I'm fairly certain that by the time I arrived, my strength was gone and no words were needed to explain when a body seems that defeated. I know my father felt like a fool—thought of all the times he encouraged me to be closer to Phillip, thought of all the times he should have known what kind of man Phillip was, blamed himself for so many things that were not his fault. I would later learn that most of that anger came from a moment while I slept, while he racked his brain for ways he could have prevented what had happened and the doorbell rang.

. . .

As I PREDICTED, Phillip had come home from work early that morning to do an inspection of us; it must have been just an hour after we left, because apparently he got back in his car and proceeded to follow us all the way to my parents' house, arriving only about two hours after we did. Cell phones were a novelty back then, a novelty I did not have. There were still blissful moments in life that were uncertain, information was slower, and there was not a lot of immediate or instant contact, so I at least had the eight-hour drive to feel as if he were farther in my past than a mere hundred miles behind me. He arrived at the door of my parents' house and my father dealt with the whole embarrassing interaction.

When he arrived, according to my father, Phillip was twitching with a kind of anger that, unbeknownst to my dad, usually resulted in my getting thrown or locked up—anger that occurred when he felt powerless. His only power play was to show up and demand things that he thought would hurt me, such as the check card for a shared bank account that I used solely to buy food for Joseph and the car I had driven down. Upon this demand, he gave my father the keys to the nearly totaled car—a car so beat up that I couldn't figure out how it had made the trip from Savannah—as a trade for the car I had driven that day. My father was now dealing with a grown man of nearly thirty years and refused to get into a dispute over property. So, to rid ourselves of Phillip as quickly as possible, he acquiesced. After that truly dick move, Phillip turned and left. My father is a stoic man. I had not yet reached deep enough into my own adulthood to see the scope of his emotional range. I don't think I had ever seen him cry. I had certainly never, ever seen him shake with rage. Until that day.

I basically slept for two weeks and took Joseph to very private parts of public beaches to let the salt water and the sunshine—which were, even in the midst of impending "winter," penetrating and warm—do some healing on the parts of my body that hurt. My shins, my hips, and my chest would forever carry the pain of that relationship, though, no matter how much I tried to let the powers that be heal them. Things get stored in your body, memories like sound waves in your bones, vibrating if the wrong frequency hits them, erupting like shock waves if you touch them or stretch them the wrong (or right) way, just sitting there waiting to be released, waiting for the moment you set them free. I would work the rest of my life to set them free. They are still in there, those memories, so deeply a part of me that they feel like marrow.

One of those mornings, as I lay on the beach next to my son in the bright early light thinking about my body and what a good sport it had been, still strong and still capable, there was, though I did not know it, a new life growing inside me from the night Phillip raped me. Rape. I hadn't figured out how to say the word to myself up to that point. And I kept replaying it, making sure I wasn't exaggerating anything or replacing truth with vindictiveness. I brutally made myself go over it, every detail, for days and weeks.

And, finally, I made myself say it to Phillip's mother, Jean, who, when she discovered that I had left Savannah and had heard his version of events—in essence, that I was a harlot who had tricked him into loving me and had been mistreating him all those years—asked me out to lunch under the guise of seeing Joseph. We met in a café in the small town where my parents knew just about everyone, the same small town where I graduated from high school and probably also knew everyone but was too involved in my own life to care or notice. I was nervous to see her, but I walked in early, got a muffin for Joseph and a coffee for me, and sat down at a table in the corner to wait. When she arrived, she came straight to the table, no purchase at the counter, negligibly noticed Joseph in his high chair, and looked me over.

"Listen, Phillip told me what happened and then he told me what you think happened," she said with nothing short of a sneer on her face and a sharp glint in her eye.

In my nervousness, all I could muster was to say, "Oh?"

"Yes. And, really, I'm just here to have you say it to my face. Because we all know it is not true. So say it. I dare you."

I sat frozen in my seat and felt tears well up in my eyes, which infuriated me. That morning, six (yes, six) tests had told me of a pregnancy I was not prepared to cope with. I had a fetus growing inside me that I could not care for and that I did not partake in making. I knew keeping it would be detrimental for me and for Joseph. I was grappling with the idea of an abortion, obviously not my go-to move, and the phone call that morning to Planned Parenthood was horrifying—the information I was given was that, by law, I had to wait until the fetus was older to abort. I did not understand the logistics of that, but it was true. I couldn't have been more than six weeks and I had to wait until I was twelve weeks. They would give me, at twelve weeks, a suppository to put in like a tampon and it would abort the baby. It would cost $350, an amount I was going to have to ask to borrow from someone, but who? I had no friends, I could not break my parents' hearts with any more of my drama, and I secretly feared they would try to convince me to keep it, a conversation I did not have the strength to face.

I had all these thoughts in my head while Jean talked at me and while my baby sat across the table, looking for someone to play with him as he peekabooed with the muffin wrapper, when she interrupted the silence with "So? Say it. Say the word, Lisa. To my face. You can't, can you, because it is not true, and you know that this is just some trap you're setting, some game so you can get rid of him. You never loved him."

I stood up, started taking Joseph out of the high chair, kept smiling and scrunching my nose at him to make sure he was not a part of this madness, and once I had him on my hip and my bag on my shoulder, I shouted, in a voice that was far louder and far more quivery than I wish it had been, in a room that was far fuller than I really think I understood until I looked at it from the parking lot, "Your son raped me. He RAPED me. IN FRONT OF MY CHILD. AND IT WAS NOT MY FAULT. IT IS NOT A LIE. AND IT WAS NOT MY FAULT."

I don't remember walking back to my car, the dented one with a bent rear tire and a driver's door so damaged I had to get in through the passenger's side. But I do remember thinking in that moment that not even fucking women would be on my side—that the world will make excuses and provide shelter for men like Phillip before they will even begin to listen to, much less believe, a moment of our pain and that we have to figure out, ultimately, how to protect ourselves.

THERE WERE NO POLICE REPORTS to file, even though my father and I tried. I would have had to return to Savannah, the "scene of the crime," and file a report, stay for an extended period of time to press charges, and see the case through, and I was not about to do that. We then went to my parents' local police department and asked about a restraining order instead; as it turns out, I had to have some kind of proof, like a police report from Savannah, to prove that I was in danger. And even if the bureaucracy had been on my side, the backward people behind the paperwork were not. Round and round it went, each good-ole-boy buffoon after another, asking over and over again, "But y'all LIVED together?" as if that were Phillip's alibi, as if that meant I was complicit in my own psychological and physical abuse. Was I SURE? Maybe it was just a misunderstanding? "He has no criminal record, we can't just go around accusing innocent people no matter how mad we are at them, now can we, little darlin'?"

I had no power. Not legally, anyway.

I did have the gifts of insight and instinct, though, two things that I figured were a woman's only real allies in the world I found myself in. While those gifts came at a great cost in the proving, I started to move back toward myself. Slowly, patiently, I knew I would find it again, the place where I had control, and that even if it happened as slowly as water changes a mountain, things would finally bend and yield the way they were meant to all along.

# 8

## STAYING

*Roots and Soil*

I TURNED TWENTY-FOUR and cut off all my hair a month after I arrived at my parents' house. I shaved my armpits, put on a pair of jeans, a bracelet, a tank top, a cute cardigan, and sneakers, and threw away my coveralls. I then made an agreement with myself to let my parents take care of me—something I was not good at allowing at first and then settled into gratefully, because, truly, it was not just about shelter and food. I needed their support and love for the first tangible time in my ragingly independent life.

Of all the terrible things that had happened up to that point as a result of letting Phillip into my world, this pregnancy was the one I was not sure I would be able to fully recover from. That, coupled with the reality of having to deal with it in a way I never thought I would be willing to entertain, was the saddest and most isolating feeling I have ever experienced. It is a significantly cornered feeling, a panic, a steel trap on your leg tethering you to something that you'd be willing to bite your own foot off for simply to survive. I would venture, safely, to say that regardless of the circumstances, it is a decision that would overwhelm any heart, burden any spirit, and break anyone down in ways that cannot be recovered from entirely. You are wholly alone in those moments. It is a loneliness, a little dark seed of defeat and desperation, that you carry with you for the rest of your life.

I went to my eight a.m. appointment alone, had the suppository inserted as I lay in the cold room of a clinic (one that was closer to my parents' house than Planned Parenthood—a purely logistical decision to help me juggle a babysitter, a decision I would later regret), with a truly wonderful woman named Ruth as my nurse, who held my hand and called me baby girl, and then I waited the mandatory five hours, mostly alone, until it was decided by the doctors that it had not taken.

They sent me home, where I proceeded to make my parents and Joseph dinner. I spent the entire afternoon and evening feeling sick, just absolutely sick to my stomach, thinking it was a sign from whomever, god or my nana or whatever was watching me from above or below, to reconsider. Abortion was not something I was against for others, it was just not something I'd ever considered for myself. I was too young and naïve and inexperienced to have much of an opinion about it politically or ethically, to be honest. I did not live in a world that required me to articulate an opinion about this particular topic. I know that seems blithe in this day and age, but other than zealots who shouted you down when you entered a clinic, I don't recall it being a threatened thing to have to fight for back then, at least not in the world I lived in. *Roe v. Wade* was an issue settled more than a generation ago. The people who threaten it now, led by small-minded fools masquerading as Christians who only want rights for people who believe in their version of god, did not have total political power then.

I did have some definite inclinations of my own, however. The Catholic Church's voice in my head was likely the one thing I had vehemently rebelled against in my life thus far. When I rejected my confirmation as a teen—the big sacrament before marriage and death, a sacrament that further saves your soul from the sin you will be awash with seemingly forever if you do not partake—it was the ultimate heartbreak for my mother. It sent her into a self-inflicted exile, crying under her sheets and in her bathroom for days because my decision meant that she had failed and that Jesus and Mary and Joseph, but most especially Mary, would never forgive her. I pulled her sheets down on the second day of her bedridden self-flagellation over my refusal to commit and confirm myself in the Catholic Church at the age of fifteen and said, "But, Mom, you should be proud that you raised me and David to think for ourselves and to want to learn more before I commit and that you've taught me to be dedicated to truth," and then she shouted, with snot in her nose and her eyes so puffy that she likely could not even make out my earnest face, "I WOULD NEVER DO THAT! THAT IS ALL YOUR FATHER'S FAULT!" After that, I kept most of my opinions about the malarkey I sniffed out in Catholicism to myself. I knew their rules to be in direct opposition to the kinds of rights I knew I and all my friends—mostly gay men or women in the early nineties—deserved. But abortion was not something that I had thought much about beyond "it's personal."

NEARLY A DECADE LATER, after I found my way out of that terrible time, I happened to be in the kitchen of an apartment on the campus of a very prestigious university, making pies for one of my oldest best friends' engagement party. The house was filled with PhD candidates, professors, eggheads, a whole collection of people who think they are better and smarter than most of the world, people I once thought I wanted to be like. The evening began with a stunning French girl named Aline, whom my friend had given my full backstory to, prodding me for information as to why I had not chosen to abort my first child. Aline—a lithe expat who helped me peel peaches and who seemed deeply unaffected by anything and everything, really—let me know squarely that, for a French girl, there is only one suitable outcome to getting knocked up at twenty-something years old by a controlling louse of a man. Aline blinked as she stated this fact very clearly to me in a way that I would later recognize as a distinctly French trait—a delightful one when it is not pointedly challenging your entire existence thus far.

"Why did you choose your path when you could have chosen freedom?" she asked. The word "freedom" was accentuated in a way that highlighted the general confusion of the matter for her, and I didn't know how to have the conversation that she seemed so committed to broaching.

I was happy in that kitchen that day, before she arrived, with just fruit, flour, and butter, everything making their way toward becoming pies. It made me happy. I was happy. My children. I adored my children—even and especially the one from the louse of a man I never loved. I felt deeply uncomfortable, did not know how to have a conversation like that and realized that, actually, Aline was the first person to ever speak to me about abortion in the way I actually believed it should exist.

Then why was it making me so uncomfortable? Was it because the honesty of the matter was that there had certainly been sweeping thoughts, mere fleeting moments (but heartbreaking ones nonetheless), in the passing years in which I had wondered about, sometimes dreamed about, the life that I could have had instead? Was Aline making me admit something to myself that made me squirm with discomfort? Or was it just the first time I had been forced to think about the actual abortion I did have to have? I certainly could never imagine my life without my children, and I was well past the point of even wanting to. How dare she? I felt. Was this her way of trying to relate? Was I supposed to envy these occasionally delightful and self-realized yet entirely overeducated, pious, well-dressed, well-traveled, well-situated, and childless darlings whom I always seemed to be encountering in the world? No. My days of envying cool, dismissive, and unaffected beauties with no actual real-life experiences to lean on ended almost immediately that day. Not because Aline was cavalier about abortion, but because she was cavalier about me.

ALINE AND I SKINNED the blanched peaches, my hands plunged in an ice-cold water bath fishing for the bobbing fruit. As she talked, enjoying hearing the sound of her own voice, I took great pleasure in the way the skins of the peaches slid off in one sheet, and instead of trying to figure out where to put Aline's voice, I became absorbed in my work, in the cosmic color a peach turns when it is fresh from the ice water, when it is an unreal shade like a southern sunset. I couldn't feel my fingers, couldn't feel a thing past my biggest knuckles. And as Aline talked at me about all the things she was so certain of, I became more certain by the moment that I had definitely not missed out on a single important thing by not surrounding myself with a life full of these chic, well-heeled, and sophisticated monsters. I felt a deep wash of gratitude that my life had sent me in the opposite direction, and as she spoke and spoke, I wished that I could put my entire body, head included, into the water bath with the peaches—plunge in so that my thick skin would go numb and come clean off my underripened, picked-too-soon body. Finally, I wouldn't feel a thing. What a gift.

I had no words for Aline. My standards for the way I chose to live my life were based solely on an agreement that I forged between my head and my heart, and that should be how every woman faces the world as a life bearer. Up to a point in life, things probably seem somewhat black and white regarding what is right and what is wrong for you. And then, one day, your life changes and you learn quickly to never, not even for a second, assume you know what someone else's life and choices are about. But those weren't the words that came out of my mouth to Aline. While we peeled the skin off the blanched peaches, all I could muster was the ability to say, "I did what I needed to do."

I COULD NEVER HAVE TOLD Aline that after the abortion I did choose to have, I went into a kind of blackout denial of what I had done, about the suppository that had been put inside me, before I had even put dinner on the table for my son that night. I could never have explained how, in the middle of that dinner, around twelve hours after Ruth had taken my hand for the first time, I was completely surprised to find myself sweating, instantly full of flushed fever, feeling like I was going to vomit or shit my pants or both and nearly about to double over in pain. I hurriedly left the table, not even having a moment to ask my parents to finish feeding Joseph, and locked myself in the bathroom, thinking that, get this, I had food poisoning.

I could never have explained to her how I truly had somehow convinced myself that the whole day had not even happened—how the mind is a funny little bitch and will play as many tricks as you want and will it to. How I found myself with the cold water running in the sink, a washcloth over my face and my body rejecting a fetus straight into the toilet, brutally remembering what I had done, what was actually happening. The fact that I was aborting the pregnancy into a toilet was even more devastating to me, as if a sterile hospital room offered some other kind of sanctity. I anguished, feeling each contraction pushing clots out of me, while I clung to the wall, gripped the toilet-paper holder, and cried, humiliated by the moment, disgusted by the way it was happening, saddened that my world had come to this, feeling so small and so helpless and so angry, just righteously angry, that any of this was happening to me. I felt so far away from the people in the next room, as if they did not exist, but, really, as if I did not exist and they were in a world that still made sense. None of this made sense.

It took about forty minutes before I could pull myself up, still bracing myself against the wall, forgetting entirely that I had a child in the other room waiting for me until my mom gently knocked on the door to see if I was OK. I said, "Yes, I'm fine," and then I quickly tried to come to, and with my knees shaking, I turned myself around to look in the toilet. It was a bloody, terrible scene, and I then did a horrific thing. I stuck my hand down to try to find the most whole piece of everything that had come out of me. I could not bear the thought of simply flushing and moving on. I wanted to face the supposedly lime-size fetus that had just left my body. Maybe I could bury it. Maybe I could remember how to pray. Maybe I could do anything besides flush and cry and give in to the feeling that I needed to set the world on fire. But there was nothing there except blood and clots and more blood. I cried into the toilet, blood dripping down my arm. I cried so hard, feeling like life was totally unfair and wrong and that I did not deserve any of this. I vomited. I cried some more. Then I flushed the toilet with such anger in my heart and, yet, still such certainty that I had done exactly what I had needed to do. In that moment, I learned one more thing about being a woman: It is only me, I am all I have, and no one will ever understand this part of me, this part that is all instinct and animal and necessary. This is the part of me that will keep me alive.

. . .

SEVERAL WEEKS BEFORE I had decided about the abortion, I sent an email to three of my closest friends outlining what had happened in Savannah, in brutally plain English, leaving out the pregnancy part, telling them where they could find me and what the soft plan was for me and Joseph moving forward—the "soft plan" being essentially "We're going to stay put until I sort this shit out."

David Earles, the kind of friend every woman would be lucky to have—the one you date just long enough to realize you are really best friends—wrote back, "Do me a favor and don't go anywhere until I get down there. It should only take me three weeks." David and I had met in high school after I moved to Niceville—his shaved head and just-dirty-enough street swagger had been such a relief for me in the crowd of Abercrombie & Fitch–clad suburbanites. A fellow military brat, he was living in Quebec at the time of the email. He was gritty and intolerant as fuck of ignorance and raw in his anarchistic beliefs. He was a drummer, read a lot of philosophical shit that I was not yet smart enough to understand, listened to music I hated, and, above all, was a very trusted friend. Since high school, he had been squatting with his bandmates and hopping trains to get wherever he wanted or needed to go. He was playing in successful underground punk bands, bands that some people might recognize if I named them, and making enough money to survive. His lifestyle was his chosen one for many reasons—political and philosophical and personal. He was not a full-blown anarchist—and he would roll his eyes if he heard me even align him with any kind of construct of thinking—but he was pretty close. He arrived at my parents' house nearly two weeks to the day of my sending him that email, smelling of diesel and as skinny as a rail.

He had spent nearly thirteen days hopping trains from Quebec to the Florida Panhandle, and when he arrived, he smelled terrible and looked even worse. My parents were horrified, and I was relieved to the point of tears. He stayed with me for ten days, making me scrambled eggs most mornings and taking Joseph for long walks so I could sleep and just generally be alone. I consider that visit to be one of the very important things that saved me, one of the greatest kindnesses ever bestowed upon me. David helped me survive. He gave me the confidence to move forward. He did a genuinely human thing, and whenever I think about it, the kind of true goodness it took and the kind of pure sincerity it required, it makes me hopeful. Never underestimate showing up for someone. Never estimate what reading Mark Twain to someone before bed, buying them drugstore lotion as a reminder to take care of themselves, or making them watch old episodes of *Murder, She Wrote* can do. Friendship like that is rich salve. David Earles showed up and was my friend when it counted, and then, ten days after he arrived, he had me take him to a train depot somewhere between Pensacola and Mobile, where he hoisted his black canvas backpack onto his shoulder and, as Joseph and I watched, disappeared in a hazy heat wave just like in an old Western. And even though we would write letters and mail each other books we had just finished reading—his always tattered and worn from a thousand reads, mine always freshly bought and just discovered—that was the last time I ever saw him.

Though he didn't know it, David had arrived just about three days after the abortion. I was nearly feral by then. He noticed, but never asked why. And after he left, I had a sense of security and optimism, even, a jolt of goodness, and, what was most important, permission to exist again in the world in a way that actually made sense. He put a pin in the map of "you are here," and I could start rethinking about where I was trying to go.

I began to make plans, began to think about my options. I'm the kind of crazy that allows for a confidence that I can make something out of nothing, so I dreamed of plenty of places to drop me and my son into and start anew. There was one place, though, that was real, a job that had been tentatively offered to me on my graduation from college. In the summer, I had a job interview for a new private high school in Nashville, Tennessee, a place I never imagined visiting, much less living, under the careful and loving watch of my old high school art teacher, Vivian Komando. She had been dutifully keeping tabs on me (god bless women), and when she found me waiting tables again at TradeWinds after I left Savannah, she vouched for me, which was everything. I was very excited about the prospect; it was a real job and a future I could potentially build on. However, much later in the process, after a bumpy interview with a pretentious headmaster who kept asking why a single mother like me was going to be anything other than a bad influence for the girls at his school and that maybe I should think about getting married before I moved to start this career— words I grinned at and blinked through without acquiescing any agreement—my enthusiasm waned and I ended up only hesitantly accepting.

STILL, SPRING CAME, and I became the first and only woman in my family to graduate from a four-year university on the same day and from the same university that my dad, a high school dropout and the first person in our family to go to college, got his PhD. We walked out of the auditorium together in our caps and gowns, his decorated, mine barely fitting, carrying such pride for each other that we could barely speak. We both had made so much happen in our lives in separate ways, despite many reasons why we could've stopped or been stopped. I am my father's daughter, deeply and proudly. Much was unsaid that day about all the things we each had had to overcome to be standing exactly in the spot we were in, but there are usually no words for those moments and it's best if you just surrender to a type of knowing.

I was pushing the ball forward. Bending that mountain. Shaping my life. I was buying new music. I was planning trips. I was making friends. I was excited about the future with my son and learning how to have and make choices.

In the midst of all this, I was invited to a beachside lunch with an old friend from my studio art classes. She heard I was in town and wanted to catch up and—strangely—asked if I could meet her for lunch, but without Joseph. She had never excluded him before, was a mother herself and always generously welcomed him, but I figured maybe some of my friends were trying to encourage me toward a little independence from him.

There had been no cooking, no reveling in baked goods, during this time. I was shockingly thin; Joseph was the only thing I was nurturing, and the only thing I was getting nurtured by; and I recognized that striking a balance was something I needed to consider. But this was not why she invited me to lunch without my child. She changed the course of my and Joseph's life forever in one small, very premeditated, and carefully considered invitation.

I arrived at the restaurant and the hostess took me to a room with a big bay window facing the ocean, and my friend was sitting there across the table from a man whose back was to me as I approached. I figured it was her husband or something, not really considering all the options, but then, just like in a goddamn movie, the man turned around, just as surprised as I was, and said, "Lisa?!" It was John Donovan, looking better and happier than ever, and I knew in an instant that I was fucked. Utterly and completely and forever fucked. She had set me, and him, up. She knew, in her clairvoyance, that our timing had been bad that first time around—he was in a bad situation of his own with a job he hated, a skinny rock-and-roll girlfriend who worked in a record store, took a lot of pills, and screwed a lot of other boys, thinking all the while that he did not know, and me, me in all my disasters. Yet there we were, in a different time and place courtesy of someone who was paying attention. I don't remember our friend being at the lunch at all that day, even though I know she stayed. I remember only him, the color of his cheeks and the exhilarative vibrations that we filled that whole room with.

EVERYTHING I WANT TO WRITE about John Donovan is a cliché. I bought perfume. I had my mom take a picture of me before I met him alone for the first time, like a teenager going on her first real date. I did all the things except admit that he was real. He was not a chance I was ready to take. I wish I could say that I was readier, when I met him the second time, to embrace what he and everyone else seemed to already know. Instead, I kept going about my life, working toward my plans as if he were not a consideration at all—but someone whose company I could just enjoy. I still was not capable, no matter how available. I liked him, potentially was even madly in love with him, but I was not about to put any expectations on him or me—I had a laser-beam focus to get out of Florida, to find a way to support myself and my son financially and maybe have some nice friends along the way. It wasn't that I didn't want him, it was really more that somewhere along the line of becoming an adult, I had not quite figured out how to have relationships, how to let people in. Truthfully, this is basically still the case—keeping everyone at arm's length and eventually letting a few in if I start to feel terrified of having to spend my life without them. It's not that I feel exclusive, I'm just a bit dysfunctional in that way. And, somewhere deep down inside, I wonder if I'll disappoint people once they really get to know me, all full of my weird shadows and habits. Trust is not an easy one for me, still.

So I gladly "hung out" with John, going to dinner, sending fancy new Yahoo.com emails to each other, accepting mix CDs full of love songs from him—all the while, never admitting to myself that this was anything more than a friendship, new perfume be damned. One night, on our third "hang" (it was a date, it was totally a date), he tried to kiss me, and I moved away from it so quickly that I surprised even myself. He ended up kissing my ear. The rejection on his face was more than I could bear. I said I was sorry, and there was so much quizzical confusion between us that all I knew how to do was to make a joke about how I was glad I had cleaned my ears that day. It was the first time I realized that he might love me, too. Somehow, I guess I had not understood that it was possible. And this weird reflex to keep that feeling to myself was hurting him, a thing I could not live with. He proceeded to be a very patient and kind bulldozer for the wall I had built without even realizing it, knocking down one brick at a time without so much as a thought for what he wanted or for what he expected from me. There were no expectations. He just wanted to be near me. He just wanted to love me however he was allowed to, however I was prepared to let him.

Once the job from Vivian became more of a reality, I learned something about John Donovan—and fast. I had only casually discussed it, this decision to move and start my life elsewhere without him, keeping my cards close to my chest and forgetting, or denying, that he deserved more from me. He had a life I did not feel entitled to disrupt—a tenured job, good money, three dogs he seemed committed to, and living in the city where he grew up near his whole family—all things I figured were by design and made him happy. Who was I to assume that he ought to upend it all and start over?

During one difficult phone call, shit got real in a flash when I flippantly, ever so casually, mentioned that I'd be heading up to Nashville in a few weeks to officially interview for the job; even though it had already been offered, the interview was more of a prospect trip for me to see if it would be the right fit. There was silence on the other end of the phone. "So you've decided? You're taking the job?" John finally said after I said, "Hello? You there?" to break the silence. I wasn't sure, I said, as I pressed my cards even closer. Because I wasn't sure about anything, really, I shrugged off. But he knew, and he was unable to hide his frustration at my lack of reciprocal consideration any longer. I heard a crash, the sound of him throwing a wooden chair across the room (he later admitted), and then he hung up on me. He called back immediately, apologized, and said he understood. He understood my need to make decisions that did not include him, my need to be independent of anyone for the sake of my son, and, ultimately, he understood that he was not my priority—that last part piercing right through me, even though he meant it with utter kindness.

But, he said, he would really love it if we could please still spend time together until then, regardless of the decision I might make. I said of course and that I had hoped we might still spend time together after I left. "I'm not sure this has to mean anything in regard to how I feel about you," I said, terrified as the words left my mouth because I had just admitted to myself—not to him but to myself—that I was in over my head, that I most definitely could not live without this person, and that, as I had known when I first saw him again, I was undoubtedly fucked.

During the same month that this decision loomed, we'd take long drives to New Orleans, a place John Donovan had moved to when he was seventeen, a place he feels is home. These trips were to install and deinstall his sculpture at a gallery on Julia Street, to visit his family, and, as it turned out, to fall more in love with each other in a city that would stamp the kind of romance we were forging: deep, slow, complicated, sensual, soft. New Orleans will forever carry the same weight and feel in my heart as that man does; they will never be separate. She was the place where he revealed himself to me without even realizing it. His tongue, the lilt of his accent, changed almost as soon as we crossed the border into Louisiana. The timbre of his voice got louder and stronger around his New Orleans family, his presence filled entire buildings, filled entire streets. We laughed and touched more, we were more alive.

You cannot understand New Orleans, truly, until someone who was raised by her, someone who loves her and is loved by her in return, takes you there. You cannot imagine the truth she possesses, the sins she will accept within you, the forgiveness she has for us all, until you walk through her with a man who can only love you the way he does, full of truth and power, because he was given life by those streets, by the people, by the thick air that nearly chokes you until you learn how to breathe through your skin and through your bones and how to move your body in a sway instead of a strut because that is what she demands. The city sticks to you, gets in your hair, under your nails; you sweat a kind of funk that feels so real and so base that all you want is to find the man you love and devour him with your whole body and let his whole body completely devour you, let yourself get folded up inside him, make yourself so small in his arms, disappear into his belly, his legs wrapped around your whole self, his sweat and your sweat no longer different, while you're surrounded by dull pink walls in a bright purple building. And even though there is a literal parade of trumpets floating by your window, you forget about the world entirely and can only hear him breathe.

If I had been denying myself the pleasure of falling in love, I was now defenseless in the face of it, in the face of the multitudes that John Donovan contained, in New Orleans. In New Orleans he was My Man. Mine. I wanted to possess him. I wanted to be possessed by him in return. New Orleans was not going to give airspace to the other frequencies, the downright noise, I had been cocooning myself with while in the presence of his greatness. She was John's best ally, his best weapon, against it. She fought for our love, in her subtle way, with a kind of heat that had nothing to do with weather. She fought for our love with summer strawberries, served to us by a large black man who saw us from across his crowded bakery and said, "I see you two over here and I thought you might need something to quench that loud thirst," as he poured sweetened condensed milk over the berries so ripe and red that they nearly pulsated in the bowl. She won, New Orleans. She won. I owe her a debt I can never repay.

# 9

## HUNGER

*Cornmeal*

J OHN, JOSEPH, AND I MOVED to Nashville at the end of the summer in 2002. We rented a house off 12th Avenue South, a neighborhood that was built around a large park immortalizing a significant Civil War battle and was, when we arrived, known for prostitution and drug deals, and as a scouting location for Harmony Korine movie extras. That neighborhood looks a lot like a wealthy suburb now, fancy shops with fifty-five-dollar tea towels that say "Bless Your Heart" and restaurant chains selling fifteen-dollar tacos with very suspect ingredients like ancho mayo sauce or green chili tapenade that only white suburbanites who don't know any better will pay for. Bless their hearts.

When we lived there, though, it was still the place where broke musicians and songwriters and artists rented from people who owned property they were praying would pay off someday. The houses were nice and affordable, the landlords were patient and gracious. John set up a studio in the basement and worked several odd jobs hanging art at local museums or in the airport or making frames at a frame shop.

Joseph started day care at a co-op where I felt connected and where he felt comfortable, and I started my job teaching art history, fundamental 2D art, and photography. I wrote artist features for a zine out of Brooklyn and every once in a while art reviews for local shows in Nashville.

We ate a lot of black beans, couscous bought in bulk, and sautéed spinach—a lot of it. I was too busy figuring out that teaching at an obnoxiously wealthy and very conservative high school was not my cup of tea to be engaged in any real cooking, much less baking. So we continued being skinny and hungry, but not out of sadness or grief. We were happy and eager. At night we would put Joseph to bed together, reading *Harry Potter* or stories from an old Native American folklore book that John had from graduate school, and then I would sing him songs, the songs I had been singing to him his whole life, in a room we decorated with Batman and Bob the Builder paraphernalia. Then John and I would have tea on the couch, while Sonny slept between us, and we would talk about art and books and the work we wanted to do, how we never wanted to retire but how we wanted to build a life where we could wake up in the morning, have coffee with each other, go to our respective corners in the house—him to a studio and me to a writer's desk—and just work, meeting again for lunch and then later for wine.

This was our simple dream. We would listen to Miles Davis's *Kind of Blue* or Beck's *Sea Change* or Yo La Tengo's *Summer Sun* while we planned and schemed about the kind of world we knew we could finally build together, all while my son slept safely in a room I paid for, with my own money, from my own hard work. We tucked into Nashville and we tucked into one another, all three of us madly in love with no one to tell us that we weren't good enough or that we weren't doing it right—and when they did, because some did (we were broke and

John was living off the small amount of savings he had acquired from being a single professor with no expenses—a tenured job he quit to come live, recklessly his family surmised, with me and Joseph in Nashville), we didn't have to listen because we had each other and we knew better.

Even though we weren't sure how it would happen, we knew this was it, our lives ready to unfurl in front of us. This was always meant to be. This was what we had both deserved our whole lives. On a little street off 12th Avenue South in Nashville, Tennessee, while dogs howled in Sevier Park across the street and Civil War ghosts slipped between houses, the Donovan family started, boldly and beautifully ready for anything that came our way, willing to risk it all for what we knew could be. We had nothing to lose, literally, except for some Bob the Builder sheets and each other, and we knew we would never leave each other's side. So onward, and eventually upward, we went, toward something more, something right, something correct—toward ourselves.

I married John Donovan in a stained-glass cathedral on St. Charles in New Orleans across from Audubon Park on a deservedly beautiful spring day, with a four-year-old Joseph sporting a black eye and a tuxedo holding our rings by my side and me with a folded-up picture of a person we had not yet met tucked into the bodice of my dress. We were engaged in October, the same winter we cut down tiny trees from Sevier Park to warm our house because we could not afford to keep the heat on, after a sweet but serious talk on our couch about whether or not marriage mattered to us, and a decision was made that we were hungry to be a family in all the ways, a whole family in a whole home with a whole name shared between us. We set out making plans for a sweet, small ceremony with our family and a few friends in the city we loved. In February, five weeks before our wedding, we learned we would be four, and a doctor printed out a picture of the person in my womb, the picture I tucked into the silk lining of my dress, who would be Maggie Donovan.

MY PREGNANCY WITH MAGGIE DONOVAN was full of romance and excitement. Sharing that time with a man I loved and who loved me was supremely wonderful. He cared for me in small ways, always made sure my legs were rubbed at night, always made sure my favorite kind of yogurt was in the refrigerator, always spent meaningful time with Joseph so I could take long showers and have restful pauses. We were deeply in love. We couldn't keep it to ourselves. We felt exhaustively lucky. Just lucky as fuck. There was not a single doubt about where we found ourselves—we knew we had made it to the right place. We were each other's place. And as much as that pregnancy was not one of solitude, it was also not a pregnancy of carbohydrate indulgence or nostalgia. I did not have the same impulses during my pregnancy with Maggie as I did with Joseph. I baked, sure, but I eventually came back to it out of necessity, if I'm being really honest. It was purely economics. Right around this time, I realized that no one in Nashville baked and that small things like birthday cakes were a niche market. I did a few for coworkers and parents at Joseph's day care. It was mostly a side project. We had new horizons. I was building a life with a person who didn't balk when I showed him my writing and said I wanted to do more. I lived with a person who randomly emailed me submission guidelines for *Oxford American* and *The New Yorker*, no bar too high for me and my aspirations. And I believed in his work, sculpture that was winning awards in South Korea, his dedication perpetually inspiring and motivating. His knowledge and engagement in the world of clay was a playbook for me in how to build a career. We were strongly focused on putting food on the table and keeping the lights on while we aimed for those far-off places. Raising our family while we took our aim was the work we wanted to get right first. It took us a minute to figure out that dance.

The offspring of the wealthy and conservative at the high school made me distraught. Not all of them but enough of them for me to feel desperate would arrogantly walk into my classroom and talk about politics and money and get into debates about George W. Bush's good deeds and how, if they could vote, they'd vote for him because "he's for money and my family is made of money," and I, in my immature twenty-four years of life, did not know what to do with myself. I wanted to teach about the radical Judy Chicago and the ever-stalwart Richard Serra in the same reverential terms, putting radical early feminism—which no high school teacher ever talked about—on an equal pedestal to that dying twentieth-century stoicism and work ethic mostly attributed to men, which was so prevalent in history books. I wanted to talk about how important art was to religion, to building it up and breaking it down in equal measure. I wanted to talk about drag queens and outsider cultures and David Bowie and Valeska Gert and performance art and Jesco White and how it all came from something real and raw about being human at a certain point in human history. I took them to junkyards to study Louise Nevelson, to build things out of trash, leftovers, scraps from the working world, make refuse into something new and beautiful with basic tools and their hands. I took them to studio visits with artists in Nashville's Fugitive Art Center (RIP), an old warehouse full of mold and asbestos that housed a dozen artists' studios—one of which eventually belonged to John Donovan—and a gallery and installation hall that would show works from local and national artists together. It had late-night art shows that were raw and real and not picture-perfect and didn't give a fuck about who was watching but were just full of people who had to be in the process of making art that mattered in that time and place in a space that probably gave us all cancer but was unlike anything Nashville had ever seen before or has ever seen since.

There is now a fancy restaurant in that space selling thirty-dollar cocktails and hosting bachelorette party after bachelorette party because it seems those kids I was teaching ended up ruling this town with all that money their families were "made of" after all, despite my best efforts. I spent too much time in that job pontificating, perched on a soapbox in the most desperate way, shouting about how the kids in my room were not doing their jobs correctly if they were just regurgitating everything their parents told them to be true, if they were limiting their scope to the disjointed way they were being raised, to not see or feel what the rest of the world might be going through, to assume that the world is important only as far as their own inexperienced eyes could see. How can you be seventeen and not have every single idea in your head all at once, I would shout, in order to dig through it to find what you truly believe? How can you not question everything?

I had a soft spot for a few of the kids, mostly the ones who were there on scholarships, the ones who got bused in, and I tried really hard to teach to them—I promise I did. But getting so close to that fire was too much for me. It was the beginning of the end when a girl, a good student and someone I had been impressed with up to that point, came into my classroom sobbing, shielded and caressed by her best friend. I gently escorted her and her friend out of my room to find out what was wrong, did she want to talk about it, did she absolutely not want to talk about it, did she need to just sit in my office for the day, how could I help? I thought someone must have died. I really did. She was crying so hard, she could not make words. I hugged her and stroked her hair and then looked at her friend quizzically. "Is everything OK? Does she need to go home?" and her friend said, in a very simple and mournful tone, "Oh, Miss Rierson. Her father had been promising her an Audi SUV and she got the family's used Volvo instead. Can you believe it?" My eye immediately started twitching in a way that it never had before, but in a way that it would forever afterward when faced with utter bullshit that I knew I was going to have to try to stay measured in the face of. I said the words before my brain had the good sense to stop them, "Are you FUCKING KIDDING ME?!" pushed the girl from my embrace, went back into my classroom, where twenty-one other students were waiting, and said, "Everyone on their feet NOW!" I walked back out to the two girls in the hallway, who were now looking confused and maybe a little scared, and said, "FIELD TRIP! EVERYONE FOLLOW ME RIGHT NOW!"

I walked all twenty-three of them out to the faculty parking lot, one that always looked markedly different from the student parking lot full of new and slightly used luxury vehicles all freshly polished with future alma mater stickers on the bumpers (because when you're rich, you know exactly what school you get to go to even before you apply). The faculty lot was full of used, unwashed cars with coffee-mug stains on the dashboards and of vintages several years older than the kids staring at them, with dents and dings and one with a spare tire that had needed to be replaced weeks earlier. That was mine, the one with the spare I could not replace. I walked them to that car, the same car Phillip had dumped on me and Joseph only a year earlier—still broken and busted even though I had had the dents pounded out and the rear axle replaced by a close friend who did the work in exchange for the really good sound system that was in the car.

"In case you aren't clear about how the other ninety-five percent of the world lives, here is my car. In the back you will see that my son's car seat is locked in, so this is also the car I drive my child around in. I drive this car daily to come teach you kids and make about enough money to put gas in it and pay my half of the rent and can only really afford to buy an amount of food that means I usually just eat my son's leftovers." I then handed the keys to the newly sweet-sixteen girl and said, "Here, take it for a spin around the parking lot, won't you?" She took the keys and tried to get in through the driver's side. "Ahh! No no no. You actually have to climb in through the passenger's side, sweetheart. That door hasn't worked in YEARS! It's FINE! You're young and limber!" She walked up to me, started crying again because I was straight-up bullying her at this point, handed me my keys, and said, "I am so sorry, Miss Rierson. I am so sorry." All I could bring myself to say was, "You are better than thinking you deserve every single thing you want already—get back to class and get to work."

For most of the rest of that year I tried to avoid giving any more lectures about class and wealth disparity and the disenfranchisement of everyone who was not a very-upper-class white suburbanite spending their whole life existing within a ten-mile radius of people who look and act just like them. A lot of those kids were, admittedly through no fault of their own, living in a world that was not real beyond their churches and banks and perfectly manicured gated communities on every corner. I saw that year out, learned how to keep my opinions to myself, and stayed in touch with some deeply good students with whom I made real connections. And then I gladly left to find work that I might be better tempered for.

That was when baking reentered my life. After I decided I could easily replace the paltry $26K per year I was making at the high school in ways that did not take me away from my son thirteen hours a day, I informed the headmaster I would not be returning, much to his (and my) relief. Once I had made friends with a few of the other first-year teachers, I learned through our after-work bitch sessions that two of the men, men my age who had an equal degree and equal experience, were making a good $10K to $15K more than I was, had had their moving expenses paid, and had the additional perk of a living stipend to get them through the summer before payroll started. They were more shocked and surprised than I was, but I'll admit I couldn't believe that this was still the contemporary landscape for women in the workforce. They had not asked for any of those perks or benefits. It had all been offered by the headmaster without question.

I did ask—right before I got the lecture about what a bad influence an unwed mother was for the young girls at the school—for moving expenses, for more money, for all of it because I had been coached by Vivian, my old art teacher, to do so. I had been told that the best they could do was to get my paperwork pushed through quickly so that I might get my health care benefits earlier than when payroll started. I had to work double time at TradeWinds that summer to save money to move to Nashville, to have enough to cover deposits, to survive a month of not being paid, to feed my kid, to feed me. The day I got my first paycheck from that shit job, I had rolled five dollars' worth of quarters just to buy gas to drive the twenty minutes it took to get to work and I was already overdue on Joseph's day-care payment. It was my first desk job, and learning that I was dealing with antics I had been gaslit into believing no longer existed in our world, because feminism!, pushed my already aggressive fury about fairness and equality over the fucking edge. Poverty and inequality breed an unsettled nature in a person. And they breed something very dangerous and insidious in the powerful men who write the contracts with biases that they will never admit they have as they continue to decide how this world gets to go. You can't be accused of sexism or racism if you hire the person, right? Even if you create conditions wherein a person's work ethic and survivability are on the line. And then you can do it over and over again, showing how you gave women and black people a chance, and it wasn't your fault they couldn't "hack" it, so that your rooms are eventually filled only with men, men you paid very well out of the gate and gave every advantage to, men just like you, whom you actually value, whom you give every perk to without their asking— men who don't threaten your place in the world, men who give you enough of a sense of well-being and safety for all that fragile shit you will never admit you wake up in a cold sweat to every night.

After that, it took very little time for me to establish how to make money and how to help keep the family from sinking further into poverty. Not a lot of money, but more than the teaching job provided. This was in part largely thanks to my willingness to say yes to absolutely anything I was asked to do. While I wanted to stay in the art community, solely writing was not going to cut it, and baking helped, becoming a semi-stable source of income, alongside writing art features for indie rags and local papers and waiting tables. Eventually, and as our family grew, I found that I could bake while the kids slept or while they played on the kitchen floor or while I fed them in their high chairs.

I would eventually make all of Joseph's friends' birthday cakes, the only criterion being that they were never themed. God help me, I'll admit, I tried once. But the shame and cataclysmic results were something I still have nightmares about. I could promise my friends that any cake I made would be delicious and pretty, but I could never make them themed or cartooned, please god. For all the things I was good at, making a SpongeBob SquarePants figure out of fondant was not one of them. Admittedly, I was defeated by it, but also I was grossed out by it. Fondant tastes like plastic asshole, like you're eating the sole of a shoe, like gum found under a subway seat. Having to peel a heavy drape of cornstarch and sugar off your cake is a goddamned travesty. Eating it is even more of a travesty. It's just a straight-up unkind travesty.

Out loud, I tried to stay polite and nonjudgmental, and my commitment to flavor over flair seemed to be appreciated by the people around me. It was also my first indicator that I was aiming for something beyond a traditional pleasure in baking. My notebooks came back out, my trips to the library started again. I found that I had ideas and standards. I was interested in, and seemingly dedicated to, finesse and beauty and classicism—hallmark traits of a pastry chef, a life and career I still had no indication I could ever call my own. Over time, I would get requests for things more refined than birthday cake for their parents' parties and holiday get-togethers. I didn't know many people my age who had a kid; all of Joseph's friends' parents were significantly older and better established than we were. They were all record producers and famous musicians married to supermodels and lawyers and Vanderbilt University scientists and doctors. They had nice houses and new clothes and beautiful furniture. They hosted cocktail parties and drank good wine. They talked about the gold-gilded toilets they had bought in Japan that shot warm water up your ass with just the touch of a button. They had private yoga classes in their backyards. Yet mostly they were all cool as shit.

If I had a chip on my shoulder about wealthy people courtesy of Mein Headmaster und die Monster Kinder, which I did, those parents started to smooth the edges a bit (except for the gilded toilet from Japan; that still turns my stomach). When I think back about how different my life was from theirs, yet how they all welcomed me and my kids into their worlds and supported us without pitying us, I remember why Nashville was such a distinct part of who I became. By and large, these were people who also didn't come from much but worked hard to earn their way—a lot of musicians in that mix. I learned a great deal about how to foster community, no matter your status, from those people. They saw something in me and I appreciated that, qualities I had been waiting my whole life for someone to recognize. They saw my drive and my grit, and they liked my food. And they gave me a chance to support my family with that work.

Back then, Nashville was full of people who wanted you to be your best. We did it together and supported one another. Everyone was all in if you wanted to open a taco truck, if you wanted to design western wear, if you wanted to start a burlesque troupe, if you wanted to sell strudel out of your apartment. Let me test your salsas, let me buy my kids' snacks from you, let me help you build your tiny kitchen. I'll do it! Nashville was all in if you wanted to hold wine classes out of someone's living room or, say, do this crazy thing where you sell thirty seats to a dinner out of a borrowed coffee shop—an idea just starting to be called a "pop-up"—and cook for anyone who wanted to come. Nashville wanted you to win. And, though we struggled, I had generous patrons, and I sometimes made upward of two hundred dollars a week just by making bread and pastry—and back then, even those weeks when it was only an extra twenty bucks really helped.

Besides the money, I also used this as a somewhat grifter-y way to keep my own family fed on the regular. I knew I could float a check at the Bi-Rite down the street from us on Belmont Boulevard over the weekend. I learned that the store made bank deposits only on early Monday and Thursday mornings. (I learned this courtesy of a cashier who saw me postdating a check and winked with her generous information.) If I wrote the check late enough on a Thursday night, I could get ingredients for the orders as well as buy groceries for our house, and then would spend the weekend making all the tarts and cakes and cookies and breads for random people in our apartment building or neighborhood—sometimes making double just from the excess of ingredients for my own family. This would also allow me to feed the kids square and lovingly prepared meals without having to scrape as much as we did through the week. Come Monday, when the payments were in hand from the deliveries and the cash came in from waiting tables, I could be at the bank by 8:00 a.m. to make sure the check I had written on Thursday night did not bounce. We were resourceful. It was difficult, but we still did not feel desperate.

Our separate families, each thinking the other was going to be the one that brought some semblance of balance or responsibility to their adult children, realized very quickly that John and I were, by their standards, equally dysfunctional in matters pertaining to traditional, and in their minds "good," decision making. We felt perfectly matched and made sense to each other, rooting each other on for our version of success and what we deemed responsibility. John was installing art at the Frist, our local art museum, and working at a frame shop across town. He was making art at night and in the early mornings, and his sculpture was a priority for us. We each dreamed big, and while I eventually became the dedicated planner and business-minded one of the two of us—not a hard-won competition, really—we were simply simultaneously dedicated to not giving up on raising our family with the belief that we could actually make a living—a good, honest living—with the work we both knew we were meant to do.

It was important for us to make it work, the life we knew we wanted. And it was important for us to do that work and stick to it in front of our kids and with our kids. We wanted them to know that if you worked hard enough, you could do what you were meant to do, whether it was to be a banjo picker or a writer. We did not want them ever to feel that they had to give up on the thing they loved just for money, because money will come and go, and if you look hard enough, you can find a way to make a buck. We had seen too many people in our lives give up on the thing they were so clearly created to be, to do, solely for the big house, the promise of happiness from wealth, and the familial expectations, and, most of all, because the fear was too much to live with. John and I, and our kids, to be fair, sacrificed a lot, were willing to not own a home, to not have new things or the best wardrobes or the nicest cars. Those all seemed like shadows of real happiness. We tried to be makers, not consumers. We wanted stability and security, of course we did. But not at the expense of being honest with ourselves. We worked hard and believed that we could have all these things because of our commitment to our work, not despite it.

I was full of big, lofty ideals about what we could do; enthusiasm for everything just poured out of me. And when Maggie starting to actively be a voice in our family, to ask questions about me and the world and herself, it became exponentially more important for me to define what my life as a woman was going to be, especially to her. When the doctor announced, "It's a GIRL!" and John Donovan fainted, I thought I might *finally* understand some things about women, about my own mother, things that had always escaped and confused me about the way I saw women interact within my family or in the world. But the opposite happened. I became more distanced from understanding why women do what they do to one another. When I held Maggie in my arms, looked at her face, watched her breathing, I felt nothing but unbridled hope and an urge to clear every possible hurdle for her. Having a daughter brought an immediacy to a task I had been living for myself since I left Savannah, a focus I was leading my family with but had not given a name to yet. She defined my spirit very quickly.

. . .

THE HARDEST PART was that John and I hardly saw each other during those years. We were merely a tag team between working and childcare. If he was home, I was working. If I was home, he was working. That was how we spent the first ten years of our marriage. During those early years, I started to discover things about myself, found myself in kitchens more than at my desk writing, found myself in libraries looking over baking books again while the kids watched puppet shows and played in the courtyard. I found myself attaching to the idea of food as something that mattered beyond physical sustenance or a few extra dollars on the weekend. I could not have known then that the deep hunger I felt for my life, for answers, for survival, for providing well for my children from a place that felt honest would create such a definitive bigger picture. I didn't realize I was inching my way toward a career that would define so much about who I became as a mother and as a woman, much less as a person in my community.

We were teetering dangerously toward the edge of poverty, taking the car seats out of the car each night in case the car got repossessed, paying medical bills five dollars per month just to keep from being destroyed by Equifax, counting pocket change for gas money. We were working harder than ever before, but the middle class in our country was disappearing and the cost of living was going up and our paychecks were staying the same. It all led to a seminal moment in our story—the kind of moment when something was going to have to give. We had a five-month-old daughter, a five-year-old son, a dog, two cats, and a hamster named Burnt Waffle, and rented a third-floor, one-bedroom walk-up approximately five blocks from the piss- and Red Bull–soaked college bar called Jacksons (now an expensive parking lot), where I was actualizing my worst nightmare as a cocktail waitress for trust-fund frat boys and too-skinny sorority girls who thought the dumber they sounded, the sexier they were. I learned how to effectively mop up a floor at 3:30 a.m. after approximately two hundred college kids had spent their parents' money on multiple vodka drinks and deep-fried cookie-dough eggrolls. Most nights I found myself calculating the physics of vomit and how to rid my world of it as quickly as possible.

Every night, though, between 10:30 and 10:45 p.m., I would sneak off to the bathroom. Here were fifteen minutes during which I would go into a stall, try to restore my faith in myself, and remember what I was working for. I usually entered with a furrowed brow and a bit of a quiver in my lip, but there was also a kind of sanctity in that time that I now recognize as lifesaving. There were two stalls, and the left one was mine every night for a luxurious fifteen minutes. The right stall was roomier, but it was a catfight to get to it—that stall became a dressing room, a makeshift bedroom, a refuge after too many drinks, a burlesque for so many young girls, girls my age who were figuring out all the things their bodies could do alone, together, sober, drunkenly.

The smaller stall ended up being more useful to me in the long run, my experiences being very different from that of those girls in the right stall. I had my own specific needs. I could stand on the toilet seat (there were no lids), pop a mad squat, and lean my back on the cleanest part of the wall behind the toilet. In this squatted stance, I could rest my elbows on my knees and get into position. Each breast would get a less-than-adequate six to seven minutes, but it was enough to relieve the pressure. The breast pump was a manual one—meaning I had to pump myself like I was doing simultaneous hand-stress workouts: one hand on the pump handle, squeezing feverishly, and the other hand on my raging-hot, overly engorged, incredibly painful breast, squeezing as gently as I could. It sounded like a wagon wheel that needed greasing, each squeeze in half-second intervals: "squeak . . . squeak . . . squeak"—while the carnival of lipstick, cocaine, orgasm kaleidoscope rotated in and out of the right stall. My breast milk felt so dirty—simply because of the things the next-door neighbors brought each night—that I always threw it out and started fresh when I walked through my apartment door for Maggie Donovan's four a.m. feeding.

After I closed down the bar on the night when the right stall afforded me my very first voyeuristic lesbian experience as I "squeak . . . squeak . . . squeak" excreted my baby's milk and listened to what had to be the metal trash can being torn off the wall in the wake of a series of groans, giggles, cigarette drags, and the eventual fumble with tangled bras (both theirs and mine), followed by a somber four more hours of serving appletinis, I walked home. For once I was not disgusted or put out by my stall neighbors. They seemed like women I could have been friends with, based solely on their intermittent conversations between all the fingering and giggling. I felt a sadness, a loss of youth, a loss of experiences, a realization that even though I had no regrets about my life and the choices I had made, things maybe just didn't have to be so hard. That maybe in some parallel universe I was kissing a girl in a bathroom stall for the first time, or riding in a car with loud music while smoking cigarettes with a handsome boy who wanted to take me somewhere to have his way with me in the dark.

I was very tired. We were very broke. Things felt impossible in a way that they had not before. I was twenty-six years old, felt like I had no potential career path, and in that moment felt like I had nothing but hot breasts with leaky nipples and dirty sneakers to call my own. I let myself have a one-off pity party, and that four a.m. shuffle home in the dark summer heat was bleak, to say the least. I dragged my body, feeling as if it weighed twice its amount, up three flights of wooden, faded teal stairs, trying to allow a feeling of sweetness for myself and for how my lean legs in green sneakers and a white eyelet skirt looked so pretty against the peeling sea-foam paint on that staircase. I sat on the stoop outside my apartment door and tried to collect myself and force some kind of feeling of "good" before I walked into my home to feed my daughter. I admired my legs again, thinking about how strong they were. And then the music started.

ONE OF THE PERKS of living in Nashville is that no matter how low you get in your life, or what odd hour it is, chances are you'll stumble across some kind of beautiful music to remind you of how lucky you are to have the gift of all your senses. The reward for making it up those stairs on painfully tired legs was knowing that I could sit on that top step and, if I lingered long enough, get to listen to my across-the-hall neighbor play her piano. Holly was Hank Williams's granddaughter, and she never let me down when I needed her the most, even at four a.m.

I leaned my back against my door and sat with her piano for as long as I could. Suddenly, I remembered something else that brought me a sliver of joy: I was to expect a package that day, my mom had said. My dad's baby sister, Aunt Barbara, a book broker and collector, regularly sent me boxes upon boxes of books. They would come in bulk: cookbooks, art books, Joan Didion books; she sent me all my favorite things, gifts that, especially at this time in my life, felt quite literally lifesaving for me. That night I walked in to just one lone book, though. It had been wrapped in a brown paper bag with my maiden name written in black Sharpie and then scratched out with a pencil, an arrow pointing to the proper name "Donovan" written in red ink to the right of the pencil scratches. As I pulled back the wrapping, I saw the words: *How to Cook a Wolf.*

I found M. F. K. Fisher and *How to Cook a Wolf* during a time when, truly and intensely, that guy, the wolf, was at my door: fangs, claws, hunger, and all. While we were happy, we were also starting to feel a desperation that most people would have not suffered through. With all our ideals about living on our terms, the reality was that we were working harder than anyone we knew because we had to and yielding far less. I've never had a place to fall, I don't have a rich daddy to bail me out of anything, failure was not a thing I could accept. We hadn't chosen a life as entitled kids who had a safety net might have. In fact, if I know myself, I bet I clung to those high ideals to make myself feel as if it were a choice, romanticizing our bohemian ideas about being artists. But, truthfully, we were working our asses off because we had to in that moment for not just a future yield but a very immediate one, and things had gotten to a point where money was so tight and things felt so impossible that we could not work hard enough to get by, no matter how many shifts I pulled, no matter how much bread I baked, no matter if John took a third job as a Domino's delivery driver. We were the adults and our kids needed new shoes. After that long and dire walk home, the one where I seriously started questioning myself, it felt remarkable to arrive to find written words about living without, building from nothing, giving from a place of not having. It helped me define how to live and thrive and grow, not as a chef but as a woman, a mother, a human being.

That night, I scooped up the used copy, went to get my daughter out of her crib, and with tears in my eyes from the night I had just had and the pain from the engorged breasts that had crept up on me while I sat on the stairwell stoop—not to mention the sense of loss I felt for a lot of things at the moment—I held a hungry baby to nurse on my lap, and I read these words:

> There's a whining at the threshold,
>
> There's a scratching at the floor.
>
> To work! To work! In Heaven's name
>
> The wolf is at the door!

I read the entire book in the early morning with my daughter alternating between sleeping and nursing in my arms, putting the book down as the sun started rising. And then I read it again every morning at that same time for many days in a row, each time renewed by the time my son woke up to make him a beautiful breakfast of grits with sorghum and butter, sweet so he would love it, and one hard-boiled egg, feeling like a champion. There was heart in those meals, and flavor. There was something instinctual in me that Fisher poked, breathed life into. She spoke to my writer's sensibilities. She spoke to the idea that even though it felt like we had "nothing," the romance of life actually comes from the refusal to stay in the dark and craggy corners where we are sometimes put or kept. Fisher wrote simply about creating beauty from nothing by finding and preserving that ever-important generosity of spirit, even when you have so little.

This whole thing, this career, started as I worked my way out of nearly desperate times, hungry times as a mother and wife and woman in the world trying to create a life for myself and my family that I believed in. Fisher's work was my bible when I had mouths to feed. And, like any good bible, it fed me stories of how I could do more, be more, and see more in my muck and mire, the life stuff that feels at once hard and important. Stretching the food, stretching my need for it, and finding beauty in feeding others when I was both spiritually and physically hungry myself, was a pivotal moment of understanding for me, and it became the foundation for my life and career. Her words and ideas collided with the mounting desperation I was feeling. What came out was a grace that I had no idea existed in me.

My early journey with food was getting to know that proverbial wolf at the door—the one that all the good writers and singers talk about—in the most intimate and dreadful way. He's a real thing, that guy, that wolf. He comes into your life, he lies in wait for any misstep that might allow him to pounce, he reminds you every day that you're potentially at his mercy. He tries to scare you into giving up. He nearly wins. Reckoning with him brought me to a strong realization I'd never had before and will likely never have again: I could walk—even in an exhausted, milk-engorged stupor—straight into an understanding with myself about what my life had the potential to mean.

I was shown my childhood on a page. I had to grow up a little to see that this story, this whole conversation about giving of yourself, is the story of my mother, likely your mother, your grandmother, my grandmother, me. *How to Cook a Wolf* is not just a generationally specific way to talk about how to survive hard times, postwar rationing, and community-crop sharing. It is the story of how women are bountiful and generous in the face of loss and desperation and need. This story about how we have all been saving one another as women forever is the one that I never knew how to admit was already in my bones because of my mother and her mother and my aunts and how they saved us the best way they knew how.

I began to make my life's work out of the spirit of that text. It started with my babies, and it slowly stretched itself out into my community until I found myself knee-deep in the throes of a career I never planned yet felt completely destined for.

# 10

## STAMINA

*Buttermilk*

S CHLEPPING PASTRY AND BREAD and cakes out of an apartment on the west side of town, waiting tables at a shit-hole tavern, I was very far from Margot McCormack's world. All the while, on the east side of town, there was a restaurant serving classic French food, simple and fresh and perfectly executed. I did not even know restaurants of that caliber existed until I walked in to apply for a job at hers. If I remember correctly, I had heard from a friend of a friend that Margot was hiring but that she was, notably, "a battle-ax" and "a straight-up bitch." I would soon learn that this meant those with that opinion simply did not have what it took or were not passionate enough to deserve to stay in her orbit. She had high standards, and she did not care if you liked her. Thank god. I was immediately attracted to Margot's focus. And completely intimidated. Gratefully, I'm not easily scared off.

Margot Café is known as the South's Chez Panisse and Margot its Alice Waters. Born and raised in Nashville, Margot was a chef in New York City when being a chef in New York City meant something. She came up in the era of *Kitchen Confidential* lore. And she behaved like it. She opened Margot Café & Bar in 2001, and it is still a pillar of high standards and delicious food to this day. I wandered into that restaurant in 2005, a few months after Maggie Donovan turned one and when the restaurant itself was just four years old—which is a strange thing to realize in retrospect. Four years into a new restaurant is its mere infancy— you're just learning to walk, just learning how it all works, just learning how to maintain your vision. It felt so established already to me, like I was walking into something that had existed for decades; that is how clear Margot's vision was, and that was how strong a leader she was. Yet looking back, she was really just finding her feet as a chef-owner, and that changed my perspective on so many things I felt at the time.

Standing all of maybe five foot four, Margot wore a tight, curly, black haircut and a perpetual disapproving squint, her apron high and tight and a pair of black, plastic slip-on Birkenstock kitchen shoes that she always slid off and on her white crew-socked feet while she sat with us during lineup, her legs always spread wide and her torso hunched over them with a menu in hand and a cocksureness that I could only dream of having. When her business partner, Jay Frein, an affable guy with a lot of money (hence his perpetual good mood, I figured), hired me, Margot was not the slightest bit interested in me or my shit. Jay hired me even though I lacked so much as a drop of knowledge on classical savory French food or wine or professional service. But he thought there was something there, which Margot, it became apparent, did not.

There was a requirement to purchase and study the *Food Lover's Companion* so that we knew exactly what Margot was talking about at every lineup and, of course, to actually know what the hell we were talking about tableside. I could not afford it, the book (or, if I'm being honest, the time to study), and never could find my way to purchasing it during those first few crucial months. She knew it. And, even though I borrowed the book from a fellow server who had been working there since the first day and knew every possible menu variation, I simply could not learn fast enough. The menu changed every day, and every day there were new things about which I knew only the basics—I certainly could have been better prepared each and every time. She relentlessly grilled me during lineup some days, asking me, with a pretty impressive snark in her voice, to detail the ingredients and preparation of every single menu item, stopping me short and lecturing me when I would forget there was lemon juice in the aioli or for stating that the ice cream was made with both whole milk *and* cream, not just cream, and how could I, how *dare* I, mix up gribiche with escabeche, what was I? An idiot? She frequently brought me to tears over details that I now know are crucial to a decent server's basic arsenal about a chef's repertoire.

I do not get brought to tears easily. Yet Margot got me there at least once weekly, often thrice weekly. I was frustrated by my inability, by how professional and experienced everyone was at their jobs, by how long it was taking me to catch up. They were able to talk about wine as if they had all been fucking vintners in the vineyard while eating and studying every variety of grape at the same time, bent over an oak barrel, little wine whores who could tell you about a Uruguayan Tannat grape as if they were as common as a Concord, me never thinking about it beyond the "this is good, see if you like it" education that Tom had given me. Their whole lives seemed to be about studying food as if they themselves were going to be the ones to cook each dish.

It was fucking terrifying. And thrilling. And I was proving to be fucking terrible at it. This was a very big step from serving twenty-year-old fornicating-under-the-table Vanderbilt students who were high or drunk and just wanted to lick alfredo sauce off each other's faces for a laugh and leave two-dollar tips on a hundred-dollar tab, but it was a step I cared about and tried to take as steadily and as sincerely as possible. Even in my TradeWinds experience, I had never seen this world before. No matter how much I had studied and obsessed over baking, that was a wholly private—even emotional—education. This job was a crash course in getting my shit straight and learning about a food world that was real, that was dedicated to the same things I was dedicated to without even realizing I had a place I belonged to. I had a chance to be a professional if I wanted it. And there I was, fumbling every day in front of an audience of intelligent and bright humans whom I desperately wanted to count myself among.

I had a lot to learn beyond the actual trade and technical points of the work, and that was where I may have found the most trouble. There was an entire dance of restaurant industry social protocol that I was also messing up left and right. I basically kept to myself in the way of personal information and what I was willing to give of my free time, and I tried to just focus on the work when I was there. This is a major demerit in any restaurant, but especially in a small, chef-owned one. Margot Café was a world, an entire world, she had built for herself, and it seemed expected that everyone, every single person in that building, would share their lives and off-duty time like a family. This seeming requirement was bizarre to me. Even with all the beauty that Tom and the TradeWinds crew brought me, we still had lives outside of that trailer that had nothing to do with our coworkers. At Margot, being pals and hanging out with everyone outside of work was not something I realistically had time or energy for, but it was something that they all did, routines they all naturally fell into. They all went to get beers and smoke cigarettes across the street at a bar called 3 Crow nearly every night, or they lingered on the patio at the restaurant to wind down after work—the most pressing things they had waiting for them at home were a few Chihuahuas whom they treated like human children. There was nothing wrong with that, but I had an actual family, with real live children to take to school in the mornings, and I knew better than to think they would understand. I would calculate my till, tip out the bartender and the back waiter, make a bit of pleasant conversation, and then go home.

I left work when it was over because I had kids to care for, kids I missed every second of the day when I was not with them. I could not attend a lot of the many (MANY) work parties, and it came off as me not being a team player, as if I were snubbing them. But my life was not that of a typical restaurant worker, and that would prove to be an obstacle for me for most of my career—trying to make my family work while I made my career work was always more of a struggle than it should have been. It's very different now; everyone seems older and wiser, and they (finally) have families and seem to understand what it feels like to have priorities that don't involve taking tequila shots after a long shift and waking up at two p.m. with just enough time to shower and get to work by four p.m. I did not play the industry game right and that was in part why Margot was not impressed. Trying to have a family and work in hospitality seemed to be a fool's choice. Yet there I was, that fool, strangely dedicated and committed to making my way because I had now found the work I realized I was built for. All my past oddities actually existed in one profession and I felt I had found my people, even if they didn't know it yet because of how elusive I appeared to be.

After I had excelled enough as a server to prove to her that I cared and deserved to keep my job, Margot sat me down at my first employee review and said, "Look, Lisa, you clearly are getting better at this job, but I need to make something really clear to you. You have just walked into MY dream and I need to know that you understand that because it's not obvious to me that you do." She was no-nonsense, to put it mildly. She cared totally about her restaurant, a trait I could not fault her for. But there was still an expectation that I would fold into her life, not just do my job well. I was focused on my family's survival and trying to keep my own dreams alive while I put food on the table at home.

Years later, after she and her wife, Heather, adopted their son, Margot and I ran into each other, and she had the frazzled, exhausted, and slightly crazed look of a new mother on her face. She hugged me, not a usual Margot move, and said, "You know, I had no IDEA what your life was like until now. Good job keeping shit together while you raised TWO kids, Donovan. I'm impressed." It was a moment of recognition that I did not know I needed—not of being acknowledged as a good mother, I don't need anyone's opinion about that (they wouldn't know anyway), but of her thinking I was a good worker. I finally had confirmation that she knew how much I cared, despite how different I was from everyone else she employed at the time.

I think that as Margot watched me grow into my career she became proud of me, and even if it took some time, I think she realized what I was working for and who I was despite her initial impression of me. Under her, I worked for someone I greatly admired, someone who earned everything she had in her life, and she worked daily, hourly, minute by minute, to make sure it was protected. She had earned the right to her dream, the one I had a walk-on role in.

Not only was I inspired by the standards she set inside those walls and at every single table and with every single plate that left her kitchen, I was inspired by the fact that she made something come true for herself. The singular thing she had missed about me at first, but seemed to understand eventually, was that I was likely paying closer attention than anyone else. I watched and learned and was quietly writing blueprints for my own life. I started to dream again under

Margot's roof. I started thinking more permanently. And I became dedicated to quality and hard work for the sake of the work, not just for the sake of survival.

It has to be said, for those out in the world who don't understand what financial insecurity and poverty do to a person: almost the entirety of my ability to think better, to finally focus on the beautiful work and intentions Margot had created in the world, was because I was actually, for the first time since moving to Nashville, making enough money to do more than hustle and pivot. John had gotten a tenured-track position at Middle Tennessee State University, and all our hard work and sacrifices were beginning to pay off—it was the first time we were able to exhale as a family and think bigger. It is hard, nearly impossible, to dream and plan and dedicate energy toward successful endeavors beyond a paycheck when you are broke and hungry. It is nearly impossible to think beyond each day when you are pinching (and rolling) pennies to make it through the week. Those couple of years working for Margot and MTSU were a big shift for us. We moved to east Nashville, and my job became one I worked hard to keep. It became a job where I wanted to thrive, a job where learning and growing were given priority—and were expected, at that. Margot and I would find our way to a long, very loving relationship full of mutual respect and mentorship. I now carry her voice with me as a guide. And, when I can't guess what she might offer, I call her to have her tell me.


MY TIME AT MARGOT CAFÉ led me toward more. It led me to the first place I ever worked pastry—a place called City House. And City House happened for me because I met Anne Kostroski at Margot Café & Bar. A decidedly local place, but not one without big-time ambitions, City House was helmed by Anne and her then-husband, Tandy Wilson, a prodigal son raised in the high-cotton suburbs of Nashville, who returned home to do good for his town—and he certainly did, with enormous help from his very well-established father. I was invited to help open City House in 2007 with and by Anne, a pastry chef trained at the CIA (Culinary Institute of America) who had moved to town with Tandy from California. We all worked together at Margot, where Tandy was the sous chef and Anne took a job as a server, making more money than being Margot's pastry chef would have provided so that they could save and afford to take time off, eventually, to build their restaurant.

Anne became a work acquaintance and the first coworker I started to talk to about the little makeshift bake shop I was running out of my apartment. Margot had agreed that people could pick up their orders from me at the restaurant if it was before five p.m. Anne started to take an interest in what she saw. She was curious where I learned how to make what she deemed a professional-looking product, and I think she was interested in my desire to learn from her every chance I got, every conversation being a strange and overly eager picking of her brain (I asked many questions and she was very patient). The day I made a birthday cake for a fellow server (and a dear friend), four layers of red velvet, decorated and sculpted to look like Dolly Parton with giant cupcake breasts wearing a strapless gown with a flame job, the only "themed" cake I would do, her interest piqued. The day I brought a stone-fruit strudel to a staff party, with damn-near-perfect flakes of pastry braided and egg-washed, baked to a beautiful golden color, filled with roasted plums and apricots, however, she wanted to know what the hell was going on and why I was not doing it more and professionally.

This was my first relationship as a baker with a baker who actually knew that world. Anne had been a pastry chef at Tre Vigne in Napa Valley, working in the glamorous vineyards under and around other professional cooks who ran in the same circles as Thomas Kellar and Alice Waters. Now here she was, excited and impressed by me and the things I was cobbling together out of a small, antique oven in an out-dated kitchen with whatever ingredients I could afford. So when the offer was made to try that career on for size, I went along with Anne and Tandy when they decided to start City House, the primary school where I cut my teeth and never looked back.

City House undoubtedly helped put Nashville on the map as a culinary destination. It is a beautiful space, once the home and studio of an important Nashville sculptor named Alan LeQuire. The kitchen served smart and very pointedly beautiful but never pretentious food, something that, besides Margot Café, was new to Nashville. There was a dedication to local ingredients that Nashville hadn't yet seen. Inspired by Italy's decidedly simple yet perfectly executed style, with things that mattered and were honest to our region, City House thrived. My role was marginal at first, assisting Anne, organizing, cooking, training, and learning—first by her side and then, within a few weeks, mostly on my own while she trained servers and dealt with the wine program. She gave me a lot of room to learn, to ask questions, and to settle into my new place, my new career. The restaurant was widely praised and nearly an immediate wild success in town and there started to be hints of national recognition. Their marriage, however, didn't last, and Anne would leave within mere months of the restaurant's opening. My career, though, the one I finally admitted to myself that I wanted, got started because Anne asked me to join her and proceeded to give me a space—and a small starter pack of a dozen or so beautifully written recipes to grow into. Our time together was short, but those few months were a crash course in technique, quality control over large batches, math, balancing a menu, and tasting everything you touch, from your ingredients to your final products.

Things happened very quickly from there. Once the dust settled from Anne's sudden departure, Tandy walked in through the back door and took me aside to say, "You have big shoes to fill, can you do it?" I said, "Yes, absolutely," went out back, called John and told him I could not pick the kids up from school that day, and stepped up without a moment's hesitation.

I took over for Anne in more ways than one. I was all in. She had also run the front of the house and so that was left unattended in her absence as well. Thus there were many days, many many many days actually, perhaps a whole year's worth of days, when I would arrive as soon as I dropped my kids off at school and preschool, work pastry alone alongside two men who ran the rest of the kitchen—the sous chefs, who would become my brothers forever, Aaron Clemins and Sal Avila—and try to crank out some of the best and most welcoming food Nashville had ever seen. Then I would go to the bathroom around four p.m., wash my face, change my clothes, and get ready to help run service. I would run service, wait tables, and close the restaurant, somehow not feeling a lick of exhaustion in my bones. Everything about being there felt correct and aspirational, daily. At night I'd go home, riding high off of seeing my food served to guests, taking inventory the whole time of what worked, what didn't work, and I'd lie in my bed reading more books, taking more notes, writing more ideas into my recipe book. Then I'd get up at five a.m. to feed my babies breakfast, send John off to his day at the university, pack the lunches and get the kids to school, and I'd do it all over again the next day and the day after that. I treated that place as my own and loved every minute of it. I taped a beautiful picture of Edna Lewis above my pastry table and tucked in, learning and growing and—to the boss's credit—was given loads of room to make mistakes, but only once, maybe twice. City House became a second home and the kitchen crew an extension of my family, not out of obligation but because we really loved and cared about one another and put the success of that restaurant as a top priority. Here was where I started to understand Margot's aspirations for me in her restaurant, and what I was missing in my absence.

Aaron Clemins was the first person to make me feel wholly capable in a kitchen, and every cook needs that. He was brutally honest, something I always require of any good friendship, but most especially ones that exist inside a kitchen. For a while this meant that, if I felt I nailed something, I could only believe it to be true if Aaron agreed. Eventually, as I gained confidence, we started disagreeing. I started being surer of when I nailed something and only *wanted* him to like it. Sometimes he didn't and would push back. This was how I got better. This was how I got good. He was gruff and surly, exactly how you'd imagine a seasoned cook to be. He was also charming and funny as fuck. He may have had a bad attitude about some things and his taste in music made me cringe, but that endeared him to me even more. I learned the fine art of shit talk with Aaron, over a bowl of cheap cereal (our favorite shared vice, a secret stash we kept in dry storage and a daily moment of pause each morning), and I learned how not to bullshit myself in a kitchen. The latter would be the most important tool that I left City House with.

I was a fast learner and very dedicated: so much so that Maggie Donovan was raised at table 21, a corner banquette table, drawing and coloring and watching episodes of PBS shows on my laptop most days. We could only afford two days a week at her preschool, so John and I balanced the rest of the week out between our schedules. Even at three years old, Maggie knew the rules of the kitchen, where she was allowed to walk, how to say "corner" as loud as she could if she was coming in (thankfully, it was just me and the sous chefs prepping). I was proud of the work I was doing. I was proud of the people I found myself around, at last feeling wholly part of something that made sense to me.

I started cultivating my own style of menu there, simple desserts that focused on flavor and tradition and ingredients. We would put out a basic panna cotta, my nod to Claudia Fleming—an idol of a pastry chef who ran the Gramercy Tavern kitchen in the 1990s, whose book *The Last Course* and whose simple yet not at all precious type of dessert menu was seminal to pastry chefs of a certain age—but it would be made with beautiful buttermilk from Cruze Farm in Knoxville, buttermilk so important and otherworldly that it literally changed the direction of my entire menu after the first time a friend walked through our back door with a case full of it.

We all tasted it, our eyes widening with each sip. It was buttermilk that, after you tried it, made you realize that you had to rethink everything about what you were doing in order to accommodate it. It was robust and clean, rich and tangy but not too tangy, and the most beautiful color of cream you'd ever seen. The yellow was just subtle enough that you wondered if you'd ever own a house just so you could paint all the walls the same shade and live inside the creamy thought of buttermilk for the rest of your life. The farmers who made it, Earl and Cheri Cruze and their daughter, Colleen, would joke about how their buttermilk not only accounted for a good, sturdy long life but also for Earl's sturdy constitution and constant fire for Mrs. Cruze. As they spoke that day, sipping buttermilk, talking about how "fresh" Earl was, I suddenly remembered my first job in Dahlonega, Georgia, at a family buffet right on the town square called Park Place—a thing I strangely hadn't thought about since I had left it twenty years earlier.

. . .

PARK PLACE WAS OWNED and run by a man in his late sixties named Obie who stood about seven feet tall and had a stomach as round as a full-term pregnant lady's, with a pair of suspenders pulled to the point of uncertainty over it. He always wore a black trucker's cap that had "I'm Not Playing Hard to Get, I Am Hard to Get" printed on it. I would arrive early in the morning during the summer days, around seven, to peel potatoes in the corner by the dish pit. I'd sit on two egg crates stacked into a short stool and peel three cases of potatoes, enough to replenish the mashed-potato bin through supper. After peeling all those potatoes, it was my job to fix up the buffet line, fill the steam tables with water, and then keep an eye on the food, making sure nothing ran out or got too sad looking from sitting too long. After "potato peeler," "refill and stir, Lisa Marie" was my official job title. But every day before the crowds arrived, around nine a.m. as I was setting up the buffet tables, a crooked-bodied man would walk in wearing the same small black cowboy hat and the same worn-out western shirt, sit down at exactly the same table and in the same chair, and Obie would bring him a tall glass full of buttermilk, which he would down in less than three sips every time.

I was too young to understand what the relationship was between those two men. The man was a mystery to me. I could never figure out if he was homeless or just lonely. Looking back, I now know he must have suffered some kind of moderate to severe stroke, one that left him unable to really speak to anyone. I did not know what strokes were back then, to be honest; I was just a kid, had never seen someone who had suffered one, so I didn't understand at the time what was wrong with him. He seemed kind, but he also seemed very separate from the world, outside of it. He was always, somehow, perpetually three days past a proper shave, his face scratchy and unwashed looking. His movements were jagged and hard to watch—they reminded me of the toddlers I would babysit, who knew what each movement should look like but were unable to command their bodies to do it. He would sit there unable to properly wipe the buttermilk from his upper lip, and I can remember wondering how to help, but just smiling from my steam-table work instead. There was something between him and Obie, must have been a lifelong friendship, one that looked strange to a fifteen-year-old girl because so much was unsaid that it looked, from the outside, not to be a friendship at all. I always wondered but never would have dared to ask Obie. He was a kind man but very country and very private and I knew he expected me to respect him as an elder, which I did. He was not interested in being my friend, he was not of that ilk or generation. He was kind. But he was my boss. And I was to stay in my lane when it came to asking questions.

I only hope I was kind to him, the buttermilk drinker. I hope I did not look at him oddly. I hope my smiles were not pitying. I'd like to think that I knew how to handle myself, but you just never know about your fifteen-year-old self. The one thing I know I never could hide was how watching him down that full glass of buttermilk used to turn my stomach, but I could never look away. He seemed so satisfied by it, would sit for about ten minutes more before he got up, and then he would tip his hat to Obie and walk out until the next morning. The only question I ever mustered up the courage to ask Obie about that man was "How does he DRINK that?!" and Obie replied, "Oh, one day you'll know that buttermilk is better for you than your mama's breast milk, and when you're old like us, you need all the help you can get. Plus, it's goddamned delicious after all these years of living."

. . .

WHEN I MET THE CRUZES, I learned that Obie wasn't wrong. And, while I knew there was something special about the Cruzes' buttermilk, I'll admit to feeling like it was connecting me to something that I was only on the periphery of, something I wanted to be less adjacent to and feel more as my own. I was searching for that thing, that southern thing that my daddy has always carried with him, the one that encourages him to crumble cornbread into milk or, better yet, buttermilk when it's around; that southern thing in watching those two men somehow loving each other through a free glass of the stuff in a quiet southern town that they both likely have lived in since the 1930s (if my math is right); the very southern thing in the basic simplicity of how it's made, by letting the leftover milk from making butter sour to fortify and get richer with funk and fat and age—an industrious by-product that farmers figured out gave them strength and virility. Buttermilk was a key, helped me work out the weird distance that I felt from being southern. I'm faulty for romanticizing any number of things. I know this about myself. Buttermilk, though, deserves it all.

In turn, I wanted it to be center stage in everything I made. It always arrived smuggled into the back door of the restaurant, like a black-market ingredient, because no distributors carried it. We had carriers (friends we could pay with food) bring as much as they could tote anytime they were passing through east Tennessee.

Cruze's buttermilk arrived right when I found my stride at writing my menu, and it became a signature ingredient of my desserts at City House. Tandy had held my hand for long enough after Anne left, and then one day it seemed he realized the menu was mine, my voice, my style, and my way of being warm and hospitable at the end of a meal—to this day, all of my menus reflect the way the one at City House looked because it came from a very sincere place inside me. Cookies were Tandy's idea, to honor his admiration for an Italian menu, but I created a space for layer cakes, for pies, for simple and salty crumbles on top of pudding. Once I started developing the menu and writing my own recipes, I found myself building everything around a sincere style of dessert that I was really proud of, one that felt totally honest. That panna cotta, topped with just-sweetened-enough roasted fruit, or a gelée that I had to call Jell-O to get by Tandy's obsession with not seeming pretentious (and to circumnavigate his then-hatred for "fancy" French techniques), slightly salty cookies and grain crumbles with peanuts or pecans, cast-iron cornmeal cakes with buttermilk gelato and honey crunch, cantaloupe sherbet with watermelon granita and a pinch of Maldon sea salt, Olive & Sinclair chocolate pudding cups with tangy crème fraîche and a perfectly bourbon-y butterscotch gelato or pie, cookie plates on cookie plates on cookie plates—these were all things that were at once uncomplicated and thoughtfully prepared—nothing flashy, just good, just delicious, and, ultimately, just comforting.

This became the way I made desserts for life—it was me finding my voice as a pastry chef. I took the technical prowess that Anne had imparted to me in such a short time—the culinary techniques to make sure your product is consistent and beautiful—and all the things I had taught myself of French and American baking and combined it with Tandy's guidance and restraints (some good and important ones, like how to plate without overwhelming the guest, and some annoying and shortsighted, like never being allowed to use vanilla) and made desserts that I am still proud of today.

I was extremely proud of the work I was doing and was constantly engaged in it. I became enthralled by ingredients. I lived for the seasons. I had a running list of ideas in my head, in my notebooks, on the wall above my pastry table. I realized what I was good at (flavor) and what I was bad at (presentation) and really homed in on, respectively, owning this and overcoming that. There was nothing I wanted to do more than to be at my pastry table working out a gelato recipe or fine-tuning a ciabatta loaf for the wood-fired oven. I was doing right by the moment I seized when I said yes to Tandy's "big shoes" offer. I felt not only that I had found my place but also that I had earned it. One of my most important mementos from City House is a note left by Margot McCormack after she had dinner there one night, written on the back of one of my dessert menus, which said, "Perfect desserts! Keep going!" with her name written inside a heart with an arrow going through it.

# 11

## ARITHMETIC

*Bitters and Tonic*

A T THE END OF THE DAY, however, the hard and good work I loved was not enough. After two years of deep commitment, of bringing my best, I had to leave City House. Opening a restaurant is incredibly difficult, and I understand the margins, especially all these years later. I basically understood it then, too, and I tucked into the work believing that I was helping to build something bigger than myself, believing when the owner told me that my raise was coming, he promised, as soon as he could. I believed him. And I *did* feel extremely lucky to be there learning from really good cooks, having the chance to build my recipes, my skills, and my worth—working toward my own future, I thought. If it had been just me, paying rent on a small apartment and eating only at work, sacrificing my quality of life for a job I truly loved, it would have been fine—even though it should not have been. Everyone deserves for their employers to care about an idea as fundamental as quality of life.

Regardless, I had a family. A family I was 50 percent responsible for financially. They were having to sacrifice in ways that were not fair. My husband was working a tenure-track job, doubling up his salary in the summer by installing art at the airport and at local galleries, but this was barely enough to cover rent, utilities, car payments, and other essential overhead necessary to keep a family afloat. Professors don't make what you think, those days are long gone. The money I made had to cover food, day care, clothing, a flip phone, dental visits, doctor visits, gas, and the paltry amount of enrichment we could afford for the kids. I wasn't asking for much, not even a salary, but I did need something to compensate for the increased responsibilities I had been given, had stepped up to, and had been successful at. Things were tight, but the Donovan crew knows how to buckle down better than anyone when we care about something. So we buckled down. I was just turning thirty; by then I knew I wanted my own place—a bakery—someday, and I thought these were still appropriate sacrifices to make to build a future, to be determined about something with a little risk and sacrifice. We were all committed to that restaurant in one way or another, and I believed, very earnestly, that I could be there for five or six more years and then maybe open my bakery next door, to work with and near those guys for as long as I could. And so I waited.

The final straw came when I asked for my first raise for the third time over the course of the second year. I received my first yes, but to a terribly insulting raise of twenty-five cents more an hour and then was told, "That's all I can do right now. I know you'll be fine though, right? With John's teaching salary?" I know the question may have come from a place of concern (a revealing, antiquated, bullshit place of concern, but concern nonetheless). But it was salt in the wound, as if I needed the raise less than anyone else in that kitchen because, what? I was just a wife who was playing dress-up as a pastry chef? Because I was not the "head of the household"? I worked my ass off for Tandy and his sole-proprietorship restaurant. He didn't have a board of directors to answer to, just him and his dad deciding the value of everything and everyone.

So there I was, struggling to make ends meet, with Maggie Donovan on-site during my work hours because I could not afford day care or even a cheap babysitter. I'd been giving Tandy credit as a "cool" boss who let my kid hang out during my work hours, but, really, what it boiled down to was that I was not being compensated reasonably enough to justify my job there if I could not even afford proper day care for my kid. By my estimation, that raise should have been offered the moment those big shoes were presented for me to fill, and here I was groveling for twenty-five cents more an hour nearly a year and a half later. Meanwhile, the sous chefs made salaries and were taken seriously, as if their lives and expenses were more real than mine. Even though I was proud of my work and felt confident that our customers were happy with what came out of my station, I know with every fiber of my being that my work and focus and discipline would have skyrocketed if I'd had to worry less about juggling money and family issues with my work life.

If I could have afforded a basic thing like day care, that would have been a small investment for Tandy to better not only my situation but his as well. Within a week of me being asked if my husband's salary would make up for his lack of return investment in me, he bragged that he was going to spend some extra "cash flow" on building a very expensive smoke shed out back; then, four days later, he hired yet one more sous chef on salary for his own benefit (making for a total of three for a kitchen open only six days a week and only for dinner service). I realized, plainly and bleakly, that he was never going to respect me as an actual cook in his kitchen, no matter how productive

and successful I was, that he'd apparently forgotten all about the conversation I'd had with him just a week before about the trouble I was
in, about how I was reaching a breaking point in keeping everything
together for my family with this job. Ultimately, I got to a place where
I simply refused to suffer for his obvious disregard of how dedicated I
was to him and to my work.

I still did not want to buy into the narrative that I was possibly being treated differently because of my gender. And I felt guilt. Always
guilt for not being grateful enough, for not being able to just put my
head down, ignore the reality in front of me, and keep working like I
was expected to, like all the women before me had in order to earn
their place in kitchens like this one. Plus, Tandy cared about me, I
kept telling myself. He was giving me a chance, I kept telling myself.
Hell, at some point I would have considered him one of my honest-to-
god best friends. And look, Lisa, he's so "cool" with everyone else,
everyone loves him, I kept telling myself.

I replayed these thoughts for a long time, just as I had done every
other time I felt like it was easier to blame myself than to assign blame
to someone who had "given me a shot" or someone I had a drink with
every day and considered a friend, someone who, in the end, groveled
for only a minute and then changed the story in his head so he could
live with his shitty choices. Over and over I thought: Did I do enough?
Did I work hard enough? What else could I have done to earn my
place? I carried the weight of jobs that weren't even technically mine,
helping to make sure the front of house did not fall apart, picking up
server shifts when we'd get a no-show, working the cold app/dessert
station a few nights when cooks were short. And, instead of being
treated like an important part of the kitchen, of the restaurant at large,
I was treated like a sister just doing the owner a favor, helping him
through an emotionally exhaustive time in his own life instead of be-

ing a valued employee. I trusted him to do right by me and was willing to wait, willing to be dedicated to something that did not seem all that dedicated to me.

It broke my heart to leave that job and it broke the boys' hearts, too, including the one who realized too late that he had made a big mistake. He came to me after I put in my notice and admitted, to his credit, that he was wrong and that he was very upset that I was leaving, that he did not want to do without me, that he wanted to talk out how to make it work. I think I was a hard lesson for him and I think he was embarrassed that someone saw him being less than he was capable of being. We had a sweet moment and I regretted that I was having to leave. Time was up and I had to make some hard choices. That is the reality when you are a mother—shit is real and there are real consequences to decisions. I couldn't stay. And, anyway, I've learned from previous experiences that if someone values you only when you're about to walk out the door, you should definitely keep walking.

I went back to Margot Café to regroup. But this time I came back as her pastry chef, not just as a struggling young mother and server with a steep learning curve. She welcomed me, knowing I was having a hard time juggling my family with the energy of a new restaurant. Or at least that's the line I sold her. I wasn't willing, at that time, to bitch about how much bullshit I was dealing with—I could hardly admit it to myself. The energy of a new restaurant was just fine with me, I actually loved it. I was thriving in my work, at my craft, despite the very real threat of becoming shit broke beyond repair looming around every corner. Margot could pay me a little better, but the work was not the same, it was easier. She had established a routine kind of predictable menu, so this was basically a job I could do with ease and with less expectation to be "great," as it were. She let me play, she let me experiment, but ultimately I was to keep within a very simple and beautiful lane of seasonal crostata with her ice cream base, her sorbet recipes, her cake recipes. It was good practice, it was a place to catch my breath, to perfect my technique.

John and I had finally figured out a schedule that worked for our family, and throughout it all he was head over heels supportive of my work, doing the dance between our worlds so beautifully and amicably in ways I had never seen a man rise up for his woman. My aprons would be washed and folded for my next day's work and, back when I was pulling all those doubles at City House, a bowl of pasta would be kept warm on the stove waiting for me at night when I came home late. If he could carry any of the weight of how hard I was working, he did. My time at Margot was a nice reprieve for him as well.

By now, I could see what the industry gave, but I could also see what it took. So when I stepped away and took that long breath at Margot, I agreed that I would always be honest with myself about whether or not it made sense, whether or not, as a person with responsibilities beyond my own wants and needs, I was even allowed to keep trying to fit myself back into that world. There weren't a lot of mothers of two, or even women in general, hustling up in a kitchen, and I was starting to wonder if that was a sign.

I spent my time at Margot taking an honest look at the work I now knew I never wanted to be without but also wondering if I was completely out of place in that world, one that clearly needed me to forsake living a life that made any sustainable sense. I weighed my options and kept circling around the idea of graduate school, of returning to the life goals I had before my pregnancy with Joseph, so many years earlier at TradeWinds. As much as those intentions no longer felt immediate, I was tired and I wanted to have credentials, I wanted my value to be on paper, I wanted to get a job that no man could tell me I didn't deserve or I wasn't worth being paid enough to do. I didn't really want to be a museum archivist or scholar anymore. I just wanted to fuck up anyone's ability to keep me so close to poverty's edge, and a fancy degree felt like the only way to achieve that. The only thing I knew for certain was that I wanted to stay in the kitchen, I wanted to keep feeding people, and I really wanted to do it as my job for as long as I could.

Even with all that wanting and knowing, I went ahead and applied for the MFA program at Vanderbilt in art history, thinking that it was time to put aside the thing I was good at for another thing I was probably OK at and could also make the best of. Worst-case scenario, I'd go teach, and John and I could grow old as professors together—maybe not doing what I love, but doing enough of what felt right. As long as I could help support my family, that was all that mattered. Acceptance to the program meant a living stipend, thus theoretically I could be a student solely and raise my kids while maybe coming up with a clever way to cook for my community on the side. I got all my paperwork under way and baked my heart out for over a year at Margot, schlepped more pastry out of my kitchen, and taught some private baking classes, all while I applied to the program half-heartedly and feeling finally defeated by money.

As I waited to hear back about my acceptance to Vanderbilt, I came up with an idea that I stayed up at night dreaming and writing about. I started writing menus in bed after my days at Margot, after my days of being with the kids, menus whose purpose I wasn't sure of, but ones that hinted at big, incredible dinner parties, ones that led me down a fantasy of long tables and pretty flowers and boozy cocktails and lots of wine and warm people in every seat. These menus started to determine so much about what steps came next in my life. Those menus became the first Buttermilk Road Sunday Supper menus.

I'm not sure what created the perfect storm for Sunday Suppers, but fuck if the idea didn't have wings. My favorite day at City House had always been Sunday, when we would roll out our Sunday Supper menu. It was a night when the kitchen could play and take a detour from the regular menu, try out ideas that we'd been dreaming up, write a menu for Nashville that was different from the menu every other night. I could use vanilla on those nights. So, with Buttermilk Road, I basically amped up the notion of getting people together for a meal. I wrote menus, thought about wine, hunted for a good spot to feed people, and, before I knew it, sold thirty or so tickets. The Suppers filled up every time, and eventually I had to start thinking about a quarterly experience, then a monthly schedule, and soon I was turning down my own crazy thoughts of doing it weekly. It was the right moment, one where the enthusiasm was contagious and celebrated. The town's response was overwhelming and encouraging.

It was 2009; the idea of pop-ups was not yet a well-known "thing," at least not in our part of the world; and Nashville was a remarkably different place then. At its birth, though, the Sunday Suppers became a showcase for all that I loved about our city. People loaned me their coffee shops at night and their restaurants when they were closed; people volunteered in the kitchen to cook and to serve, or just to hang out and be a part of something fun; the local wine shop sold me alcohol at cost; printmakers printed my menus for seats at the dinner; musicians came and played and sang for their supper; and it grew and grew and grew. It was a distinct reflection of the spirit of Nashville, the early spirit of everyone in this town.

I liked the sense of control I had over the variables at Buttermilk Road. I liked that people were really showing up to have the most fun kind of dinner party with thirty or forty strangers from the town they lived in, sitting together, sharing family-style meals, making connections, and, hopefully, learning something about their community that they did not know before.

Our slogan somehow became "Bringing People Together, One Biscuit at a Time." Tables were communal, and you were meant to come with only one or two people whom you already knew. Then you would pass family-style plates and bottles of wine and bourbon to strangers, and you would leave as friends, feeling a deeper sense of community. All of this happened over biscuits, creamed greens, gumbo pots, whole grilled fish, brussels sprouts and Benton bacon salad, entire vegetarian menus, artillery punch, pies, more pies, and, occasionally, pie. We had post–Mardi Gras dinners called Tardy-Gras, full of gumbo and cornbread and bartenders slinging Sazeracs and Vieux Carrés, that ended in a second-line parade of brass instruments making its way down Gallatin Road in east Nashville while it drizzled just enough to make the street shine oil-slick rainbows our way. Imagine, a whole group of stuffed, slightly drunk people who hadn't known one another prior to that dinner who had all just sat down a few hours earlier, now dancing together down a busy, trashy Nashville street as if they'd been friends their whole lives. It happened once.

We had fund-raisers for local charities such as Thistle Farms—a Nashville-based charity that supports women and children—that ended with people guzzling bottles of bourbon, writing big checks, and putting them in collection baskets passed around Arnold's Country Kitchen like a church offering. We lugged vintage plateware all over town, rented real silver, pressed napkins, made wildflower arrangements out of old milk bottles and things from our backyards, and brought in anyone and everyone who wanted to join us. John Donovan washed dishes each time, unloaded truckload after truckload of equipment and decor and hot boxes full of food and dirty rented wineglasses. My best friends acted as bartenders—their real job in real life—for a pittance from me. They were servers, cooks, free advertisement agencies, and overall workhorses. We did it all together and it was fun.

The supper I was most proud of turned out to be the end of an era. And maybe that was OK. Everything has its time.

Teresa Mason, a local friend who started Mas Tacos Por Favor, one of the first food trucks in Nashville, which eventually became a brick-and-mortar space with a perpetual line down the street, let me host my favorite supper, a nod to my family and to other South and Central American cuisines, out of her kitchen:

## BUTTERMILK ROAD SUNDAY SUPPER
## AT MAS TACOS POR FAVOR
### *Sunday, September 30th, 2012*

COCKTAILS AND BEVERAGES

Agua de Jamaica:

*Hibiscus Flower Tea*

Margarita de Pina y Aloe:

*Pineapple and Aloe Margarita*

Caipirinha Punch:

*Brazilian Cocktail with Cachaca, Lime, and Sugar*

APPETIZERS

Pepitas Enchiladas:

*Chili Spiced Roasted Pumpkin Seed Mole, Greens*

Esquite:

*Warm Mexican Street Corn Salad*

Pupusas con Queso y Chiccaron con Curtido:
> *Salvadoran Street Pastries with Cheese,*
> *Crispy Pork Belly, and Cabbage Salad*

Acaraje con Vatapa y Caruru:
> *Brazilian Black Bean Fritter Stuffed with*
> *Shrimp, Hot Chili Paste, and Green Tomato Salad*

### FIRST COURSE

Garnachas con Mi Abuelita's Canitas con Chile
Verde y Ensalata de Aguacate:
> *Mexican Fried Masa Tortilla with My Nana's*
> *Green Chili Pork and Avocado Salad*

### SECOND COURSE

Guatemalan Garifuno Tapado:
> *Traditional Guatemalan Seafood Stew*
> *with Coconut Milk Broth*

### THIRD COURSE

Cajeta Ice Cream with Spiced Pepita Brittle

What started out as a scheme to keep me cooking, to keep my connection to hospitality and serving my community, became a full-time job that, honestly, someone with better management skills could have turned into a full-blown and financially stable venture. I was not, it would seem, cut out for selling my brand online—everything felt so personal to me. My world was changing very quickly from "doing cool shit" to "doing cool shit and then packaging it for mass consumption and brandability on social media." I did not like that world at all, however lamely Gen X that sounds of me. But really, what it boiled down to was: I just could not learn fast enough to keep up. Maybe it was shortsightedness on my part, maybe it was just my Luddite brain fighting against the inevitable world of social media. The idea of blogs and "influencing" things made me squirm. Aside from the new medium of "branding" human experiences, there was an additional stink of blogs for me that felt like *women talk about food "here" and men talk about food "here,"* which stemmed from an already strange feeling I had that I was somehow both failing myself as a strong woman by "going back to a kitchen" (my dad's words when I called to tell him about my sudden promotion to City House pastry) and perhaps wrongfully trying to penetrate a man's world, the restaurant world, where I potentially didn't belong because I was, in fact, a mother and had a life that mattered outside of the industry's gates and moats. I resented the idea that I had to be cute and fashionable and charming online to be successful. I didn't want a blog.

Thanks to my snobby cynicism and high ideals, I watched my career take ten times longer than I wanted it to because I was not willing to take a chance, to redefine something about myself, or to no longer rest on old ideas. If I was going to write, it was going to be printed on paper, in a book or magazine that someone could hold in their hands. If I was going to cook and feed my city, it was going to be because people really liked the food, not because they felt they needed to be in the "scene." I can eat my words all these years later. I have seen women like Stella Parks and Deb Perelman own the arena of blogging and prove that you can be tight and professional and innovative, and just downright good. But I was never smart enough to get beyond it simply feeling limiting, a space outside of the "real" world of cooking that I wasn't so sure of. I wanted and needed the tactile space where I could watch and smell and interact and engage face-to-face. And, for all my misses, I can at least attribute my stodgy ways to being the thing that really holds my own ass accountable. I guess I can't meet myself, or anyone, really, in the middle. I fucking hate the middle. And I'm too stubborn to change or apologize for it now.

On the night of the Mas Tacos dinner—when I hit a personal stride of figuring out how to simultaneously write menus and cook food that I was completely proud of while also organizing a million other things to pull these dinners off successfully—I realized that the Sunday Supper idea had lost its spirit.

During the sale of tickets for the dinner, I had to refund three groups who tried to essentially buy out the entire dinner for their friends. That wasn't the point, I urged them, but I would be glad to talk to them about doing some private events anytime—these dinners were to share a meal with a larger community, have a new experience, maybe feel uncomfortable for a moment but to have a go at learning that food is a worthy connector. The night of the dinner, though, I realized that this strange mood was continuing throughout the night, as if a new group of people, weirdly entitled people who didn't get it, people who really just wanted to go to a restaurant, had heard about this pop-up and wanted to try it out. We found ourselves with a menu we were extremely proud of, Mas Tacos decorated with a colorful and beautiful candlelit glow that was stunning with Teresa's already perfect aesthetic, me and a killer kitchen crew doing our best to masterfully prepare the fish and the cocktails, employees whom I could finally pay properly, and the event ticking like we finally knew what the fuck we were doing.

Yet it didn't go to plan. The meal was lovely, the service was, by my high standard, perfect—but the people were out of place. Within the first hour of everyone arriving, a couple on a date pulled and reset a table for two away from the communal table. One of my friends very kindly talked to them and explained that service would be family style and so they agreed to move it back, but they did not even stay through to dessert. Then I had a man come into the kitchen, just walk right in, in the middle of us plating the main course and ask me about how much these things, these dinners, cost to put on, what I was making each night, and how the "infrastructure" worked as a business model. He was thinking about doing his own, you see. Was there for research. And, oh, hi, I'm Bob, by the way.

Someone else would likely have rolled with it, and a couple of pop-ups that started around the same time as and after Buttermilk Road certainly did. For me, it was meant to be a moment in time. Eventually, I let the moniker go, even though, for a few years after, I would have "just one more Sunday Supper!" for good causes like friends' book releases or fund-raisers. But we had caught lightning in a bottle, and it was good enough for me to have been a part of something that hopefully mattered to someone. I'm OK with a moment. It mattered to me.

# 12

## DEDICATIONS

*Pie*

A LICE RANDALL, a Nashville legend, a songwriter, and the author of *The Wind Done Gone*—who was a regular at both Margot and City House and one of the first people to say, "So you can write? Well, then, write!"—wanted to know if I would like to have tea. I was not about to miss an opportunity to take tea with a woman like Alice. Alice, whose presence is like that of a Lewis Carroll character, solid feet on the ground but not of this world, was a personal hero, someone who brims with ideas, would always be fair and honest with me, and did good, hard work to connect with and inform the world around her. When she spied *Charleston Receipts*, a revered Junior League cookbook, in my bag and asked me about it, I divulged to her my new obsession, my new studies. She gave me a look I am now familiar with: the look that tells me I am about to learn something I should already know.

I had started to explore beyond pastry and bread. An obsession with old southern cookery, pickling and vegetables in particular, had arrived during my tenure with Buttermilk Road. My books were no longer professional books written by professional chefs from the library but instead old Junior League books, spiral-bound church cookbooks, handwritten note cards in boxes found at flea markets, and ancient newspaper clippings found folded up in all of the above with some woman's cursive script annotating when she made what and for whom. I had started a trove of treasures I had been collecting for years, the ultimate delights in my life. I felt like this was a weird thing, to be honest, spending hours fawning over old layer-cake recipes, giving a shit about caramel cake, trying to reach the heavens with a coconut cake, making them with a freakish kind of yearning that I had to keep to myself so no one would know my kooky leanings, my obscure habits, my over-the-top internal filing cabinet that had become a record of every antiquated dessert invented and made and bought and sold in American history and how it came to be. I lived for this shit, the stories of divinity and ambrosia and aspic pineapple molds and sugar pies and all the bars from lemon to "magic" seven-layered ones to things called cowboy cookies.

At that time, everyone was still mostly spinning the French narrative in food, obviously for good reasons. However, the era of learning French technique and applying it to, say, a chess pie or a simple cookie was not really part of the story for the restaurant industry at large. You still had to prove your worth through brisée and mille-feuille and pate a choux. But my nose was firmly planted in every church cookbook, every ladies'-guild or school-fund-raising cookbook, every old stapled or spiral-bound book of cakes and pies and divinity candies that I could find. I thumbed through Rose Levy Beranbaum's *The Cake Bible*, just like every other studious baker teaching herself to get it right. But what those recipes taught me in precision and technique, they lacked in story and real-life meaning for me. So before I started taking apart the technique of everything, hoping to make it not just nostalgic but good, I started with the other recipes, the stories, the feelings from women who signed their recipes as Mrs. Frank Jones and Mrs. William Jenkins and so on.

Alice's kitchen was painted white, with a beautiful island in the center, and, more than a kitchen, it was a library with built-in book-shelves lining the walls, holding what seemed to be thousands upon thousands of cookbooks and notebooks and books that, as she showed me, I realized were the real history books of southern cooking. Alice had old hand-bound books, handwritten, undated, and full of recipes from those women and men who never got credit, who made the cakes for the white women "hostesses" to parade out of their kitchens as their own, who wrote recipes based on their own family traditions, tradi-tions that went back to Africa, traditions that the South is built on. Here was the reveal of the Gullah traditions that lined the pages of *Charleston Receipts*, those who really wrote that book, Alice said with firm, unflinching kindness. Everything I loved and had been clinging to and had been trying to build came from the hands of slaves, from "domestic workers," from oppressed people who still did not get the credit of their contributions. My indignation came only because I was ignorant. This was obvious information. How did I need to be shown this? I wondered.

I had to ask myself what it was about my life that enabled me to evade those conclusions on my own, to not see the real history of the place I was working so hard to understand. Did I think my limited studies of Edna Lewis allowed me to check the box of "southern racial understanding"? I knew nothing as I sat there thumbing through Al-ice's books, hearing her talk about the diaspora, the Great Migration (a thing I never, not once, learned about in school or from my white, southern family), and her own family's journey, seeing recipe after recipe from some woman's beautiful handwritten notes, notes that weren't meant for tourists or voyeurs to buy or sell but were meant as directions from one cook to another about how something worked, what to do when provisions are low and still make it good, recipes that certainly were not meant for a white woman to center herself within. Should I choose to sidestep this education, I would merely be carrying on the tradition of erasure penned by Mrs. William Jenkins and her ilk. I could go on my merry little way making my cakes and having all my big feelings about being a southern baker, sure. But Alice taught me that I needed to know and honor these things, the real history, and then decide how I wanted to tell the stories of what they were worth.

The trick was a simple one: undo your miseducation. Not everyone has an Alice Randall in their world. And Alice Randall should not have to do this work for us. My relationship with her was built on her kindness and her generosity; I am fortunate. And I am proud to say that, after our tea, she became one of my biggest clients and supporters for many years. To this day, we talk about being mothers, being women in this world, and she never flinches in a moment of honesty. The last time I was with Alice, she said to me, "Lisa, sweetie, let me tell you, we are all each other's mothers, all of us women, we have to take care of each other in that way."

I KEPT LEARNING, I kept reading, a little more broadly than before, and I started connecting to the recipes that felt familiar to me, trying to forge an understanding about the South that I could allow to creep in finally. It was a slow build, one that felt suspect to me in some ways. Being southern feels like a religion, and even though I was raised far away from the South for most of my childhood, it still stood strong in my bones—no matter how hard I tried to be separate from it. Had it not been for a kinship I felt for my daddy's family in Virginia, so much would have gone undiscovered about my truest gifts as a baker. Sean Brock entered the picture while I was having all these conversations about my southernness with myself. And Buttermilk Road was how, eventually, he came to know me. This was how I came to be the head pastry chef at what is considered one of America's best and most innovative restaurants in culinary history. At this point, early courtship conversations were just unfolding about potentially working with Sean to open Husk in Nashville. I was still on the fence but was having some deeply peculiar and annoyingly constant daydreams about all the things I could do if I said yes. Back then, even the popular kids in the food world had not yet started paying attention to the capital stories being told through southern food. When I met Sean and he did not balk at the idea of a slice of pie in a fine-dining establishment, I thought it might be time to reconsider my hiatus from restaurants.

Sean and I realized that our Appalachian families were a mere holler away from each other up in those mountains. We talked about ways our families likely knew one another. We talked about dried apples. We talked about hand pies. We talked about Sunday suppers. We talked about moonshine hidden under family floorboards. We could barely keep up with the similarities in our family histories from that world. We could literally be kin, and Sean had found a way to make something beautiful and lauded from that shared heritage. I lived for our talks, for hearing his loud, enthusiastic laugh. His questions were deep and thoughtful, and he'd start writing as soon as I started saying anything that mattered to him. He valued my thoughts at every single turn. What the fuck?

Sean was a full-fledged star at that point, and Husk was an idea and an ideal for him. He believed in the South so much that he created an entire restaurant, started in Charleston, that would celebrate that story, the ingredients, the farmers, the terroir.

I'll admit, my relationship with being southern has never stopped being a frustrated and tangled one, but Sean gave me a way to work with it. With the exception of the buttermilk at City House, being southern was not something I embraced or felt very connected to in my life. It was complicated and dirty, it was the part of me that felt unattached to the world I longed to be a part of, the one that was forward-thinking and progressive and that cared about equality and fairness and worldly things like art and beauty. It took me some time to want to come around, even though I could see the beauty in things like my daddy's demeanor, in the way a loblolly pine drips with moss, in things like industrious buttermilk and cornmeal. All the same, the South can be a hard pill to swallow. It may always be. But I believe that southerners have an ability, and a strength, to dig deep into those waters in order to keep going.

I see the right people telling the stories now. I see the voices getting bigger, more accurate. That's something. And, not for nothing, in the process of getting down into the nitty-gritty of being southern, of learning how to accept it for what it is and for what it tries to be despite itself, I discovered that I had some secrets up my sleeve with regard to baking that I didn't even know about. Figuring out that I had some serious ancestral magic lying dormant in my hands—the kind that steers you toward a damn fine pie—surprised me more than anyone.

A couple of years before I met Sean, right around the time I became deeply entrenched in all those old recipes, I had been back up to Floyd, the place where my daddy grew up, to attend my grandfather's funeral. I arrived in Virginia after an intense mountain drive through some truly shitty and terrifyingly heavy snowstorms mixed with just enough random sunshine here and there to keep it interesting. The drive lasted nearly three hours longer than expected, partly due to the storm and partly due to my trepidation with the intense mountain terrain. Both of my small children peered at me through the rearview mirror from the back seat, their eyes wide at the curtain of winter doom surrounding us. My patience and love extended beyond my fear—I was on my way to say goodbye. More important, I was on my way to see my daddy and be with him while he said goodbye.

Floyd, Virginia, was a place I had not been to since I was ten, but it still seemed deeply familiar. This was where my father had been raised—on a farm by Aunt Annie and Uncle Hobe, my father's great-aunt and -uncle. My grandfather had left my father here, in this town, with them when he was a small boy some forty years prior. Just left him. He and my grandmother had taken my father's three younger siblings with them overseas for many, many years and they just left him in Floyd. This place, where my little-boy daddy had been left for most of his upbringing, was now holy ground for him. It had defined him. And me. And my children. And we are all better off for that heartbreaking exchange made sometime in the early 1960s.

When my daddy would tell stories of walking ten miles through the snow to school, it wasn't hyperbole. It was a serious life, with serious consequences. The cow needed to be milked at four a.m. Chickens were slaughtered weekly, not by ax but by Aunt Annie's strong hands with a tight wringing of their necks. Food was put up all summer from the family garden. Aunt Annie and Uncle Hobe had kind eyes and adored my father. He was, after all, the only child they ever raised—even if just for a decade. I'm told that the time seemed for them too short of years. With all their kindnesses, they were firm, strict, and unyielding. They were simple and conservative—traits, to this day, that my daddy maintains. Being raised by honest, hardworking farmers and carpenters changed him in ways that were important. His siblings would attest that they themselves struggled with years of addiction, crimes, bad decisions. My daddy has always been steadfast, honest, unyielding to what is right and what is wrong—an unflinching understanding of the circumstances that life can hand you and how, no matter what, the cow still had to be milked before the sun came up. He learned how to survive. He learned that, daily, you had to make a life from what you had, not what you wanted. And he learned these things from Aunt Annie and Uncle Hobe.

The night I arrived in Floyd, as I sat with a family I had not seen in twenty years at a table full of rolls, fried chicken, dumplings, a big pot of green beans that had been stewing all day in anticipation of our arrival, sun tea, pies, and dump cakes, we looked over old photographs and I quickly saw that my great-grandfather Berkeley looked frighteningly like my daddy. Not just the strong chin that prevails in our bloodline, but rather their eyes, the creases in their faces, the brow furrow, the glint, and the glare. The person showing me the photos from her piles and piles of scrapbooks of images carefully dated and pasted and protected by thin and slightly cracking acetate was my great-great-aunt Ruby.

Aunt Ruby was Aunt Annie's baby sister. She was born in 1917. "1917!" I thought to myself that night as I played little scenes in my mind of what her early romances and dresses and books and friendships must have looked like when she was a young woman. She and I were immediately inseparable. Our sudden kinship, I think, took us both by surprise. We talked until the late night and early morning, she in her wheelchair and me sitting cross-legged like I was around a campfire hearing ghost stories. I had never asked so many questions or come to such calm realizations about so many indescribable emotions. With each story, I felt more like I had come home. Stories about our secret family moonshine ring, which was how "Christmas was afforded and done." She knew just how many times her brother Berke-ley and the boys got "nabbed" for "the likker" they were making—a total of nine times among the lot of them. She shared stories about Aunt Annie and herself as sisters growing up—those were the stories I was hungriest for. She was the baby in the family, and I believe she felt a duty to remember as much detail as she could. I didn't know Aunt Annie, but I dreamed of her as a lost mother. I wanted to know the woman who took so much time and care with my father, the woman who seemingly saved him.

Before I saw it coming, Ruby changed my heart forever, solidified something inside me that was already squarely on the table when I met the likes of Sean. Aunt Ruby asked me what I did for a living; she had heard that I was successful and wanted to know more, changing the subject so rapidly that it took me a minute to catch up. She was fasci-nated by my ability to have children and work, and she wanted to know what that looked like. She liked that I cooked for a living. And I began to tell her, with a bit of uncertainty about how much I should share, that I was doubting my place in a professional kitchen. I talked about how I was hungry to find my own voice and that I loved the work. She shrugged it all off in the most refreshing way. And then she declared that she felt like maybe cooking was the thing she was best at. And then she talked about her dried-apple hand pies.

She made a piece of paper and a pencil materialize from a kitchen drawer for me to write notes. On that day, Aunt Ruby was ninety-one years old. She talked about how she had peeled three bushels of apples from the family orchard every year since the day she could hold a knife, slicing them better than a mandoline could, and set them out to dry on old screen doors propped up on the porch, by her daddy many years ago and by her sons and grandsons later in life. She would set them out every morning in neat little rows, one by one, and bring them in every night, unless it was a warm dry night, in which case she would let them stay with a white sheet on top to shield them from the night bugs. The process would take a week or two, depending on the heat and humidity. And she'd keep them all year in bags in her cupboard to make dried-apple hand pies that would hopefully last until the next harvest.

Our family recipe, over one hundred and fifty years old, includes cream and black pepper. At some point in that history, nutmeg and cinnamon (basic pie spices in general) were difficult to come by. What they discovered through not having nutmeg and cinnamon was that they did have a hell of a lot of black pepper, a little cinnamon from the one stick they might have had lying around, and cream from the cow, which needed to be used up on the regular. Black pepper and cinnamon do an odd thing in concert and it's a beautiful thing—they taste like clove and nutmeg. Adding the cream after the apples cook and before filling the pie rounds to crimp and fry, she said, balanced out and softened the black pepper. It was, and still is, the smartest and most exciting thing I've ever heard anyone say about baking. Aunt Ruby and I talked about food like little girls, wide-eyed, until almost morning. That night is still so alive in me, every single day, but most especially when my hands are in flour. I understand now why it has always been a transcendent experience for me—how I'll find myself with an incredibly stoned joy and a dumb grin on my face even in the muck and mire of industry toil. It is a muscle memory that goes well beyond my short life and one that connects me to a certain feeling that is distinctly my southernness, slow and intuitive and clearly something I was a fool to fight off.

The next day we said goodbye to my grandfather. It was cold, and wet, and dreary. The flag was folded, the seven guns were fired three times each, and he was sent off properly as a war veteran. We all shivered and stood still, not sure where to look besides the gray sky or the ground, and we all felt alone, as that's how funerals tend to work on the human heart.

My grandfather was a man I used to cuddle with—the one I used to admire in that girlish way that you admire any man who loves you when you're young. But I didn't know what to do with the years of sadness that he left my father. I know this was a rejection that my daddy's good heart never mended. It was, I think, the heartbreak of his life. It's a rejection I can't even imagine and one that I can still feel in him when we speak. I didn't hate my grandfather for it. I loved him. I missed my grandfather deeply. But, honestly, on that day, all of the turmoil and self-doubt I realized he left my father made me miss him less. And whether or not that makes me a good daughter or a bad daughter didn't really matter to me. The sadness I felt about his death was more about realizing that after a lifetime of knowing him, I couldn't find the same affirming love and connection that I found in one singular night with my remarkable aunt Ruby.

Meeting Aunt Ruby and experiencing that flood of self-discovery was like meeting Aunt Annie. It was a glimpse into my daddy's "chosen" and real family. In losing his father and my grandfather—something I didn't know how to reckon in my head or in my heart on that day—I felt like I had met the real part of my father's soul—the place where you might imagine his parents residing. I looked at the faces, even if only in pictures, of the people whom I had always missed as links to who my father is. And who I am. My father never carried himself the way my grandfather did. He never had the same grifter bravado, he never had the same false pride.

I remember going back to my hotel that night. I bathed the kids and tucked them in. For a minute I sat and tried to untangle the heartache that funerals always bring, then washed my face and proceeded to drink the Floyd, Virginia, water right out of the tap. It ran down my face, down my neck, and fell onto my body. It was my father's water. My grandfather's water. Berkeley's water. Aunt Annie, the woman who made my father the brilliant, beautiful, quiet man he is—it was her water. And it is Aunt Ruby's water. The water, so clean and sweet tasting, couldn't come fast enough to cool off the hotness that my tears brought that night. It was a flood. And yet I was still thirsty.

AN APPALACHIAN HEART is a very specific thing. And when you meet one, you'll know that to be true.

Sean Brock has an explosive laugh, one that feels like it's been brewing in his gut for hours before he lets it erupt. And when he does, it's contagious. He can be standoffish but also warm and attentive. He can be too intense but is focused and dedicated. He's so complicated that, as soon as I start writing these things about him, I think of fifty ways someone could disagree or, hell, fifty ways I've seen him prove me wrong. Yet there is an equilibrium in his complexities. I seem to give him a lot of room to disappoint or disrupt a way of thinking, which is not typical for me. I guess I just never felt that any of the frustrations Sean presented to me in our personal or professional relationship outweighed the parts that inspired. He and I became fast friends. We seemed to be on similar journeys as cooks and as humans. He was the first person to care about the deep and true leanings I was having in my baking world, and as we got to know each other better, a certain understanding evolved that there was more to our connection than just location, than just being southern.

He invited me to oversee pastry for Husk, and I said yes to the job on the heels of all these overwrought feelings I was having about the South and my place in it. He seemed to be the perfect maestro to help me channel these discoveries about myself into food. Part of me wondered how much this invitation came as a way to soften the stance that I think he was concerned about Nashville taking toward him. Even though he started out in Nashville, I think he worried greatly that the tight-knit community would resent him for being a "celebrity chef" coming to show Nashville how it's done—as that was beginning to be a trend. Part of me, not wanting to be skeptical about his intentions, did know that some of my allure was that I was an insider in Nashville, that I had a wide audience, and Sean probably wisely assumed that if he aligned himself with me, it would make for an easier transition. But I never allow myself to start relationships on lowest-denominator skepticisms. It's bad practice, and if you can get out of your own way, I've learned that people will more often than not surprise you and prove you wrong, thank god.

Before I accepted that job, though, I was warned. Sean did have a reputation. "Getting Brocked" was a "thing"—stories of late-night drunkenness gone bad, stories of high-intensity work met with higher-intensity play wrecking the novices around him who all thought they could keep up. The fistfights, the disappearing acts, the drunken arrivals to important events, the thrashing anti-authority-redneck-fuck-you-I-won't-wanna-do-what-you-tell-me bravado was practically legendary. I was fully warned, with tale upon tale of ways he had not been honorable or admirable. People, friends with whom I had worked long and hard in kitchens before Husk, warned me away from it, from him; they came out of the woodwork to say, "Lisa, what are you actually thinking?" It's not your kind of kitchen, they would say. It's not your kind of life, they warned.

Those friends had walked away from the same kinds of opportunities already, once or twice, in their lives. They knew Sean to be dismissive and rough, hard on everyone, a perfectionist at his best and completely wrapped up in being wild and destructive, self-important and irrationally dismissive of his commitments at his worst. And they knew me. They knew my heart. They knew my intentions. They also knew I was a stubborn little shit who wanted new experiences more than I wanted to be comfortable. Also, I was still harboring some frustrated feelings about having to leave a kitchen I felt successful in and really thought this was my chance to become as good as I could be, with someone who seemed to value me from the start.

I decided I would take the job and make it work within the parameters of who I was becoming as a cook. Maybe those friends didn't know me as well as they thought they did, and, anyway, the Sean Brock they seemed to be talking about was not the Sean Brock I was getting to know. All we did was sit around and talk about food, cakes, pies, ideas, and books like excited children. He believed in me.

It would work for me because I knew exactly what I wanted, I thought. I knew where I was going with this. I just needed a bigger space to move around in and Sean agreed and wanted me to have that. I wasn't scared. I had read all the caricatures of the world they were talking about. I thought the whole thing was a silly testosterone charade that I could easily pop the bubble of or at least maneuver with skill. I thought I could break down the walls once I was inside. I wasn't a fool. I wasn't scared. I took the job, learned more than I ever imagined as a cook, and also proceeded to have my whole world turned upside down, for better and for worse.

Mostly, I believed in Sean's ideals. All our ingredients would have to be sourced within one hundred miles of the restaurant's front door. This not only celebrated the South, it tried to have a conversation about sustainable food practices, keeping the restaurant industry's footprint small, doing away with all the damage that transporting food thousands of miles does. I got excited about standards that seemed like they were not gimmicks but honest attempts to do right by our community. And his food? It was fucking brilliant there at the beginning. I can honestly say, to this day, I have never met anyone with a brain like Sean's. The complexity with which he followed a thought through taught me more about how to cook than, likely, anything before or since. He took my emotional foundation of thinking about and cooking food to another level, one that started with seeds and origin and historical relevance. My enthusiasm became effective action, real work, the ability to think bigger than the plate. I started looking deeper, more closely, more broadly.

The kitchen was massive, the staff was many. We had upstairs kitchens and downstairs kitchens and backyard kitchens and we had *stagiaires* working with their heads down every day and night. It was a boisterous space, everyone at first full of enthusiasm for simply being there, no amount of tedious work putting a person asunder. The walk-in was organized three times a day, and the blue kitchen label tape was cut with precision. We wore ironed white shirts and stylized gray aprons, and we harvested food out of a beautiful and thoughtfully planted garden out back.

Initially, it all felt like a whirlwind, but eventually I found my pace, at least when it came to menu writing. During this time, I developed what became "the thing," the recipe I will not outlive. It's both a blessing and a curse to make the "best" version of something—"best" being debatable I'm sure by anyone who has their own version of it. Not debatable was the fact that my buttermilk chess pie took hold, grabbed the attention of all our customers and, less important, the media. I had discovered a few recipes for chess pie while I was working in the kitchen at Margot. I was intrigued by these "sugar pies" but had not found a recipe that actually made me love anything beyond the "idea" of it. So I futzed. I worked with the ratio until I had just the right combination of custard and buttermilk and until the texture was spot-on. I would never claim to make a "perfect" version of anything, but this pie comes pretty close.

Despite my pride for it, I tried to take it off the menu once at Husk, determined to keep building similarly inspired desserts, moving on to other things, other projects. But that lasted only one day. The demand was too strong and I was forever tethered to that pie as an identity of sorts. Because I was proud of it, I came to terms with it being a constant in my life. And, in some ways, this became a relief, as the pace at Husk and the systems I was now a part of were not what I was accustomed to. Not having to think about the success of a menu item was a visceral relief. We were cranking out two services a day, seven days a week, trying for three turns each service with a dining room that had nearly a hundred seats and a private dining venue out back. Keeping that pace while being at the top of your game creatively was challenging for us all.

We were all there to work with Sean, who was becoming known on an international scale at this point as a prodigy of the South. But for those of us who worked with him, there were things behind the scenes that would destroy the sanctity of what kitchens were supposed to be, of what we were supposed to be, of what we all came there to do. I did not know that when I agreed to work with Sean I was also agreeing to his world, a world I was not wrong about, one that was based mostly on passion and genius and, even if hard to manage sometimes, a perfectionism that I still do not resent.

However, I also did not know that I was agreeing to work with a company that cared more about its investors getting rich, and fast, than with the well-being and health and careers of its employees. Suddenly I had a front-row seat to the potential cause of Sean's terrible antics and reputation. Sure, he had a choice. And, sure, I blamed him for plenty and still do. Our relationship took many hits and twists and turns, and we had to get over a lot of pain in the end. But, I will argue, for as long as anyone will listen to me, that I'm not sure what anyone should expect when millionaires find a genius boy who doesn't come from much, with big aspirations and a good, strong mind, and make him do impossible math equations with his gifts. If there was another thing I recognized in Sean, it was his hunger—a kind of hunger that only comes from loss and not having. He and I were similar in many ways, but this one might wholly be where my heart strings stay tethered. So little of what was expected of Sean and everyone under his direction had to do with talent. Rich men will do anything to get richer. Wars are fought, people killed, to make sure our barrels of oil don't go over fifty-five dollars and that when they do, the rich men don't make less, we just pay more. It's no different in the restaurant world.

My daily work life was belittling—the head chefs, all young guys, seemed jealous of my relationship with Sean, one where my opinion was sought after when he was recipe testing, one where I never had to ask for permission in the restaurants he built. They were kind to my face but did not support me in ways that really counted. I started to find that cooking was different in this kitchen. It was competitive, mean, aggressive, not about hospitality but, instead, about everyone's ego, about *StarChefs* magazine coming to interview people, about PR, and about who was impressing Sean the most at any given appearance he made. I didn't give two shits about his fame or his approval. I appreciated him for his brain and his childlike enthusiasm; we trusted each other and that was all that mattered to me. I wanted to do right by this opportunity and I wanted to do my best. And I wanted to learn from his giant abilities to think through food. This, I would come to find, set me apart in the kitchen, and it led to jealous whispers by sous chefs about how I must have gotten my job.

Years after I left Husk, I found myself reminiscing about the "good times" and, naturally, the "hard times" with someone who occasionally used to work pastry but mostly worked on the line during service at Husk. We opened the Nashville Husk together, had seen it all, and, after we both had time to catch our breath from our shared experiences, we decided to catch up over a few beers. When we got on the topic of the "hard times," he casually said to me, "It must have been especially hard with yours and Sean's situation."

I leaned in, thinking I had misheard him, and said, "I'm sorry, what?"

He seemed confused. "Oh, you know, his divorce and you and your marriage."

I stopped dead in my tracks. "I have no idea what you mean."

He stammered, feeling rightfully embarrassed. "Damn, sorry, Lisa. We were just told that you guys were a thing and, shit, I'm sorry. Fuck. Man. God. I'm such an asshole."

I paused for a long time, already knowing the answer, and asked, "Who told you that, exactly? And in what way?"

He was sheepish and pissed for me, but mostly just sheepish. He did not want to be a rat, and so he left it at "we all just took it to be true but I don't remember who told me." Apparently it was easier for some of those guys to say that I had gotten my job because I was fucking Sean than to admit that he simply valued my talent and ideas equally to or more than theirs. I let the poor messenger off the hook, told him I was glad for the information, basically suspecting that this was what people thought, because it explained quite a lot regarding the resentment and battles I found myself fighting for no good reason in that kitchen.

The kitchen at Husk became toxic in such a way that my family never even wanted to come near the place. People were so bitter and unhappy, loathsomely so, that it just seeped into everything you tried to do. An eventual darkness loomed and settled over everything, a meanness you could not escape. John stopped by one time to bring me a coffee, to say hi, as he had done in previous kitchens—a small chance for us to reconnect during our busy schedules—and left within five minutes. He sent a text when he got back to his car that simply read JESUS FUCKING CHRIST THAT PLACE FEELS TERRIBLE I AM SO SORRY YOU HAVE TO BREATHE THAT AIR.

For some time I continued to believe I could do good work and make an impact that was positive and strong, figure out how to be a good leader under pressure. I failed. It was a failure that took me a long time to get over.

I was a nationally recognized pastry chef, published in "best of" rundowns, asked to submit recipes to the world. I was asked to speak about what I knew, had people come into the restaurant just to have my dessert, and saw firsthand how much money I made that company on a daily basis with just my product alone. By my second year there, when I was flying back and forth between Nashville and Charleston to run pastry at both the Husk restaurants—and, in turn, giving up my entire intellectual property to a company—I was still only making fifteen dollars an hour. When I asked for a higher salary and my title to be executive pastry chef—a job I had been performing but had been asked to do just as a "favor"—I was told I was no longer needed in Charleston (hell, they already had all my recipes and six months of nearly free staff training) and, beyond unbelievably, I was told I would have to cut one of my pastry cooks down to less than part time, essentially firing her, in order to get my raise. That was when I left. That was the crux of my professional life not making sense any longer.

I was burned out. I was no longer making food I was proud of. I was detached from my community, a community within which I had built a good name and had made a lot of important friendships. I had not learned how to be the kind of manager I could be proud of. I had no examples of leadership in front of me that were not aggressive, angry, fed up, or physically and mentally soaked with exhaustion and alcohol.

I had been a witness to and an active participant in a world that would easily kill me if I let it—a world that was driving away people who were smart enough to say that they deserved better within the first few weeks of employment there. *Stagiaires* stopped coming as frequently as they had previously. Chefs de cuisine cycled through at an alarming rate, even for a new restaurant. And yet I left feeling ashamed of myself, ashamed of my inability to carry all the weight, to make it all work, to be better for my cooks, in ways that now make my own heart break a little. I carried that for a long time. It took me nearly two years to see it for what it was and to see just how swallowed up I was within that dark, dank belly of a bloated beast that was work I once loved and lived for.

13

## FINDING

*Layer Cakes*

I T FEELS REALLY NICE to be good at something," I told
Angie Mosier as I worked cold butter into gold-flaked schmears
in the flour, a thing I've done so many times that my hands go
into their own kind of daze, movements I don't have to think about,
much less try to get right.

About a year after I returned from Costa Rica, Angie and I were
hosting a workshop to benefit Hambidge, an important artist's retreat
in the foothills of the Blue Ridge Mountains that has come to mean a
lot to my work. After I left Husk, these kinds of moments became
more plentiful—the kind where I would be laughing and singing and
wearing lipstick without scrutiny in a kitchen if I goddamn wanted to
and reveling in being a girl who could cook again. I had my hands in
dough for the first time since leaving Husk. I was relieved that these
hands still knew what to do, relieved that I had not completely lost my
love of this, relieved that it wasn't all a fluke or some weird fever
dream. Whatever it was that I had promised myself I was going to do
when I left Costa Rica a year or so earlier, all that "get back to the

work you were meant to do, Donovan," I realized I had absolutely done it.

I was also smart enough to count my blessings. Saying yes to Sean had brought an entire world of opportunity to me. It brought me the chance to prove myself an expert in my field, to talk in public about what felt like my weird obsessions, to feed my community and reach a far larger one, and to work with younger cooks who wanted to learn about the odd shit I had collected in my brain. Saying yes to Sean had taught me about a convoluted faction of our industry that I had not bargained for, yes. But it had also brought me the friendship of practically everyone I truly love today. It was a cascade of hardworking, focused, dedicated humans who were all bright lights in this world, lights I never want to be without.

My work with Husk led me toward women in my field, the kind of women I had never met before—women who would stabilize me when shit got really bad, women who stood stronger than anyone I had ever met, women I would find myself in sisterhood with for the rest of my life. The irony is not lost on me that I was delivered to these women after years of trying to tap dance around so many misogynistic foibles and fumbles in my life and my career, after so many moments of pivoting around ego-driven and clueless men to survive.

No one ever tells you how lonely being a woman who is dedicated to her career, either by choice or necessity, will be. Other parents whisper about your absences, other women whisper about your fidelity to your husband, some people guilt you directly to your face about all the things you leave behind every time you go out to do the work you do. Worse yet are the women who find your career to be a commentary on their failures or ambitions, or see you as some kind of competition, and that equation has never made sense to me. Finding a friendship with women who had to hustle just as hard as I did, with women who might understand that my priorities and my responsibilities went beyond social scenes, was something I had started to think I might never have. It sounds simple, but before I met the likes of Angie Mosier and Rebecca Wilcomb and Ann Marshall and Cheetie Kumar and Ashley Christensen (and, trust me, the list goes on), I had a horrible fear that as an adult, I might not have the ability to make a true friend who was a woman.

Angie, whom I once dubbed the Patron Saint of Layer Cakes, pays attention and champions all. She is a quietly revered southern baker who has carried the torch of our traditions with such goodness and skill that people don't even know they are replicating things that she buoyed and researched for her Atlanta bakery in the very early 1990s before I even had the good idea to do this work. I met Angie for the first time in Florence, Alabama, in the basement of Billy Reid, where I sat alone and watched a literal parade of every kind of layer cake—coconut, chocolate, strawberry, caramel!—on beautiful antique cake stands appear from nowhere and make their way through a large crowd of mostly hungover chefs and writers and musicians. It seemed to happen in slow motion—as most really important things do when you get at remembering them—the cakes moving toward a table to be served for that day's brunch. It was the early days of a now-famed weekend called Shindig, put on by Billy, the local menswear designer and connector of many good things.

As I sat on a step of the stairs leading down into the basement with a plate of food on my lap, not knowing, really, a single soul, I caught the tail end of the cake parade and rushed over to the first familiar face I could find. I found John Currence, from Mississippi by way of New Orleans, the rogue Oxford, Mississippi, chef and the first friend I made that weekend. I grabbed his shirt and probably shouted that I needed to know WHO had made those cakes. "Who?!" I demanded with a desperation that, when I think back, was probably alarming.

He pointed to the fieriest mane of red hair cutting down the middle section of the back of a slight woman's bright white shirt and said, "That's Angie Mosier, she made them all," and shook himself loose from me like I was some kind of crazed fanatic or bully.

I worked my way through that crowd like a lovestruck girl in a John Hughes movie, my eyes fixed on a person I had never met, making sure she did not wander off, out of the door, onto the street, out of my life forever—as if she were some kind of mythical creature that might not be real. I had not met, at that point in my career, someone who could DO THAT. I did it. This was the amazing thing that Sean Brock saw in me, and he was the first and, I thought, only person to truly appreciate it the way I did. I tapped Angie on the shoulder, and she turned around with the brightest face and the smartest southern drawl I'd ever heard.

"Did you make those cakes?!" I said, probably still shouting.

I didn't embarrass myself because Angie is not that kind of person, but I was beaming. I can remember her smile in that moment, a little crooked but big and wide and eyes all squinty and shiny. It was likely one of the kindest faces I'd ever seen. Still is.

That weekend, we swam in the Tennessee River, listened to people talk about sustainability in our work, and shared ideas about how to keep bringing the South up and over the cultural bumps of our region. We listened to Jack White and the Alabama Shakes and Jason Isbell play live to small crowds of mostly southern folks who spend their lives making things, folks like me who cook, folks like Natalie Chanin who make clothes, and folks like Angie, who, I would soon find out, makes every chance she gets an opportunity to celebrate the people around her. That weekend would be my true introduction to the Southern

Foodways Alliance, which for twenty years has done its best to document the oral histories of the South's foodways, to bring people together over food and words about food and to ultimately get to the heart of who southerners are because of it. Founded by mentor and friend John Egerton, it has almost single-handedly brought the southern food community together in a way that seems unnatural for an industry known in other regions to be competitive and bitchy. (New York photographer Penny De Los Santos once leaned in to me at breakfast at a Knoxville gathering and said, "I mean, all you southern chefs can't ALL be friends—right? I mean, this isn't really how chefs behave, you can tell me—it's all a bunch of bullshit, right?" She was genuinely perplexed and meant no harm. But she was absolutely incorrect.)

ANGIE AND I BECAME INSTANT FRIENDS, and it did not take long for us to feel like family. Right away we were finding reasons to cook together. We would take over kitchens as fine as McCrady's— once Sean's macro-gastronomical playground full of fanciful, haute cuisine—to make Lane cake for three hundred, asking sous chefs and line cooks who usually carried things with tweezers to carry five hundred pounds of Lane-cake goo in a thirty-gallon mixing bowl up three flights of stairs, which they did. We would travel around, putting cracklins on caramel cakes, deep-frying saltine crackers to serve with key-lime pudding cups, making our own parade of layer cakes for crowds. Angie would get up after we had served people cake and pie and sing in front of the crowds "Angel from Montgomery" and "These Days," all the songs that break your heart, with a voice that can pierce through you. And then, most nights, we'd leave the party and go sing for hours into the night, just the two of us together in a car, in her living room, on the porch of a cabin in the woods, losing our shit about the perfection of Elton John's *Madman Across the Water* album (except that one song), howling Steely Dan songs at the full moon after too many glasses of bourbon, me always playing the air organ and Angie religiously singing only backup vocals—because that is the real genius of the *Aja* album, we decide each time, always as if it's a new revelation.

After she had recovered from being a professional baker, Angie became one of our industry's best photographers, whose beautiful work helped to catapult the books of Eric Ripert and Sean Brock and beyond well past "successful" and straight to "important." She worked hard to settle properly into the career she deserves, taking every opportunity to grow as a professional, to learn from those around her, and to bring people up and help them move forward in their own ways. Truly, the kind of person you can't help but admire a little more every time you meet her.

I can be an insufferable and intolerant freak show. I will be the first to admit it—I'm sometimes dreadfully hard on people, incapable of letting bad manners slide, and even more incapable of letting it go unknown when I've sniffed out that you're a fraud or a generally bad person. I can't suffer a fool, or a person with bad intentions, and I have a big mouth about it. But Angie Mosier gives everyone grace and kindness, and she is a salve and a relief for me. She makes me take my time, makes me think about the person and their circumstances. She talks me down long enough for me to soften my edges. She and the rest of the women who have come into my life have bettered me, have bolstered me. Have loved the nasty bits and have brought out the best bits. They are my reward, proof that—even if I feel I have never done enough—that I have at least done something worthy of their friendship.

So there Angie and I were, at Hambidge, in the same place where the beloved Miss Edna Lewis and the venerable Scott Peacock wrote and completed *The Gift of Southern Cooking*. Miss Lewis, a woman I believe to be the reason the world has ever paid attention to southern food, proper southern food, is an undeniable hero to anyone who cares about seasons or "farm to table," the sincerest tradition of the southern table. Scott Peacock became her late-in-life companion, and together, after Miss Lewis's long tenure in New York as a chef at Café Nicholson to the likes of Truman Capote, William Faulkner, and Harper Lee, and nonsouthern expats like Marlene Dietrich and Diana Vreeland, they created a part of our history as southern cooks who forever set a tone, one that many of us would spend a lifetime honoring and praying at the altar of. They spent their time up at Hambidge foraging for wild sorrel, which still grows next to a small but enthusiastic creek that cuts through the land. They spent their time writing their book in between strolls and cooking meals with and for each other. What was written in that book is a story so deeply of this region that it feels as if it has always been around, even though it came into this world in my actual lifetime (2003, to be precise).

I sat in those woods at Hambidge, in the exact spot where I knew they used to wander, trying to absorb some of their sense and feeling that I hoped they had left behind. I realized very quickly that it was, naturally, everywhere all the time in this South—from the man at the gas pump in Mississippi to the woman at the counter selling sugar pies—and was embedded in me and almost everyone I found myself cooking alongside.

Scott Peacock later told me that, yes, there was magic in the moments in those foothills, moments of inspiration, connectivity, and energy that were like lightning striking. But the magic was also the experience of learning how not to miss details and of finding the good work within their long and deep relationship—those are the things that felt real. He didn't say so, but I surmised that he was eager to demystify some of that lineage, to give me permission to add my words to the story. He seemed to want me to believe that we are all cooks of a certain place and time, that we all deserve to share in shaping the historical record. The complexities of who gets to tell these stories, who gets a seat at the table, is rich in our story of the South. I want to be careful with the space I take, and I also want to claim some of that space in equal measure. Maybe the word is "honor": maybe what I really want is to honor it from the place it actually comes from with no need to own the narrative.

I huddled in that wood, alone, thinking about all the ways my career had disappointed me. But then I started to take some responsibility for how I had let things unfold. I had made my choices. And it was my responsibility to unmake them. These weren't choices about jobs or restaurants. These were choices I had made to coddle the powers that be, to let myself be less than those around me, to be afraid of seeming ungrateful to the men who "let" me into their world, the same men who incorrectly decided what I was worth, time and time again. I had to undo that. That was on me. So, in some ways, I found more than I bargained for by that creek. I tossed a stone and it landed in a bed of new sorrel. I picked at the sorrel for a few minutes, snacking on the peppery leaves, and was glad that I was thinking about my mom and not Edna Lewis for the first time in my whole career.

THE DAY I STOOD in a cabin next to that creek with my hands in a giant ceramic bowl of flour and salt, two pounds of cubed, cold butter, and a giant mason jar full of ice water next to me, Angie sat nearby drinking a beer, pulling boiled peanuts out of their shells so we could make a boiled-peanut hand pie—because, first, necessity required it and, second, "why not," our only rules of thumb when we cook to-

gether. There is a farm stand that sits right on the Georgia–North
Carolina border, not far from Hambidge. They sell the best boiled
peanuts either one of us had ever had; we couldn't get enough of them,
those peanuts, and so, when the wild mushrooms that we had originally planned to use to make the savory hand pies turned out to be
much less than we hoped for in the way of wanting to put them in our
(or anyone else's) mouths, we had to look around and use what we had.
And we perpetually had about two pounds of boiled peanuts on us at
any given time.

Unflinchingly, we put them in. They were delicious, an unusual
"meat" for a savory hand pie that only required some caramelized onions and a buttery cream sauce cut with a very small amount of sharp
cheese and a lot of black pepper to bind it all together. We sat there,
talking about the ways in which we had found ourselves in that place,
at that time, able to play with food and each other. However strange
people might have found those pies, they devoured them instantly.
They shoved the second (and third) one in their mouth with a "Huh!
Who knew?!" expression. Angie and I had a private sublime moment—
not uncommon for us, when she and I get to cooking together—where
we drank another beer and felt lucky. Finding those moments of joy in
a kitchen again adjusted something inside me, replacing the anger and
rage I felt for all that came out of my experience at Husk. I started to get
back to what I had loved in the first place and to be ever grateful for the
culture of food that I was a part of; I settled into that, tucked myself
right in, and let myself be folded into a community, an entire group of
people I trusted for the first time in my life.

Inasmuch as Husk broke my heart, it eventually brought me an
opportunity to walk into a kitchen with confidence about my contributions and tell my story in my own way. The pantheon of women
in my work who kept me connected and present in a world we all

believed in helped me navigate those tough years. I found myself in a space shared by chefs and writers, men and women alike, who leaned in when I spoke, who talked numbers with me, who gave me a stage to speak, to write, to contribute. I could never have known how deep the rewards would get.

KELLY FIELDS, a New Orleans pastry chef and my very dear friend, and I were invited to cook dessert together in San Francisco for the leather-pant-wearing goddess who is Diana Kennedy. It was an honor of a lifetime. If I had any lingering doubt about my place in the food world—or, moreover, my right to exist out loud within it—Ms. Kennedy kicked the shit out of it in one fell swoop.

Diana Kennedy is the kind of chef and food writer so epically legend that, no matter how hard you work or how successful you become, you will never feel you have the right to be in the same orbit to even cook near her, much less for her. Ms. Kennedy is the real deal. In a time when women mostly stayed at home and Phil Spector was spinning hit after hit about women's main vocation being adoring and marrying a man, do-lang, do-lang, do-lang, Diana Kennedy would get into an old Nissan truck with a knapsack full of notebooks and drive down vast dirt expanses in Mexico, where her husband was a *New York Times* writer and correspondent, and go, just drive down vacant swatches of land until she ran into people she could talk to. She would then set up camp, stay for a while—everyone was so gracious and welcoming—and cook with them. This was how an entire generation of Americans learned about Central and South American food, because a wild British dame refused to keep her wanderings bottled up, refused to squelch her curiosity, and refused to wait for anyone to give her permission.

Writing these words even feels like nonsense because I do not believe she ever thought that to be an honest option for herself—no one needs to give Diana Kennedy permission to do anything; she is her own planet and makes her own rules. She then proceeded to write a few dozen of the most important cookbooks ever written. Being in the same room, sitting on my hands with my eyes wide, full of the thrill of recognition, of finally feeling like I had just met my proper leader, my queen, while she spoke about her gumption and her assertions in life was as close as I'll come to screaming at a concert like all those girls did for Elvis or the Beatles. To me, Diana Kennedy never seemed to give a fuck about the "wrong" things, about being palatable to anyone. She just focused 100 percent on the work in front of her and her curiosity, both of which were certainly bigger than anybody else's expectations. I was so relieved to see her in action that summer in San Francisco in leather pants and with turquoise jewelry dripping from every possible appendage. What a goddamned hero.

Kelly and I had cooked together before; we pastry-flirted via email and would visit each other's restaurants, eventually growing our friendship into something real and meaningful. By the time we were invited to San Francisco, we had a certain amount of confidence about the kind of magic that comes out when we're together. Kelly knew some folks in San Francisco from her many years as a chef there, and so we had kitchens, and friends, we could count on to help us spin ice cream and otherwise pull our shit together. We both arrived a few days early and did our separate, various things to get ready.

To honor Ms. Kennedy, Kelly made a dense and moist cornmeal cake, while I made a cajeta ice cream—a traditional Mexican caramel made of slowly cooked goat milk, also fondly called (by me) "milk jam" in the South—that was just salty enough for my taste. Then we topped it all off with my buttermilk cream and vanilla-roasted apricots. It was interesting to find that West Coast chefs were not accustomed to buttermilk in desserts, and so, to my surprise, my simple whipped cream with buttermilk and just enough vanilla, sugar, and lemon juice was their main object of interest. As it was summer and California chefs had assured us that peaches were "great" at this time of the year, I thought we would do a simple process of some peaches— if they were sweet enough, just a little lemon juice and sugar to macerate for about an hour before we were to plate up, and if they weren't, more sugar and a quick, super-hot roasting of them. Kelly had made and shipped her cake; it arrived in all the right pieces. I had made and packed my Tennessee buttermilk from Cruze's dairy in Knoxville and my cajeta ice-cream base in a cooler with ice packs and vac-sealed bags of ice and checked it like luggage for the seven-hour flight. I would get my fruit in California and work with it there.

I landed, had just enough time to clean up, and rushed to Chez Panisse, where I met Samin Nosrat for dinner. Samin was one of those women whom I recognized when I first saw her years prior as a familiar and as a kind of ally in my efforts. We had met several years earlier at our first Southern Foodways Alliance symposium. For a debate, Pie vs. Cake—a Lincoln-Douglas-style debate between Kat Kinsman and Kim Severson—I made Aunt Ruby's apple hand pies and a coconut cake that I was very proud of. I prepared the pies and cakes in a kitchen I shared with Vivian Howard while she made her family's chicken and rice in a giant tilt skillet, openly fretting and problem solving with me and others about how best to protect her rice, to keep it from overcooking. This was a moment in time, a clatter of cooks and storytellers, all women, all together, making righteously good food, the kind of food that mattered to me, with zero ego, all heart, and delicious. Samin and I clung to each other all weekend. She was magic, she was overwhelmed—as I was—at the crowd, and we hunkered down and shared our projects, talked about our histories, the people we had worked with, what we hoped to grow into, what we hoped to leave behind. Zero small talk! This came at a time well before I met Kelly or Angie or any of my other important women. Samin was my primer to them; she warmed me up and gave me such hope and excitement about my place in the food world, like we were building our own industry within an industry and like we finally had voices and we heard each other loud and clear.

The Diana Kennedy dinner in San Francisco was the first time Samin and I would see each other again after that symposium. If you eat at Chez Panisse with Samin, the place she worked and learned and taught, you will be sitting with Chez Panisse family and you'll sit at the kitchen table, a two-top next to the chef's pass. She worked hard at Chez Panisse to build her career and her knowledge of food, and she is, hands down, one of the smartest cooks in this country, if not the smartest. Samin and I talked about her book, which she had been working so hard on over the course of those years, something that seemed such an unyielding and relentless process, a process she was wholly committed to, that it did two things for me: it made me question my dedication to every single thing under the sun I had ever done and it made me respect Samin with such a deep care and love that I knew I would want to know her forever. We ate a beautiful meal, yet the thing I remember most was her incredible laugh resonating in that cozy room and, ultimately, just being glad to know someone like her. I walked away from that meal feeling certain that the food world was moving in a direction I would want to keep aligning myself with, no matter how hard things were getting back home in my own restaurant world.

At the risk of saying all that has been said about Chez Panisse before, there is only one detail I really want to mention, a very important detail: the fresh apricot that I was given for dessert with one bahri date next to it.

Samin noticed right away and grinned at my first bite. I started to babble about apricots in general. I could not find words other than "Why doesn't this taste like shit?!" Apricots do not grow properly in the South and, therefore, taste like mealy ass—if I were to bother imagining what mealy ass tastes like. I never understood their appeal and never had to worry about it because, well, we had peaches and, having never been out west before, I just assumed that people who liked apricots had never had a good peach and were suffering through their best idea of what delicious was. Idiot assumption. I was aghast. I was reborn right there next to some very cool cooks and chefs who all likely thought I was ridiculous, who all thought, Poor redneck from Tennessee has never really eaten good food—at least that's what their eyes said.

But there was no real embarrassment, not in front of Samin. She laughed her beautiful laugh and let me reel. All my life I had been the victim of bad, truly terrible, nearly offensive apricots, and I believed them to be an unreasonably nasty fruit, a thing people must have discovered had caloric merit but were forced to eat. I had not only *not* had a real, absolutely important California apricot before, but now I was having it served to me on a plate as a treasure, a treasure on an antique plate with a price tag to match. I had stepped into a world, for the first time, where a chef, literally, had to do *nothing* to the food that was around them. All they had to do was to hold out their hand and say, "Here! Eat this!" and then watch someone roll into a haze of (slightly) controlled euphoria.

I immediately changed my plan for Diana Kennedy's dessert. I asked Samin where I could possibly get the same apricots, to which she said, "Oh, anywhere really . . ." in such a cavalier way that I got angry at the easy access, the no-big-deal-ness of it all for locals. I mean. What the actual fuck, I kept thinking. You *live* this way? All the time??

She directed me to the Berkeley Bowl, and so the next day I saw myself to the Berkeley Bowl as eagerly as a kid waking up on Christmas day.

It was a good thing I discovered the apricots because the peaches, which I tasted once I arrived at the store, were shockingly bad and did not pass muster by my southern standards (can't win 'em all, California!). Once I was in the Berkeley Bowl, I was overwhelmed—I had no idea what to do with myself. Not only was there the best-looking fruit I'd ever seen in my life, but there were no less than five different varieties of each kind. There were seven apricot bins, all from different places, all with slightly different shapes, all with slightly different flavors.

I started to bag dozens of them like a goddamned rookie. I figured I would ask Samin to get the Chez kitchen to order me cases, but first I wanted to try each kind. So I bought several of each, took them outside, found myself a sunny spot on the curb, and proceeded to have a private apricot orgy as people walked by me wondering why the hell I was squatting on the sidewalk moaning and shouting, "You should definitely GET THE APRICOTS!"

After picking the two superior varieties (because you should always combine texture and taste if given the chance), I bought seven cases of each and, with Kelly, made the dessert I am literally, still to this day, most proud of.

I made my tres leches mixture, with raw whole milk, buttermilk, and sweetened condensed milk, and soaked Kelly's beautiful and very dense cornmeal cake in it. The cajeta ice cream was spun. I made the buttermilk cream, and then I took those apricots, pitted them, macerated the ripest ones in just a bit of sugar and vanilla bean, took the underripe ones and roasted them on high heat with a squeeze of lemon juice, sugar, and more vanilla bean, and then, once they were cooled, combined everything to make one delicious apricot creation to put on top of the tres leches cake.

Kelly and I knew what we had. Bill Corbett, a pastry whiz with impeccable taste in music, came with our ice cream and a big bottle of bourbon. We washed dishes and helped any cooks who required it, but mostly we ended up staying in our corner. There was an intensity to the rest of the kitchen that we tried to participate in, to be helpful, but they seemed to have it all under control—more hands than were needed to make sure nothing was unattended. This dinner was a big deal, so the organizer's stress and high intensity were understood and appreciated. But when it came to the cooks we were working along- side, there was a nervous air of uncertainty about getting too close to us—what if we were flops? And what if they had been nice to us? They couldn't seem to bring themselves to risk it. West Coast chefs don't bother getting to know chefs who aren't in their region, unless it's New York City, so they didn't really seem to know that Kelly and I were stalwart, ass-busting professionals—not "big deals," mind you, just capable—and our southern quips and easygoing cadence must have terrified their crisp white tweezer hearts. The younger cooks basically ignored us, rolled their eyes at us when we cut up, and just generally dismissed us. At some point during plate up, Kelly and I were doing our best to maintain good attitudes and be cordial—you know, have fun. But when everyone was being a bit too stressed and tense for their own good, we finally stopped engaging and just kept giving each other wide-eyed looks of "yikes." I went into my own zone and plated up, not wanting to rock the boat. But, suddenly, Kelly tossed her saucier spoon into the bowl and said, "Damn, y'all! I'm not sure how I became the asshole in the room but y'all gotta lighten UP!"

We laughed most of it off and then, when dessert time came, flexed.

The young cooks who previously had been too stressed or could not imagine wanting to know anything from a chef from Tennessee or Louisiana perked up when we started plating. To their benefit, they started asking questions and softening their cold, hard stance once they had a reason to engage with us, bless 'em. Once they saw our food, they became interested. They especially perked up when two people rushed back separately from delivering dessert, shouting, "Chef Lisa! Chef Kelly! Diana Kennedy wants to see you two NOW!"

Kelly and I looked at each other. I was initially terrified. I don't think Kelly is scared of anything, so it's hard to say what was going through her mind at that moment. I went through every possible thing that could have been wrong. Maybe the cake wasn't soaked enough. Maybe the ice cream had not been temped as well as we thought. I had come up with no less than twenty-five possible disasters by the time we arrived at her table, escorted by the host of the event, Caleb Zigas of La Cocina.

Diana Kennedy was, as always, wearing her black leather pants, but she had upped her silver jewelry for the special occasion and even looked to be wearing makeup. She wiggled her finger for us to come closer, then, when we had our heads up by hers—a threesome of strong women faces all collected in a circle and it felt like we were all truly mind melding—she whispered, "That was the FINEST dessert I have ever, EVER had." Kelly and I both stood upright, straight as arrows, and looked at each other as if we had just met, just seen the light, just gotten some kind of anointment from the universe that not many others had ever received. She asked about details, about the milks, about the apricots, about the cornmeal. We talked out our dish with her, Goddess Supreme Being Kennedy, every once in a while catching each other's gaze to say "What the ACTUAL FUCK" with our eyes. Then she asked us to sit down. Kelly got accosted by a fan, because she is famous, and I sat down with Diana Kennedy for approximately four minutes before she got swept away in her honorific night.

In those four minutes, Diana Kennedy seemed to want to make a point to me, a point I can't quite figure out how she knew I needed. She asked if I had heard her recording her podcast the day before. I said yes. In the podcast, she talked of the women's spirit in the kitchen, how it rules Mexican culture, how it rules the family, how it rules the hearts of those who get to come close to the magic of a mother or an *abuela*. She asked if I was a mother. I said yes. She asked if I cooked for my family. I said yes, of course. She then asked if I had told that story to the world. I said I had not yet told any stories to the world. She then asked me why she had never heard of me if I was capable of making these desserts. I said I did not know. And then, as she got up to leave the table, she said, "I do. Stop letting men tell your story."

Diana Kennedy knows what she is doing at all times. Nothing is an accident, and she is certainly not just trying to be sage or look cool. She actually is sage and cool and can fuck you up with a word. My frustrations with my career must have been visible all over me. This was at the height of hearing man after man on NPR and in *The New York Times* telling stories of their mothers, their grandmothers, anyone whom they felt gave them clout or a sense of humility and whom, I'm certain, they honored and cherished and wanted to shine a light on, hold up high on that pedestal. The thing is, women are revered straight into abjection, useful only as a totem of inspiration. When we go to make that work our own, we are unable to survive in the industry the men built, the one they sell our wares within.

In that moment, I accepted that I would no longer allow myself to feel that my sense of womanhood and motherhood is the part of my identity as a chef that I have to undersell and downplay for fear of my professionalism being shrugged off, as it has been in the past. I will no longer be afraid to talk about how my strength as a cook rests almost solely in my strength as a woman. I am a mother and I am a daughter. I am a granddaughter who learned at my nana's polyester-panted hips, curvy and full of Mexican juju and mysticism. I have grown up in kitchens with women and I am now a woman who cooks from that place, in my heart, for a living. I am not driven to be better than any other cook around me or even to make a "perfect" version of something. I want to give people food that tastes of our past stories and of our present now, like the good food that all these chef boys' mothers used to make. I want that food to be respected and honored in our world from its true origins, not solely from a male chef who has figured out how to build an entire brand around what he learned from our hands as he stood by our strong, life-giving hips watching and wishing to god he had some kind of magic that even came close.

# 14

## REMEMBERING

*Masa*

I KNEW THAT MY MOTHER had handwritten recipes from my
nana tucked away in a *Southern Living* cookbook somewhere in
her house. I remembered seeing them during one of our many
moves several years after my nana died. Her masa recipes, her flour
tortillas, her chile verde—always served with shredded pork and
stored in gallon-size ziplock bags in the freezer because she would
make such large batches—were all written in her beautiful script on
folded-up index cards and torn scraps of college-ruled notebook paper
in the most conversational tone, speaking directly to my mother in
each line, sometimes by name.

## GREEN CHILIE [*SIC*] FOR BURRITOS

3–5 little cans of chopped green chilie
1–2 lbs of hamburger or chopped pork or beef pieces
   (your choice)

*Fry meat, drain grease, add chilie (water to cover meat and*
*chilie), garlic + salt cook on low heat till ready for use.*

*Now then, the meat is already cooked, so is the chilie, so you wouldn't think that it needs all the cooking. But, the longer it cooks the better the flavor.*

*Mary Ann, you know I always add pork skins (cracklins) to my green chilie cause we love it that way, but that is your choice baby, some like it, some don't, Ronnie sure doesn't ha ha.*

The recipes tucked into those books preserved the voices of my mothers. Yet I had avoided them for as long as I had been cooking professionally, and all the questions that they demanded I face—the lost identities, the sadness, the fear-ridden lives that all the women in my mother's family seemed to have lived that I'd never understood or wanted to understand, the painful stories that were never consistently told, the urge of every generation to move beyond what and who the previous generation did and was. Even though they, the recipes and the women, are undeniably the richest part of who I am.

Here are things women do, even and especially when no one is watching. Women support their families with food, slinging Sally Lunn loaves and birthday cakes out of their kitchens to neighbors, selling pies out of the trunks of their cars in parking lots for Thanksgiving and the Fourth of July, everything prepared in the middle of the night when there aren't babies to feed and diapers to change. Women build businesses out of nothing, no loans, no mortgages to lean on, and they save money in skillfully "shrewd" ways, as the word properly connotes, no taming required. Women pick wood sorrel together while their cast-iron biscuits bake in the oven, showing one another how not to mistake it for clover. Women talk about their own sadness and joy as they brush off the chanterelles found on their morning walks while simultaneously counting the few spiders that come forth from their stalks, giggling as they prepare a lunch for others awaiting them in the formal dining room, knowing that most of those fancy people would balk at the fact that bugs sometimes live inside our food. Women share recipes like they share love stories, sometimes with great tenderness and sometimes with great sadness, because our recipes tell the others who we are and where we came from. Women talk about their mothers, it's true. But we do so quietly, and we do so protectively, because it is a sacred thing that many of us don't know what to do with until the day they, or we, die.

ONE MORNING I DROVE UP a steep mountainside with Angie, bouncing up and down until we reached an old cabin built about a hundred years ago, give or take a decade. We met more friends, two women who have also worked hard in their professions and have succeeded in many ways, all of us doing different work but somehow on the same path. Rinne Allen, a writer, photographer, and general savant idea generator, and Natalie Chanin, a protector of American threadways, seamstress, designer, and artist—both acclaimed in their respective fields—are the kind of friends you learn from every time you sit down with them. All four of us shared a breakfast on the screened-in porch where a brief mountain rain gave us a fresh waft of calm that felt bittersweet because we were each, that morning, heading out of the nestled valley that had been home to us for two weeks, heading back to our busy lives managing companies, raising children, paying bills, hiring new employees, fixing marriages, calling accountants, and meeting deadlines. It was a breakfast full of ideas, full of love, full of watchful care and consideration of one another. It was also a reminder for me that everything that comes forth in a kitchen is buried inside me from the women before me and sometimes even the women around me.

Being around women like Angie, Rinne, and Natalie drew something out of me, made me realize that I had been avoiding parts of myself that were there in conversation with the women in my family. I had pushed those voices to the side. Not because I do not love them, but because it was simply too much to bear most days and I could not get past the anger I had about the way they had left me to carry the burden of all their unresolved suffering. All I knew was that I didn't want it, had no time for it, and did not find it useful.

When I dug deep into my women and the stories they seemed to have buried, the ones I am made of, the well was full of a kind of generational muffling, a gag order on the most beautiful things about my own person, things that had also been buried but that I was now working hard to be allowed to use out loud. I can go backward in time and find almost exactly when the shit went down. I can only go as far as I can see; what remains beyond is a mystery that no one in my family will talk about, the past being littered with so much pain and regret. But I believe this burying at least flourished, if not began, under my grandfather's oppressive voice, bred in that archaic, early-twentieth-century Mississippi space that he imposed on everyone around him but especially on my nana.

In this new way, I became the excavator, the archaeologist, digging and sorting, trying to find the correct answers and sometimes getting buried myself under all that my women tried to unbecome.

*Be invisible, be whiter, be prettier, don't take up any space, you're stupid, stupid, stupid.*

The excavation site became littered with markers. Every once in a while I would uncover a key, a Rosetta stone that helped me decipher what I knew in my bones to be true. Food always seemed to bring me safely to those dark places, its graciousness first welcoming me sweetly and then hitting me with an avalanche of feelings I hoped I could avoid being eaten alive by. This was never just a casual feeling, what my women left me. It was a haunting, a rending, a kind of exorcism that usually resulted in me yelling at the sky, at spirits, that I did not want their shit, that they were motherfuckers for assuming I did, that I was just fine not sorting through their ancestral baggage, thank you very much, and that they could keep it, check it at St. Peter's gate, burn it in an astral fire, I didn't care. Just leave me out of it. We all know that isn't how things like this go.

WHEN I WALKED into my first *panadería* and a recognition sparked inside of me, I realized I no longer had the strength to keep it at bay. This was a markedly different moment than when I had discovered my daddy's Appalachian family, the hand pies, the dried apples, the generous spirit of giving even in lean times, and how technical handwork managed to genetically find its way into my natural skill set without otherwise having a reason to. Those were so basic and easy. But these stories, this pain, this is what I had been avoiding my whole life. It wasn't going to be as simple as assigning it a technical skill in my bones or even a lost hurt that belonged to my daddy.

My mother, her family, the spirit of them, I've kept it all at a very long arm's length—deflecting it with a type of manic industriousness, working hard so I could do that trite thing that every woman does: fighting with the ghosts of who our mothers were so we "don't become them." I knew it was too much to try to understand until I found a little more capacity for tenderness, until my heart opened a few more of the chambers that I am known to keep tightly sealed and protected. The emotional habits of my dad's people felt safe. Their frontier prowess, their stoic and useful mountain ways, their complications always easily on the surface with no time for the impracticalities of feelings—less time wasted spent burying them—were much easier to explore than the tangled, muddy, cavernous, and deeply vulnerable world from whence my mother, and I guess I, came. This was the part of me that I did not yet know how to translate, but it makes up most of my sum as a woman, as a mother, as a daughter, and as a person who makes her living feeding people.

There was nothing familiar to me about the actual pastries I found in that first *panadería*. The colorful bleached-flour concoctions, the white, pink, and yellow sugars, the piggy cookies—none of it was nostalgic. But as it happens, the *panadería* I first walked into was also a tortilla "factory"—the term "factory" loosely meaning two guys and a woman behind a deli counter cranking out tortilla after tortilla by hand with three teenagers packaging the product before they took it to the storefront or to the restaurant next door.

I watched them for a long time. The woman's hands were mounding masa, small and deft and fast—dipping her fingertips into a bowl of water first and then, as if she had done it a million times a day over the span of a million years, pressing and slapping the masa onto her skillet, contributing to the smell already consuming the space, a smell I hadn't been filled with since that morning in my aunt Rose's kitchen when I was alone with my nana. My blood recognized itself in the hot ground corn, a smell that is undeniably one thing and one thing alone, and it felt like a train hitting me square in the chest; my face immediately became hot and wet with tears that I didn't even realize I was making until I felt them sliding down my neck, down onto my suddenly heaving breasts, soaking my bra and skin.

When I think about my nana and the women she begat, how their lives have impacted me, it is not simply a longing—I am overcome. The inaccessibility of information deliberately hidden, burned, discarded, or told inaccurately from generation to generation, the information never the same, the stories told differently my whole life and their whole lives, this is a wound that seems to bleed fresh every time it is opened. My nana became a martyr, a saint, an icon—practically a version of the idol I palmed for dear life when I was a kid in bed, afraid of the dark. How was I supposed to know who she was, who my mother was, who I was, when all I knew of their stories was their pain? This was not my religion and I was not trying to spend my life painting stations of the cross to pay homage to the dowry of suffering they left me. I had a lot of resentment to get past; that's what happens when you gift your daughters with fear and heartache, mistaking it for protection. Could I find a place to hold them, give them shelter once and for all? I had no idea. But the corn was telling me I should consider it.

The pain of my women goes beyond my grandfather, beyond the shame he built within all of us, the shame it took me years to undo so that I could make the life I deserve. It goes much deeper. My mestizo nana, her Zuni mother, Anita, her Mexican father, Pablo: they seemed to have a plan to transition their family from something deemed lesser in the world they lived in, to bequeath more to whoever came after them. Burn the records, assimilate, pick lettuce, find a man, a white man, who can take you away from your brown life, no matter how bad he is to you. I cannot claim to understand how this feels, but I know what I feel, and it is a great burden for me to try to understand that these choices were made with any amount of kindness—because I have seen the fallout. It has been the opposite of healing, the pain of that erasing ferried from one person to the next in my family the way most families share love and support. Instead, we share shame and guilt and misery, none of us certain why or from where it came. But the more I dig, the more I see that this motivation to protect a daughter, in this case my nana, mutated into a great deal of suffering and martyrdom that I have avoided, and in essence avoiding my women in turn.

I don't want to move past those recipes any longer, I don't want to erase anymore. I want to write them back into my narrative, I want their lives to be fuller in my mind, but mostly I want them to have a place in my heart that feels safe. I don't want to trade their voices in my head for a space in a kitchen, or in a world that will give me only enough room to apologize or give me enough of their supposed "power" to build up the men around me. I want to be finally strong enough for all of my women to carry the things they were not allowed to. We deserve to see who we truly are, because of who we come from—the indigenous, the immigrants, the builders, the lettuce pickers, and the women, most especially the women. I want to be strong enough to let them in, to take it back for them, for Anita, for Mary, for Rose, for my mother. I will wade through the mud, I will try to honor what they felt they had to bury, had to hide in order to get by in their lives, what was never a stain, but what I have always been and what I will always be made of.

I will do the work to make the masa into a beautiful thing for them again.

# 15

## DEATH

*Lamb*

TWO YEARS AFTER leaving restaurants for good and approximately a year after I pulled myself from that warm salt water in Costa Rica, I found myself in a cold barn in Vermont standing in front of a man wearing rubber pants and holding a rifle in his left hand.

He used words like "shot" and "stick" instead of "shoot" and "slit," as in "First we'll make a shot and then we will stick the animal," but what he really meant was "First we will shoot the animal and then slit its throat." It is easier on the ears, I suppose.

Language is important when you are "harvesting" an animal. It serves as a navigation tool, a way to ease an experience where the concepts are too hard on our hearts, too jagged for our brains. I had been anxious about this moment for weeks, knowing way too far ahead of time that this was going to be a part of the weekend that I had been invited to attend. Thirteen chefs on a sprawling farmstead in Vermont, on James Beard's dime, learning from more experienced folks how to be advocates for a better world through our industry. It was two days full of long, important conversations and then this one afternoon full of silence. There is an intense reverence and a certain kind of understanding that only comes when you witness and participate in taking a life.

The kill did not go well. Our farmer and butcher, Mike, did not tie the thirteen-month-old lamb up to the green tractor correctly at first and it struggled, trying to find a place to hide between the few crevasses behind the front-loading scoop. The tractor was the same color as my sneakers that day, a paltry point of distraction that kept me from focusing wholly on the anxious lamb crying out with ever-growing frequency. When she realized there was no space to wedge herself into and no way to slip her rope—accentuating the fact that she was not accustomed to a rope being tied that tightly around her neck—the cries turned into wails. She had come from the farm's petting zoo, had lived with several other lambs her age her entire life, and when she was not surrounded by small children stroking her softly (perhaps her worst moments were experiences of them tugging at her wool too firmly), she was out to pasture with other grazers basking in a Vermont life free of trauma or pain, which I'm pretty certain made this exact moment all the more terrifying for her.

Now she was being tied tighter than she'd ever been to a strange big machine, with a circle of humans around her and a rifle trying to steady itself on the top of her head. She was so scared. I cried into my scarf but would not let myself look away. When you are with an animal that knows it is about to die, you realize very quickly that you have a responsibility to hold steady, to honor the life that is about to be lost by not flinching, by not looking away, by not denying the truth of what is happening in front of you, the sanctity of what life is and of what death is, too. So you hold your eyes fixed, you accept the moment, and you steel yourself against fear almost as an offering to the animal, as a hope that she might take some of your strength at that moment and not be afraid or "be not afraid," as my priest always said. The moment took too long. And then it was over, with a shot and a stick.

Mike was kind and steady and displayed a dedication to killing this animal properly that almost broke your heart as much as hearing the animal cry. Almost. I stood there, hearing only my own heart pound, no more cries, with a cold Vermont breeze, which I was not accustomed to, chilling my ears, the only part of my face besides my wide, still unblinking, eyes not buried in my woolen scarf now soaked in tears. I stood there in the moment before I volunteered to skin the lamb with my own bare hands and thought about all that I was now responsible for. I would put my bare hands under a warm pelt and peel it off the sinew and muscle of a lamb, as if this was a task that had been waiting for me my whole life. I did not hesitate. It felt like a rite of passage, an initiation into a world where you had to admit to yourself that seeing a thing, a death, a rape, an exploitation, an abuse, makes you responsible in a way you cannot dodge. You have to look it straight in the eye, you have to bear witness, to act on it. I had to skin the thing, feel the warmth of it still, and carry it with me forever.

I balled up my right hand and, while my left hand pulled the pelt tight, proceeded to wedge my knuckled fist between the layers of pelt, skin, sinew, muscle. I felt strong that day, stronger than I had in the days past, like I had a sense of place and a responsibility to protect that place. Blood dripped onto my green shoe, but I got closer. The body was warm, the smell of lanolin rich, the feeling of its form heavy. My hands would smell of her fat for weeks, a reminder to hold myself responsible. Because at the end of the day, it doesn't matter who shot the lamb. I saw her die.

· · ·

FOR A LONG TIME it wasn't cool, or even correct, to ask the kinds of questions that might make things better in our industry, to change the way things were going. The expectation was to adapt, to fold in, to hold your breath if things got bad and then drink away the fear you swallowed after you finished service. Nothing was sane about it. Nothing was productive about it. But it was the way we were told it should be. So we wrecked our nervous systems, destroyed our guts, taxed our mental health to the point of potential no return, and we just hoped to live another day to cook. Of course this has to change, and of course it will. Yet, and by god, you can rest assured that there will definitely still be an army of young mini-machismos willing to go down with that ship of ego and insanity, in the name of all the gods who came before them, so help them, Michael Pierre White.

After these last few years of playing all the moments back in my head, wondering what I could have done to change the thing, wondering how, if at all, I could have pulled the brakes and made a significant enough change to my own immediate world, I come back to only one thing with such frequency that it is starting to feel like a mantra in my head. There is a tender, heartbreakingly sensitive vein running through our industry, one that makes us all pretend we are tough, one that makes us all work harder than any human should. I see immigrants who are trying to support families, who want to build better lives for their children, who will work three jobs to make it count. I see young kids who are searching for a path come into these kitchens and discover a whole life around a sauté pan, around a clean station, around others just like them. The best people in kitchens believe in showing up for the work. We want to cook. We want to work. We want to provide for our lives. Kitchens serve that need for a living and a call to hard work, and we show up. Within our exhaustion, some of us even dream about what we can accomplish the next day. It's what we wake up for, yes, even if we have children. And with this understanding, I get tired of people asking what chefs can do to cope, to manage ourselves better, to survive. Why is the question: How do you, Chef, survive an exploitive industry? Why isn't the question: How do you, investors, dismantle the historically exploitive system you and your ilk have built?

Here's the thing: if you're pretending you care enough about these people and this world to invest in a restaurant, you can't spend hundreds of thousands of dollars on art and sconces and a PR firm and then argue that a pastry chef or a line cook is only worth a few nickels and dimes. How can you justify creating salary structures that are built simply to legally allow your cooks to work longer hours than any human should for way less money—selling them the idea for the faux prestige of a bullshit, antiquated brigade title like chef de partie? I have a lot to say about those greedy "developers" and so-called "restaurateurs" who exploit hardworking cooks and scullery workers, but the most polite sentiment I can find for them is: fuck off out of kitchens already.

The restaurant business is notoriously hard, but when you are sensible about how you grow and serve, you can make it work honorably and sustainably. I've seen it done. I see it done all the time now, thank god. People who give a shit, who put their people first, are opening restaurants and growing companies that start from the right bottom line. You can be a smart investor and also be dedicated to putting health care, fair livable wages, and the well-being of your staff before anything and everything, even the food. Then build from there. Are there Mario Batali–style and –size cultural problems? Yes. Is he the base of what the actual problem is? No. Investors have created a safe haven for bullshit people like Batali, egomaniacal, accused rapists who don't have to answer to anyone if they are raking in enough dough for the sugar daddies to look the other way. Investors make room for snakes who pretend they are allies for women when really those kinds of chefs are just opportunistic liars who pretend they have been on the high road their whole careers for women—using an important moment in media as a way to get out of contracts they no longer want, indicting others, and shouting online about their names being stolen from them—and then center women in their new restaurant group to save face and continue their masquerade as soldiers for equality. In the midst of all this current talk of women in kitchens and women getting their time in the restaurant industry, investors still can't seem to see their way to actually funding us women, but holy shit are they suckers for boys who pretend they are feminists in a very all-of-a-sudden way. It only took me walking out of my fifth meeting with potential investors in Nashville to realize that the game wasn't changing. The only thing that has changed is the story men are spinning to get what they want. And bankers and investors are still lapping it up and pouring money on their projects like water on a grease fire.

While I was figuring all of this out, realizing that it was going to take so much more than outing a few disgusting trolls who never deserved our respect to begin with, I was asked to speak in Copenhagen at René Redzepi's MAD Symposium. We were discussing how to keep conversations about our industry going in the right direction, how to better them, how to make sure we were all thriving and supporting one another. The organizers brought chefs in from all over the world but predominantly American chefs to talk about some serious and hard issues. And we did. It was important on many levels, but for me, it was especially important to realize how significantly "American" these problems were. People were shocked, perplexed, at the stories we told. From Australia to Germany to Denmark to England, they all wanted to hear more about the insane way we run restaurants in this country, and to kindly and generously offer practical, and basic, solutions to what I realized was mostly "our" problem.

In the same way that I had decided I could no longer ignore the power of my mothers in my life, I decided Copenhagen would be the last time I stood in a room in front of people and talked about what does not work. Instead, I would talk about what does work. I would not turn a blind eye or be afraid to call out bad behavior (obviously), but I would also work hard to protect and contribute because that is what you do for the things you love. I decided I would try to always bring women with me wherever I went so they could chime in about their work, their mothers, their places of inspiration, their bottom lines and business structures and priorities. I decided I was done adding more noise and instead would add more good work. I see a lot of people doing the same now. That is what chefs do, we get to work. I want to talk about the food, the finding of it, the preparation of a meal, the spirit of service, and the celebration of the whole process, from picking the first vegetable for the meal to washing the last dish. And I want to be really honest as often as I can about who I think deserves to have a hand in building this world with us. Spoiler alert: it's not a bullshit millionaire who wants to spend thousands of dollars a month on PR but haggles your already stellar 27 percent food costs down to 25 percent.

I feel ferociously protective of this world. The truth that I have found as a person in hospitality still feels important to me, despite the reality I can see very plainly now. I have found a sense of self and connectivity in this work and in the people I cook with unlike anywhere else in my life. I believe that is true for most of us who have truly put in the time. We made this our world, and if you think about how complicated and beautiful that world is, how it's really just a collection of tenderhearted goons out there trying to love and be loved, it's enough to break your heart. We settled into the weird routines, resting when everyone else was working and working when everyone else was resting, never having a holiday off, never sitting down to eat our own meals, making our lives out of the moments when food comes out of a kitchen, leaves our station, and is placed in front of another human to whom we feel so grateful to have the honor of feeding. That's the thing right there, isn't it? Those moments? That's what this whole damn thing is, right?

# 16

## REBIRTH

*Burgundy*

L AMOTHE-GOAS IN THE SOUTH of France is almost
equidistant between Paris and Barcelona, deep enough in
the ambling hills of the country that it masterfully lulls you
into its green pastures and simple farm food so that you spend the
majority of your time doing the very American thing of dreaming up
all the ways you can trade in your rough-and-tumble life full of
Kroger rats and processed foods and sporadic farmers' market novelty
weekends for something as real and as seemingly basic to sanity and
well-being as the life people lead in places like that. When you come
out of Paris, you realize that French people are boisterous and kind,
even if you are sloppy with their language. And their eyes sparkle at
your terrified attempts to communicate, them probably knowing full
well that it is a fear won at the hands of a well-heeled and perfectly
coiffed Parisian at a wine bar or cheese boutique who could not believe
the vulgarity of your accent or the vulgarity of just you in general.
Not that I ever mind the spirit of Paris. I love their cool disregard
as much as, if not more than, the comforts of the countryside. I even

appreciate my own American sensibilities more when I'm in Paris, when I see someone trying to eat a burger with a knife and fork, preferring to fumble through it instead of having sticky fingers to lick—a deeply satisfying and deeply American thing that no one, least of all an American, should be willing to forsake, no matter how many beautiful and thin French women are glaring from across the café as you catch the mayonnaise sliding down your chin with your tongue and you take a big swig of wine before you're even done chewing just to help you wash it all down, satisfied and beaming. In France, I swiftly realized that you are allowed to contain multitudes. It is, in fact, glares aside, deeply encouraged.

I was far away from Paris, though, with only a thirteen-year-old Maggie Donovan and a thousand fields of wheat and French cows and bucolic vistas next to and in front of me as I drove from Goas to Toulouse. I was also far away, in both time and distance, from Niceville or Husk or Costa Rica and from the person I had been in any of those places. It was eighteen years since I took that phone call in Tom's office at TradeWinds. Joseph had graduated from high school and was on his way to spend the final two weeks in Barcelona and Paris with me and Maggie. John was at home, his hands in clay in our backyard, both of us doing the work we said we wanted to be doing—sacrifices paid off. But, mostly, our love and support for each other was so otherworldly that we knew, even during all those times we had struggled, that we would not fail. Failing would have equaled something much bigger than money problems or other petty bullshit. Failing, for us, would have been letting each other down, letting the other's dream die, not keeping careful watch to protect the real part of each other that mattered beyond "success." John Donovan has never, not once, let me down.

But at that moment, in Goas, I had only my daughter next to me. We had just cooked for a bunch of artists for a week, painters who had retreated to a quiet corner, hoping to find some kind of inspiration, I guess, while I huddled in the kitchen making summer vegetable salads with zucchini and herbs from the garden and honey vinegar from a thousand-year-old pantry and Îles Flottantes bobbing in their ocean of vanilla cream while I attempted to get it as right as the one at Bistrot Paul Bert in Paris (and nearly landing it perfectly) and clafoutis made with plums from the neighbor's château and coq au vin from just-killed young roosters I found in the adjacent town of Fleurance, making two-day stock from the head and feet and other parts that never come with the chicken I buy at home, which is usually wrapped in plastic with its blood-soaked pads.

I needed very little that summer and was given an abundance of things that I had assumed were forever gone from my landscape as a cook at some point in my career. I had freedom, I had a chance to make and serve people food, to be hospitable in a home that wasn't even mine, to forage, to find, to learn, to explore, and to be in an environment where I was valued and treated as simply as I needed to be, with kindness and with proper pay. Mostly, though, I had my daughter with me. All the other glorious things were dim lights by comparison. I never make Maggie Donovan responsible for my happiness, but the fact is that she is a buoy in this world and a light so bright that all you can do in the face of her is to be lighter, to be glad you are alive. She is singular in her ability to right my ship, to straighten my spine, to quiet the static.

I had decided that my career, a career I really cared about and did not want to forsake, would and could and should include my actual life as a part of it. I realized that this likely meant, sadly, that I never would go back to the restaurant industry, where I could never make a decent living, where I might always be seen as a tool for someone else's success. Instead, I started finding ways to cook whenever and wherever I could. And I started bringing Maggie Donovan with me everywhere, just as I had when she and Joseph were small, and I refused to let the world dictate to me that being a mother was somehow an obstruction to how good I was at my work or to my goals. In some ways it felt radical to simply decide to show up with my kid in tow, in a way that did not feel radical when I was a scrappy young kid who seemed to know better, who insisted that people, professors, and deans get the fuck out of my way so I could survive. I accepted that, if cooking was my gift, the thing I could give the best of myself in, then I would have to, again, make my own way. Baking workshops, private chef jobs, consulting, recipe writing and testing and editing: I could do it all, work twice as hard, manage my own shit, and still not be as frustrated or sad (or drunk as a result) as I was when I was trying to play the game their way. Part of me, which was fully breaking away from the weird, totally invasive, and toxic patriarchal culture I had let myself get tangled up in, was now showing the fuck back up with my kid on my proverbial hip, daring anyone to question it, daring anyone to suggest that my work might suffer. And no one did. And, if they did, I worked around them. I have always known what I am capable of, and it is, in fact, multitudes.

My dear friend, a baker named Julie who used to be my sous chef, had been living in France as a working musician. She had moved there not long after leaving my pastry kitchen. I told her I was coming to France to cook, and she came, with zero hesitation. The three of us, me and Julie and Maggie Donovan, made some beautiful things happen in a château kitchen together, windows opened wide despite the summer flies, music playing, songs being sung both quietly and loudly, dancing, brushing mushrooms clean, picking herbs, drinking wine from a box, and moving in rhythm together like we'd been there forever. And this was the first time I started to feel like things made sense again. I was not lonely for very long with Julie by my side. Her steady skills and her even steadier heart grounded me, and a few memories of those days when we worked in a bustling kitchen of a fancy restaurant came creeping in every once in a while, for better and for worse, little flashbacks of urgency that we no longer had to feel for our lives, that were gone.

On the last day we planned to prepare a simple dinner, which we would set at a table outside for all our guests, and then watch the sun set from the roof before driving to Toulouse to drop Julie off at her train back to Angers, her home. That morning, after we had made the coffee and set out a service of bread and butter and cheese and fruit for our guests, I went upstairs to start packing. I was tired; it had been an intense and full week of cooking three meals a day for twenty people; I discovered I had some kind of hay-fever allergy to something in bloom; and the previous night, I had had a nightmare unlike any I'd ever experienced. Julie, Maggie, and I were sharing a room with three beds, and I had woken them both up by clawing at my headboard violently, screaming and sobbing in my sleep to not bury me, please to just save me, please to just keep me from being swallowed whole by the pit I had found myself in. Julie jumped onto my bed and held me and shook me awake, wiping my tears away, and then we all kind of chuckled about how I had shrieked a crazy shriek that sounded like I was being murdered. "God, I felt so hopeless and so scared—I was being buried alive," I said, trying to laugh along but still feeling terrified. Maggie got in bed with me and held my hand, and I fell right back to sleep. I could not stay asleep, though. Something felt desperate and I felt very shaken by it.

So when I went up to pack and be alone for a moment to drink my coffee and catch my breath after serving breakfast, I opened my phone to pull up emails and texts and the news, just to distract myself, to catch up on the life I had been too busy to keep track of that week. There were nearly a hundred texts from just about every person I knew, all within the last couple of hours. I could only see their names and the time they texted. It took me a while before I got up the nerve to open my phone again. I was too terrified to look. When I did, it was full of pictures, full of links, full of heartache. Anthony Bourdain had hanged himself. He had succumbed. He was gone. My eyes did that funny thing where they get fuzzy and out of focus and you can't tell what you're actually seeing, as if they are trying to protect your brain and heart from the shock, filtering it with feigned dysfunction, pretending to not work for the sake of the whole.

I knew Tony the way I think a lot of people knew Tony. We worked together on some projects, he offered himself generously in person and in emails and over texts to make me feel welcomed in his world with cameras and producers, he said my name on television a few times, we drank a few beers together, and we had important, for me, conversations that gave me pause and changed my mind.

But I would never dare to call him a friend. We might have been on our way to friendship, but I considered myself lucky just to be in his direct orbit, lucky to have a chance to share space and time with his kind of heart, feeling seen by him, feeling wholly connected in ways that didn't exist out in the "real" world.

We had all become lost orphans overnight, no matter how hard we had worked to find a place for ourselves, no matter how I had spent that last week feeling proud and confident in the way I had built my life, how I had reclaimed the right to cook and be in a kitchen in a way that felt right to me. None of that now mattered. It all felt lost in that moment. We were all lost. Tony had been the one to give any of us derelicts some hope to begin with. It felt unjust. It felt heartbreaking.

It felt outrageous. And then all I could feel was deep sorrow. The kind of sorrow that seems to form only when someone you know and love takes their own life—a feeling of loss and guilt and confusion for the kind of pain he must have felt, which I have no right to speak to, all those feelings vying for equal time.

When I put my phone down, I looked up, not realizing that Maggie had walked in and was leaning out of the window across from me, like a picture, her elbows perched on the window ledge, the wooden shutters splayed open, and wearing a yellow dress with orange flowers on it that we had just bought the day before at the market in Auch. Her golden hair was literally catching and throwing sunshine and reflecting it so that it looked like she had a halo—or maybe it was the tears that had formed in my eyes making everything a bit hazy.

I walked over and stood by her, still stunned and unable to say anything. Long moments passed quietly.

"Mama, you good?"

Sometimes I don't speak, and I keep my feelings very close to my chest. And sometimes the words just fall out of my mouth before I know they are coming.

"I'm OK, baby. I just heard that someone I know, someone I loved, someone everyone loved, died. He must have had a terribly broken heart, baby. Please. Remember. Please. You come find me if your heart ever feels broken, OK? Promise me. Please."

This urgency to make sure everyone who mattered to me knew they were not alone, not scared, and not beyond repair, pushed past the sorrow. And then I felt Julie's hand on my shoulder.

I turned to her and she hugged me and we each took a deep breath and packed our bags silently. Every once in a while one of us would stop for a moment and look around, lost, because that's what happens when the questions get too big and you feel that making eye contact with another person is the only thing that will keep you from sinking beneath the feelings.

We finished our day, packed our things, said goodbye to the guests and the wheat fields and the cows, and drove north toward Toulouse and a train for Julie.

We said our goodbyes in the car, Julie grabbed her bag from the back, and Maggie and I headed back out into the late night to find our hotel.

The streets of Toulouse were packed, friendly, and full of pedestrians. I was driving a little car, but by my estimation not little enough. I hadn't realized Toulouse was such a raucous college town, and it was full tilt by the time I shoved that tiny car, which still felt giant, through the magnificently small cobblestone roads that the map swore would lead us to our hotel.

It was dark. I was tired. I was overwhelmed, and all I wanted to do was drink the very nice bottle of Burgundy that a wine vendor had given me as a gift for buying so much product that week. I could not make heads or tails of where to go or how to bob and weave a car through the thicket of crowds and scooters who seemed to own the roads along with the drunkenness and the fun. I could not bring myself to find any foreign joy in and of it, not that day. I emerged from a dead-end alley; I could only go left or right and both ways were full, shoulder to shoulder, of humans dancing in the street and hanging on each other's shoulders and otherwise not looking like they were prepared to deal with a car. There was a man smoking a cigarette and watching me. He was leaning on the wall of the alley, just the three of us staring at one another in the darkness with a world of light and joy just feet away, like we were behind a movie screen, living on the periphery of everyone's easy fun. I wanted his cigarette and would have asked him for it had my daughter not been there. She's never seen me truly frazzled; it doesn't happen very often. But I was exhausted and lost and sad and tired. And I wanted his cigarette in my mouth. I rolled down my window and sputtered my one French phrase, *"Je suis désolé, parlez-vous Anglais?"* He stood up from his long, hard lean against the wall, threw his cigarette on the ground, and walked over to the car window. He was wearing a chef's coat. And he was overwhelmingly handsome.

"Yes, hello, of course I speak English. You are lost, can I help, please?"

I went on to explain that I felt like maybe cars did not belong on these roads full of people. They do, he assured me. You just have to go slow and tell people to move.

OK. Yes. Good.

Then, also, where do I park for a hotel that is supposedly just two blocks that way? He directed me away from the center of town and suggested I walk. Telling me it would be good for me after a long drive and a hard day.

OK. Yes. Of course.

"Is that all? You are comfortable now?" he asked.

I said, Yes, thank you, and asked where he was a chef. He pointed, said some name that I did not pay enough attention to to remember, and I replied, "So weird that you'd be the one to help me. I'm a chef, too. Funny."

He said, in the same curious tone, taking out another enviable cigarette and lighting it as he spoke in the most indubitably French way, "Yes, somehow I knew that. We just know each other, yes?"

"Yes. We do. We're all from the same planet."

He seemed to like that and made Martian antennae with his fingers.

I drove off, parked five blocks away, and then Maggie and I grabbed our bags and walked, becoming a part of the thick crowds, making our way to our bed, a shower, and a bottle of Burgundy that felt very important.

Maggie was quick to fall asleep. We were in a lovely small room with one bed, a bathroom, and a small table that, if you moved it just enough out of the way, you could open up two windows and be on what felt like a balcony overlooking the still-busy late-night streets. I was hungry, but all that was available were some macarons left on our bed. Despite the carnival-style festivities below, there was not a single place still serving food.

I ate a green macaron hoping for pistachio but got a misguided mint and opened the bottle of wine.

My brain spun through it all: taking moments to reflect on how I needed to keep to the center of my life, to never let it get out in the fringes again; making lists of people I needed to call immediately, people who I knew were suffering in that exact moment. But mostly I settled on thinking about how tender we all are. How absolutely tender every single person I ever met in a kitchen was and is, no matter their mocking tone or their fuck-you gaze. Maybe we could each just take one another's tenderness and protect it, protect it with all our strength. Maybe that tenderness could prevail for once and fuck all if we just stopped being so ashamed of it. Maybe we could just feed people and be seen and maybe be loved and maybe that tenderness could find a home and maybe that was enough.

The streets were quieting down in Toulouse and the air was warm. I had bummed a cigarette off the front-desk clerk while Maggie was pushing the elevator button, and I lit it, leaned out of the window, and noticed that the sun was starting to creep over the horizon. It was nearly morning and I was still drinking a bottle of wine. And smoking a cigarette. Vices I had for the most part put away but now felt like the only proper solution to the way the week in France was ending. We had to drive to Barcelona to pick up Joseph in just a few hours. We would all be together soon, me and my two kids, in a small café in Spain, and I wanted to be present and ready for it. I put out the half-smoked cigarette, poured out a sip of wine onto the street below, washed my face, brushed my teeth, and looked at my tired eyes in the mirror as I, however futilely, put on antiwrinkle cream.

I decided on a moment of pride, refocused my brain. I was about to be in Europe with both of my children. Where I was at that exact moment in time mattered. The sun was rising on Saturday, June 9, my daughter was sleeping in the bed next to me, and my son was on a plane headed to Spain from Nashville, a grown man, a strong, beautiful, grown young man who deserved a life unsullied by small, terrible people and who got exactly that, because I fucking fought for that, for him and for me. And Maggie, with a heart of gold, ready to be in the world the way she was born to be, the way I was born to be but had to fight my whole life for, for her and for me. I fought for every goddamn thing in our lives. And I won. I earned the right to be where I was, earned every dollar and every feeling and every bit of pride I felt for my family and for myself. There was no more shame in my heart to devalue my hard work. There was no more burden of my womanhood. I would not succumb. I would not submit. My womanhood was the reason these things existed. My world was fully my own because of it, not despite it.

I climbed into bed with Maggie. I had two hours to sleep but mostly I just stared at her. I remembered how proud she was to be in the kitchen with me and Julie, how she carried herself like a young woman, her hands stained with plum, a bandage on her thumb from a small knife cut, her hair still in a bun from washing the dinner dishes before we left Goas—all these things giving me glimpses into the future but she was still carrying her own deep mysteries, ones that I will watch and not be a part of, ones that I will have to let her manage, ones that will be her own story. And I felt a deep sense of wanting to make her proud. Wanting tenderness to win and wanting to make Maggie proud were the loudest voices in the room. I thought about my own mother. Thought about how hard it must have been for her to have a daughter like me, one who just would not take my medicine and go to bed. One who asked too many questions, demanded answers, but not just any answers, the "right" answers. I thought about how challenging I must have made it for her being a woman, a girl raised to believe she could be nothing but a body, a pretty face, an apologetic dreamer. My relentlessness must have broken her some days. The strain it took on us, time and again. How my insistence on finding the answers to make everything easier on her by holding everyone, including her, accountable, believing that somehow, somewhere, there was a code to set her, us, free and how that must have made her feel so small, like she had not done enough. I wondered how hard and cold the world must have felt for her once I realized after having my own daughter that it was no longer my job to save us all. How, overnight, the realization that if the choice came down to making my mother proud or making my daughter proud, I would choose my daughter every time. Maybe, I thought, if my relentlessness could do one thing, maybe it could break the boulder that my mothers carried for so long into small enough pieces that it no longer would feel like any of us were being buried alive.

I wasn't going to pass that on to Maggie Donovan. If all my questions led me anywhere, it was to that understanding. As I lay in that bed beside her, I decided that the old baggage would be set ablaze, right there, right then. I leaned into her, smelled her hair and her face that smelled like French hotel soap and lotion, and I whispered my mother's name in her ear that night. I whispered my nana's name, Mary Cordova Gutierrez. I whispered a Hail Mary for the first time in thirty years but stopped in the middle, none of it feeling real. It was no longer my prayer. I could let it go. I looked at my daughter, an entire universe that had everything yet nothing to do with me, and I sat with the trick of that understanding, the trick of holding her up while also letting her loose, never making her responsible for my expectations but still giving her the power of the things I had learned and fought for. And then I kissed her and, before I fell asleep with her in my arms, whispered one last, real prayer into her ear.

"*Mija*. Go wild."

# ACKNOWLEDGMENTS

It's funny and odd to start adding up the reasons, the small intentional moments, the transformative conversations, and the chances people took on you—I promise you it is an emotional avalanche of gratitude that you don't know how to begin to categorize or communicate. It makes your brain do seemingly impossible somersaults in order to get it all down thoroughly and clearly. But here we go anyway:

David Black, you scared the shit out of me when we first spoke those many years ago. You cut through my bullshit with a hot knife and waded through a lot of moments of growth and becoming with me. You were exactly what I needed, and I am grateful I was somehow smart enough to keep you close to me. I am grateful for your voice in my head and I am grateful for your mentorship. But mostly I am ever grateful that you believe in my writing and that you refuse to let me see anything other than my utmost potential. I'm not scared anymore. I adore you.

This book, and my still intact sanity and emotional constitution, would not have been possible without everyone at Penguin Press getting behind me and enthusiastically supporting this book so graciously and fervently. I am especially forever indebted, though, to my generous editors, Ginny Smith Younce and Caroline Sydney. You took me so far over these last few years and over all these pages and iterations—learning about this work from you has been the honor of a lifetime. You both brought such skill and talent and love to this process, and to my life. Thank you for believing in me. Thank you for this chance. It is, truly, a dream come true. I hope I have made you proud.

To my first two editors ever: Kate Krader and Kat Kinsman. You have been so important to this, so important to me. Thank you for being two of the first people to put my writing into the world. Thank you for seeing something in me that was ready to take up space and thank you for providing that space.

To everyone at *Food & Wine* magazine: your enthusiasm and full-on support of chefs, your good intentions, your dedication to telling the right stories, and your warmth and sincerity are going to change the world.

So much of our life in the South is based on connections and friendships and lifting one another up. When I think of the two greatest and nearly visionary connectors in that world, I think of John T. Edge and Ashley Christensen.

John T., you have a habit of kicking down the gate when you have the power to do so, the gate that usually keeps a lot of us out, and I love you for it.

Ashley Christensen, you have been a standard-bearer for so many of us for so long and you have shared your success and your opportunities with so many of us, especially your womenfolk compadres, with the most generous hand. You radiate kindness and you bring people together in very big and important ways. You've made us all so much richer in our work and relationships. Those of us who get to call you a friend are fortunate indeed. I love you very much.

Angie Mosier, Ann Marshall, Cheetie Kumar, Rebecca "Quiet Riot" Wilcombe—I don't even have words for how much your friendship means to me. It's funny that we say "TNB!" because I would trust you bitches with my whole, entire life. I can do anything knowing you all are out there, behind and beside me. I am so grateful for our love and trust and honesty.

Yve Assad, you are my favorite collaborator and daydreamer. You and your whole team went the distance to make the cover of this book something I could get my head around and be proud of. Your friendship, hilarity, joy, and light in this world mean so much to me. Let's keep going!

Ronni Lundy, Leah Chase, Diana Kennedy, Alice Randall, Alice Waters, and Annie Quatrano—you have lit the path every step of the way, you have reached back to make sure we knew we were welcome, and you have all showed us how it can best be done. But mostly, you have given us the power of your grace, strength, and love in a world that does not necessarily cultivate those things for or in women. Thank you for being dedicated to building the world we all deserve.

Timshel Matheny, Heidi Ross, Emily Leonard, Robin Riddell Jones, Libby Callaway, Vadis Turner, Kelly Williams, Mary Arwen, Barbara Mountenot, Joy Shaw, and so many other women in Nashville: thank you for keeping me fed and loved and supported and energized and for making me feel, for the first time in my life, like I have a hometown.

Lolis Eric Elie, Tony Earley, Ruth Reichl, Kim Severson, Margaret Renkl, Mary Laura Philpott, Dorie Greenspan, Keia Mastrianni, Charlotte Druckman, you all show me what hard work and dedication mean in writing. You are all inspirations. Thank you for gracing my life with your generous words, support, and friendship.

My kitchen family, Margot McCormack, Sean Brock, Anne Kostroski, Sal Avila, Aaron Clemins, Brian Baxter, Morgan McGlone, Davis Reese, Molly Levine, Sean Ehland, Katy Keefe, Sam Jett, Colby Rasavong, John "Buddy" Sleasman, Mike Wolf, Dano Heinze, thank you for opening doors, and for being teachers and touchstones in times of both failure and great success.

I get to exist in a community so large and so loving that this list feels incomplete. But during this process, my career, and my life at large, these people have been guiding lights and true loves and have done so much, either up close or from afar, to keep me afloat and joyful and full of hope—true friends and inspirations, as they say: Natalie Chanin, Alex Raij, Eder Montero, Kelly Fields, Johnny Mosier, Paul Silber, Scott

Blackwell, Julie Saunders, Mashama Baily, Katie Button, LeighAnn Smith, Osayi Endolyn, Allan and Sharon Benton, Bill Smith, Jason Stanhope, Nick Pihakis, Charlotte Coman, Judith Winfrey, Tamie Cook, Vishwesh Bhatt, Katherine Miller, Frank and Pardis Stitt, Dolestar Miles, Pableaux Johnson, Vansana Nolintha, Matthew Kelly, Sloan and Wendy Southard, Mark Nash, Skip Matheny, Bob Durham, Glory Dole, Jenny Le Zotte, Andrea Fehl, Anne Phillip, Francis Lam, the Lee Brothers, Tallahassee May, Hunter Lewis, Diane Flynt, Judy Pray, Rene Redzepi, Melina Shannon-DiPietro, Sarah Abell, Soa Davis, Lisa Geffen, Kelly Clarkson, Brandon Blackstock, Allie Kearns, Tricia Farrow, Ava Brock, Chelsea Kramer, Lily Aldridge, the Kings of Leon, Dave Chang, Arielle Johnson, Angela Dimayuga, Mike Solomonov, Samin Nosrat, Marc Vetri, the Arnold family, Caleb Zigas, the La Cocina family, Julia Turshen, Mayukh Sen, Jessica Battilana, Pat Martin, Jennifer Justus, Erin B. Murray, Kim Greene, Susannah Felts, and, most definitely, Kevin and Nancy Murphy.

Big love and gratitude to Fred C. Donovan and Susie Spellman Donovan—my mother- and father-in-law, who remain two of the loveliest humans I know. I'm forever in your debt for your love and support and, ultimately, for having raised the very good human who is your son.

My sisters, not by birth but by the grace of whatever god is out there—Dana Grace Murphy and Alisa Love Martin—you are my family. This book is wholly possible because of you both. Thank you for taking me on long drives, for letting me lose my shit on you on the rainy streets of Paris, for tolerating my insufferable self-involvement over these last few years, for making me laugh through the tears and talking me through all the crippling self-doubt that comes with writing a book. You've seen it all. Somehow you still love me. I will never not feel like the luckiest human in the world to get to love you back.

Elsie and Mary, my grandmothers, I know are never far from me. I carry the great weight of their love and protection with me everywhere I go, a thing I feel an overwhelming sense of pride and responsibility toward. I owe a great deal to both of them.

My brother, David Michael Rierson—I could write an entire acknowledgments page just on you alone. Your golden heart is one of my favorite things floating around this planet. You will always be my best friend, and you will always be such a big part of who I am in this world. I love you.

William Michael Rierson, my father, my hero, my truth teller—when I feel the most lost in the world, I remember that I belong to you, that we belong to each other, and then I remember I can do anything because I am your daughter. Thank you for showing me what true strength of character looks like. Thank you for hearing and seeing me, all of me, my whole life, even when it was hard.

Mary Ann Rierson, my mom, you carried me under your big, important, and boisterous heart when you were just a young woman in 1977 and then continued to carry me inside of that same heart every day after I was born. Your love and prayers mean more to this angsty, stubborn fool than you know. I would be lost without them. I would be lost without you.

John Donovan, what can I say that hasn't already been said? I don't know who deserves the kind of love you give me, but I will take it and I will cherish it, and you, forever. Our marriage and our hard work together make me so proud. We're just getting started, so I hope you've napped.

Last, but most important, my two children, Joseph and Maggie—you have always been the reason. Being your mother has been the privilege of a lifetime. You two are the absolute lights of my life. There is nothing we can't do, the four of us. I know it to be true, because I've seen it. I love you both with everything I've got.

There is no luckier woman walking this planet than me. I am grateful for it all.